THE POLITICS OF LANGUAGE

Byrhtferth, Ælfric, and the Multilingual Identity of the Benedictine Reform

The Politics of Language

Byrhtferth, Ælfric, and the Multilingual Identity of the Benedictine Reform

REBECCA STEPHENSON

UNIVERSITY OF TORONTO PRESS
Toronto Buffalo London

Toronto Buffalo London
www.utppublishing.com

ISBN 978-1-4426-5058-9

Library and Archives Canada Cataloguing in Publication

Stephenson, Rebecca, 1975–, author
The politics of language : Byrhtferth, Ælfric, and the multilingual identity of the Benedictine reform / Rebecca Stephenson.

Includes bibliographical references and index.
ISBN 978-1-4426-5058-9 (bound)

1. Aethelwold, Saint, Bishop of Winchester, approximately 908–984 – Language. 2. Byrhtferth, approximately 970 – Language. 3. Benedictines – England – Winchester – History – To 1500. 4. Languages in contact – England – Winchester – History – To 1500. 5. Literacy – England – History – To 1500. 6. Great Britain – History – Anglo Saxon period, 449–1066. I. Title.

BR754.A1S74 2015 942.01'7 C2015-902599-0

University of Toronto Press gratefully acknowledges the financial assistance of the Centre for Medieval Studies, University of Toronto in the publication of this book.

University of Toronto Press acknowledges the financial assistance to its publishing program of the Canada Council for the Arts and the Ontario Arts Council, an agency of the Government of Ontario.

Funded by the Government of Canada
Financé par le gouvernement du Canada

For my husband John

Contents

Acknowledgments

As with all books, the writing of this monograph has been a long and circuitous journey. This path has been made easier by the generous help of so many members of the academic community, and I certainly cannot name every person who contributed to this volume with an insightful idea or even just a listening ear, but I will endeavour to try, with apologies to anyone whom I have forgotten. I would not be able to understand the difficult Latin styles of the late tenth century, if it were not for the careful attentions and instruction of Michael Lapidge. Katherine O'Brien O'Keeffe was my first teacher of Old English and has been a mentor and inspiration throughout my academic journey. Beyond the walls of my alma mater, I have been richly blessed with the support of many other mentors and colleagues, who have read drafts, written letters, and generously offered support, particularly Helmut Gneuss, Mechthild Gretsch, Roy Liuzza, Andy Orchard, Robin Norris, Elaine Treharne, Elizabeth Tyler, Paul Szarmach, and Emily Thornbury.

Many at my current institution, University of Louisiana at Monroe, deserve special thanks for supporting me while I rambled on about this for so many years, including Mary Adams, Julia Guernsey-Pitchford, Helen Lock, and Janet Haedicke. Melinda Matthews is an amazing wizard of Inter-Library Loan, and she always ensured I had any title I needed. It goes without saying that this project would never have come to completion without Kilian Garvey's Nespresso machine.

Long projects such as these truly show the devotion of friends. Nicole Guenther Discenza deserves special thanks for reading so many drafts and so patiently saving me from countless errors. And to my dear friends Jacqueline Fay and Renée Trilling, I cannot say enough about what your help, support, and constant encouragement have meant to my work.

This project has received substantial material support. Awards to Louisiana Artists and Scholars provided funding for a year's research leave to write the text and a trip to London to examine computistical manuscripts. The Deutchser Akademischer Austausch Dienst (DAAD) funded a two-month trip in 2002 to Georg-August-Universität Göttingen, where I was generously hosted by the late Mechthild Gretsch. It was there that what is now the fifth chapter of the book was drafted, and the kernel of an idea began to form.

An earlier version of chapter 2 was previously published in *Anglo-Saxon England* 38 (2009): 101–35; it is used here with permission. Portions of chapter 5 were previously published as "Ælfric of Eynsham and Hermeneutic Latin: Meatim Sed et Rustica Reconsidered," *Journal of Medieval Latin* 16 (2006): 111–41; it is also published here with permission.

I am grateful for the scholars whom I cannot name, who wrote such thoughtful readers' reports, all of which improved this book substantively. I am deeply indebted to Suzanne Rancourt and the University of Toronto Press, who have been tremendously helpful throughout the process of preparing the manuscript. And to my family, and especially my husband, I am thankful for your patience and support; I know this has been in the works for a long time, and I am glad to finally present it to you.

THE POLITICS OF LANGUAGE

Introduction: The Literary Context of the Monastic Reform

The Translation of St Swithun

St Swithun was an obscure ninth-century bishop of Winchester without much to distinguish him, until Bishop Æthelwold (963–84) translated his relics from the graveyard to a prominent shrine inside the Old Minster on 15 July 971.[1] Through this elaborate ceremony, Æthelwold made Swithun both the patron saint of the monastic cathedral at Old Minster, and the perfect tabula rasa onto which reformers could project the ideals, anxieties, and preoccupations of the Benedictine Reform, since little is known of his life, other than the dates of his episcopacy, 852–63.[2] The movement of the relics was commemorated in a very elaborate work, the *Translatio et miracula S. Swithuni*, composed by Lantfred (fl. 975), a monk, possibly from Fleury, who was living among the community at the Old Minster in 971.[3] Both the translation and the literary work that memorialized it were intended, in part, to heal a rift in the community created by Æthelwold's expulsion of the secular canons (priests who served the cathedral) from

1 The sources on Swithun have been gathered together in a single volume by Michael Lapidge, *The Cult of St Swithun*, Winchester Studies 4.2 (Oxford, 2003). The legacy of Bishop Æthelwold is detailed in Barbara Yorke, ed., *Bishop Æthelwold: His Career and Influence* (Woodbridge, 1988).

2 Lapidge discusses the few details of Swithun's biography that are extant, *Cult of St Swithun*, 3–7.

3 For an edition, see Lapidge, *Cult of St Swithun*, 252–333. For a reconstruction of Lantfred's biography, see ibid., 218–24.

the Old Minster in 964 in order to replace them with Benedictine monks.[4] Somewhat later, Wulfstan of Winchester (fl. 996) recast this prose *translatio* into dactylic hexameters, arguably the most elevated literary form in which a saint could be memorialized.[5] In 998, Ælfric of Eynsham (c. 960–c. 1010) translated Lantfred's work into English, as part of his *Lives of Saints* collection, thus spreading the account of Swithun's miracles to a wider audience.[6] In the shadow of his conflicted position as a secular cleric, yet patron saint of the Benedictine Reform, the narratives of Swithun's translation and ensuing miracles offer insight into the language politics of the Benedictine Reform.

Lantfred's description of the invention of Swithun's remains performs an important role in tying the newly refounded community to their past, while suppressing the memory of the role of the secular clerics in the monastery's history. The reformation of Winchester in 964 was not without a certain amount of drama, if the *Life of St Æthelwold* is to be believed.[7] According to this text, Æthelwold arrived at the cathedral with a loyal following of Benedictine monks and an order compelling the monastery to follow the Rule of St Benedict. As Æthelwold approached the doors, he heard the monks within saying the mass, "Seruite Domino in timore, et exultate ei cum tremore, apprehendite disciplinam, ne pereatis de uia iusta" [Serve ye the Lord with fear, and rejoice unto him with trembling: embrace discipline, lest ye perish from the just way].[8] The newly appointed bishop interpreted this statement as a divine order to cleanse the monastery of the negligence of the secular clerics and reinforce monastic discipline. These

4 D.J. Sheerin, "The Dedication of Old Minster, Winchester, in 980," *Revue Bénédictine* 88 (1978): 261–73, at 267. For the date for the expulsion of the canons, see the discussion in Michael Lapidge and Michael Winterbottom, eds, *The Life of St Æthelwold*, Oxford Medieval Texts (Oxford, 1991), xlvi–xlvii.

5 For an edition of this work, see Lapidge, *Cult of St Swithun*, 372–551.

6 Before Ælfric translated the *Translatio*, he first made a Latin epitome, which abridged Lantfred's work and excised the distinctive vocabulary. For a discussion of Ælfric's characteristic methods of abridgment, see below, chap. 4. For Ælfric's authorship of the epitome, see Lapidge, *Cult of St Swithun*, 553–61. An edition of the epitome can be found ibid., 564–73; an edition of Ælfric's English version from *Lives of Saints* appears ibid., 590–609.

7 An edition of this work can be found in Lapidge and Winterbottom, eds, *Life of St Æthelwold*. An epitome by Ælfric is also published in the same volume.

8 Ibid., 30–3 (their translation).

cathedral canons,[9] many of whom were connected to local powerful families, were replaced *in toto* by Benedictine monks brought by Æthelwold. Although Æthelwold did have some kinship ties to the inhabitants of Winchester,[10] the monks were unlikely to have relationships with the local population as strong as those belonging to the evicted clerics. Therefore, the translation of the relics of Swithun in 971 connected the monks to Winchester's past and to the local community by creating a narrative that united the monks and clerics under the banner of monasticism and erased some of the effects of the radical disruption created by the forceful eviction of the cathedral canons.

Lantfred's *Translatio* in 975 recorded and memorialized the important rituals of Swithun's translation in a very specific register of Latin that included esoteric and recherché vocabulary that could potentially limit its audience to only an educated monastic elite.[11] This particular style seems to have been something of a coterie language designed to show identity among an elite group of reformed monks, and thus, the style of the *Translatio* enacted linguistic acts of community building that paralleled what Æthelwold attempted in the ritual translation of Swithun's remains. Winchester monks, however, did not always prefer such stylistically complex texts and were not always exclusionist in their linguistic policies. The same community of monks for whom this work was composed were also instrumental in an English-language educational revival in the late tenth century that included a strong emphasis on religious education in the vernacular.[12] In short, Winchester found itself at the centre of expanding and contracting circles of literacy, which could easily be – and often were – exploited for tactical and political purposes. While English-language education was expanding, the difficulty of Latin texts was limiting their readership to a monastic elite. In this book, I will examine the political context that encouraged the simultaneous development of a simple English style and an esoteric Latin style. The tremendous growth of vernacular language texts in the late tenth

---

9 Canons are secular clerics who are part of the bishop's *familia* and serve a cathedral. For more on the distinctions between secular clerics, canons, and monks, see chap. 2.

10 For a reconstruction of Æthelwold's career, see Barbara Yorke, "Æthelwold and the Politics of the Tenth Century," in *Bishop Æthelwold*, 65–88.

11 For more on the details and history of this style, see below, pp. 14–27.

12 For more on this education revival and its connection the Alfredian renaissance of the late ninth century, see D.A. Bullough, "The Educational Tradition in England from Alfred to Ælfric: Teaching *utriusque linguae*," *Settimane di studio del Centro italiano di studi sull'alto medioevo* 19 (1972): 453–94.

century must be read against this sociolinguistic backdrop, since these English-language works were written by monks who also cultivated a very distinctive Latin style that greatly limited Latin readership. And while the bulk of my book will focus on the incredibly prolific writers of the second generation of the reform, namely, Byrhtferth of Ramsey and Ælfric of Eynsham, who can each offer a substantial corpus about which strong conclusions can be drawn, it is useful to return to the example of St Swithun, since the school at Winchester plays a foundational role in the development of stylistic choices that predominate in the late Anglo-Saxon period.

St Swithun's Translation in English and Latin

Notably, no accounts of Swithun's life survive, since, according to Lantfred, the secular clerics who were in control of Winchester were too negligent to record any of his great deeds. Instead, the substance of Swithun's hagiographical materials comprise the saint's invention, translation, and subsequent miracles, all of which occurred as a result of the actions of the reform. Although all the recorded deeds happen after the advent of the reformers, Swithun is not a monastic saint imported from elsewhere, like (say) Cuthbert. Rather, he is a local saint, whom the reformers monasticize and thereby obfuscate the crucial truth that his background was in all probability closer to that of the evicted secular clerics than of the newly arrived reformers. According to Lantfred's invention narrative, the relics are not found by a monk, but instead, Swithun appears in a dream to a smith, who in turn tells Eadsige, one of the evicted (and indignant) clerics. After much protesting, Eadsige humbles himself and tells his kinsman Bishop Æthelwold about the dreams concerning Swithun's relics. Once the two churchmen have settled their differences, Eadsige and Æthelwold lead the procession during the translation of the relics, thus creating a precedent for the former secular clerics to rejoin the cathedral community and accept the kind of monasticism now practised there. The reunification of the kinsmen Æthelwold and Eadsige metonymically stands in for the possibility of restoring many other kin relationships disrupted by the reformation of the monastery.

While Lantfred's *Translatio* can be seen as unifying the monks and the former secular clerics under one banner as newly reformed Benedictines, Ælfric's English version cements this connection by explaining how monks should relate to many segments of society. This English work is drastically shorter than any of the Latin versions that preceded it, and the meticulous selection of material reveals a hierarchically ordered society in which both secular clerics and the laity are subject to a monastic priesthood. Following his source in Lantfred's version, Ælfric's rendition first inscribes the close connections between the monastery and the lay population. The basic outlines are the same: Swithun announces his presence in a dream to a certain smith, who in turn must relate that dream to Eadsige, his lord, a former secular cleric and kinsman to Bishop Æthelwold. When Eadsige announces the vision to Æthelwold, order is restored, establishing a hierarchy in which a lay person corrects a (former) secular cleric, who in turn accepts the authority of the monastic bishop.[13] In the end, this secular cleric accepts the tenets of the reform and the yoke of monasticism, and in Ælfric's version the secular clergy are effectively erased from the remainder of the narrative. Ælfric's narrative differs from Lantfred's in that it is not concerned with affairs at Winchester, but rather speaks to a universal ordering of society in which the secular clergy are subject to monks.

Benedictine monks stand in effectively for secular government as well. Lantfred's version was heavily populated with miracles that freed those held in bondage. Ælfric seems to have been uncomfortable with the wholesale amnesty such miracles offer to convicted felons, and thus he limited himself to three: two in which the punishment is disproportionately heavy relative to the meagre nature of the crime and one in which someone is falsely convicted.[14] The latter of these is a particularly dramatic miracle in which sight is restored to an innocent man's eyes despite the fact that they had been put out and one hung on his face suspended by the optic nerve. Although Ælfric is known for his reticence in recounting miracles,[15] his zeal in repeating this particular episode seems to be related to the role of Swithun in correcting earthly justice gone awry. These stories reveal the

13 This is possibly analogous to Robert Upchurch's suggestion that Ælfric emphasized chastity in order to encourage the laity to question the moral imperatives of the clergy. "For Pastoral Care and Political Gain: Ælfric of Eynsham's Preaching on Marital Celibacy," *Traditio* 59 (2004): 39–78. More recently, Upchurch has suggested that Ælfric revised the homily for the second Sunday after Easter in order to criticize an unruly witan and negligent pastorate, who did not follow the appropriate role of supporting the king. "A Big Dog Barks: Ælfric of Eynsham's Indictment of the English Pastorate and Witan," *Speculum* 85 (2010): 505–33.

14 Mechthild Gretsch, *Ælfric and the Cult of Saints in Late Anglo-Saxon England*, Cambridge Studies in Anglo-Saxon England 34 (Cambridge, 2005), 186–7.

15 M.R. Godden, "Ælfric's Saints' Lives and the Problem of Miracles," in *Old English Prose: Basic Readings*, ed. Paul Szarmach, Basic Readings in Anglo-Saxon England 5 (New York, 2000), 287–309.

monks' control of even secular matters through their ability to intercede with a powerful monastic saint.

The miracles connected to Swithun touch those from all walks of life, ranging from slaves, to free men, to wealthy landholders, and Ælfric emphasizes that even very wealthy thegns benefit when Swithun is paid his proper respects. Ælfric recounts the story of a rich thegn who went to Rome in order to find healing. Despite his vast expenditure in travelling to the holy city, he did not find the miracle he sought until he returned to England and visited the shrine of Swithun at Winchester. And while no miracle directly touches the place of the king, the narrative ends with a nostalgic tribute to the great days of King Edgar, reflecting the reformers' political theology. Swithun's translation of 971 was the first in a series of elaborate events that celebrated and cemented the close alliance between King Edgar and the Benedictine reformers, Dunstan (archbishop of Canterbury, 960–88), Æthelwold (bishop of Winchester, 963–84), and Oswald (bishop of Worcester, 961–92, and archbishop of York, 971–92).[16] In 973, the Council of Winchester ratified the *Regularis concordia*, a document that standardized monastic practice throughout England and established the monarch as the patron of the monasteries.[17] In the same year, Edgar was coronated at Bath in an elaborate event, which was likely a second coronation since it occurred a full fourteen years after he had assumed power.[18] The imperial connotations of the belated coronation and the close relationship between the crown and the Benedictine reformers can be seen in the iconography of the *Benedictional of St Æthelwold*, a richly illuminated

16 For an overview of the monastic reform see David Knowles, *The Monastic Order in England: A History of Its Development from the Times of St Dunstan to the Fourth Lateran Council, 940–1216*, 2nd ed. (Cambridge, 1963), 31–82.

17 T. Symons, S. Spath, et al., eds, "Regularis concordia Anglicae nationis," in *Consuetudinum saeculi X/XI/XII monumenta non-Cluniacensia*, ed. Kassius Hallinger, Corpus Consuetudinum Monasticarum 7.3 (Siegburg, 1984), 61–147; establishment of the monarch as patron at 75–6. For the evidence for the circulation of the *Regularis concordia*, see Joyce Hill, "The '*Regularis concordia*' and Its Latin and Old English Reflexes," *Revue Bénédictine* 101 (1991): 299–315.

18 A discussion of the coronation can be found in Simon Keynes, "Edgar, *Rex Admirabilis*," in *Edgar: King of the English 959–975: New Interpretations*, ed. Donald Scragg, Publications of the Manchester Centre for Anglo-Saxon Studies (Woodbridge, 2008), 3–59, at 48–51.

book produced for Æthelwold's personal use.[19] The prominent placement of an illumination of St Swithun in this benedictional commissioned to celebrate Edgar's coronation shows the central position of both Winchester and its patron saint in the political machinations of the late tenth century.[20]

The emphasis on the king's contribution to the reform can be seen in the prologue of Lantfred's *Translatio*, which carefully situates the miracles of Swithun among the great events of Edgar's reign in the flamboyant Latin style typical of the period:

> Post cuius ergo ineffabilem mirifice humanationis adunationem, transcurso nongentorum curriculo annorum cum bis septeni reuolutione lustri, quinetiam ferme annum Phoebo rotante medium, aetate sexta (quae est caducorum nouissima), indictione quartadecima, Eadgaro regnante, basileo insigni atque inuictissimo, prepotente ac clementissimo, necnon gloriosissimo sceptrigera ditione et feliciter gentibus imperante compluribus, habitu distantibus, uoce atque moribus, diffuse in insula commorantibus quæ "Albio" nuncupata legitur ab Anglorum fore ueteribus: ipse Dei cuncticreantis unicus, lucis assidue splendor sempiternus, dignatus est suis largiri Anglis-Saxonibus celeste munusculum, per gloriosi precipuum antistitis Suuithuni meritum, ægrotis aethereum conferens beneficium, quia in presignata tempestate pontificis huius almi reliquie conuocationi catholice caelitus Deo largiente mirabiliterque sunt reuelatae, quinetiam multiplicibus prodigiis ac uirtutibus comprobate, miraculisque inenarrabilibus luculenter adornate.
>
> [Therefore, after the inexpressible union of Christ's wondrous incarnation, with the passing of the cycle of nine hundred years together with the revolution of twice-seven *lustra*, in fact with the sun nearly revolving half the next year, in the sixth age (which is the ultimate for transient creatures), in the fourteenth indiction, with Edgar reigning, that renowned and unconquerable king, powerful and most merciful and fully glorious in his sceptre-bearing sovereignty blessedly commanding several peoples distinct in appearance,

19 Robert Deshman, *The Benedictional of St Æthelwold*, Studies in Manuscript Illumination 9 (Princeton, NJ: Princeton University Press, 1995); see esp. "The Royal Program," 192–214. See also the discussion in Deshman, "*Christus rex et magi reges:* Kingship and Christology in Ottonian and Anglo-Saxon Art," *Frühmittelalterliche Studien* 10 (1976): 367–405.

20 Plates of the benedictional's illuminations can be found in Deshman, *Benedictional.* A facsimile of the full manuscript is available as Andrew Prescott, *The Benedictional of St Æthelwold: A Masterpiece of Anglo-Saxon Art* (London, 2002).

> speech and custom, dwelling widely scattered in the island which was reportedly called "Albion" by the early English: Jesus himself, the only Son of all-creating God, the eternal splendour of perpetual light, deigned to grant to His Anglo-Saxons a heavenly gift, bestowing an ethereal bounty on the sick through the outstanding merit of the glorious bishop Swithun, since in the aforementioned time the relics of this holy bishop were divinely and miraculously revealed to the catholic congregation through God's agency – moreover, they were confirmed through manifold prophecies and portents and were splendidly adorned by indescribable miracles.][21]

Even before one can wonder at the glory of Edgar's reign, however, the passage strikes the reader with its inflated style. Rather than the simple *anno domini* formulas that appear in other Anglo-Latin works, such as Bede's *Historia ecclesiastica*,[22] this passage begins with an elaborate dating formula, including the *lustra*, the indiction, and the age, writing the elaborate phase, "post ... humanationis adunationem" [after the unification of humanity (i.e., the incarnation)] in place of the simpler words "anno domini." As a further indication of the date, the reign of King Edgar is also given, who ruled 959–75. The remainder of the passage contains four appositive phrases modifying "Edgar," two appositive phrases describing the people that he ruled, and a relative clause naming England, before the main clause is reached. The grammatical complexity of this style joined with its predilection for rarefied and esoteric vocabulary connected to the arcane knowledge of medieval chronology is characteristic of a style that came to dominate Anglo-Latin texts in the late tenth and early eleventh centuries.

The excesses of this elaborate style of Anglo-Latin saints' lives is contrasted with more simple vernacular lives and homilies written during the same period, even in texts with similar connections to the Benedictine Reform and filled with praise for King Edgar. When Ælfric abbreviated Lantfred's passage in his homily collection *Lives of Saints*, he eliminated most of the unnecessary repetition, condensing the passage to its barest elements:

21 Lapidge, *Cult of St Swithun*, 258; translation by Michael Lapidge, ibid., 259.

22 For instance, Bede begins book 2, "His temporibus, id est anno dominicae incarnationis DCV" [In these times, that is in the year of the Lord's incarnation 605]. Bertram Colgrave and R.A.B. Mynors, eds, *Bede's Ecclesiastical History of the English People* (Oxford, 1969), 122.

On Eadgares dagum ðæs æðelan cynincges, þa ða se Cristendom wæs wel ðeonde þurh God on Angelcynne under ðam ylcan cyninge, þa geswutelode God þone sanct Swiðhun mid manegum wundrum þæt he mære is.[23]

[In the days of Edgar, the noble king, when Christianity was flourishing among the English through God under the same king, then God showed that St Swithun is great, with many miracles.]

Although this passage indicates the same respect for Edgar, Ælfric made no attempt to approximate the inflated diction of the Latin text. For instance, Lantfred chose the Grecism "basileus" in place of the more common Latin word "rex" [king], but this is rendered in English with the common word "cyning" [king], instead of a more flamboyant synonym. Equally, the wordy phrase "multiplicibus prodigiis ac virtutibus ... miraculisque inenarrabilibus" [with many prodigies and signs of power and indescribable miracles] becomes simply "mid manegum wundrum" [with many wonders] when translated into English. Many of the repetitive clauses have been eliminated as well. Despite the simpler register, however, this work decidedly emphasizes Edgar's role as an ally of the monastic reform, even surpassing his source in some places. Michael Lapidge characterized Lantfred's description of Edgar as less effusive than that of later writers like Ælfric, arguing that "there is in his wording none of the extravagant eulogy which is customarily found in English monastic authors writing after the king's death in 975."[24] Ælfric's more enthusiastic praise of Edgar can be seen in his tribute to Edgar, which he added to his homily, but did not translate from Lantfred's *Translatio*:

We habbað nu gesæd be Swiðhune þus sceortlice, and we secgað to soðan þæt se tima wæs gesælig and wynsum on Angelcynne, þa ða Eadgar cyning þone Cristendom gefyrðrode and fela munuclifa arærde; and his cynerice wæs wunigende on sibbe swa þæt man ne gehyrde gif ænig scip-here wære buton agenre leode þe ðis land heoldon; and ealle ða cyningas þe on þysum iglande wæron (Cumera and Scotta) comon to Eadgare – hwilon anes dæges eahta cyningas – and hi ealle gebugon to Eadgares wissunge. Þærtoeacan wæron swilce wundra gefremode þurh þone halgan Swiðhun (swa swa we sædon ær).[25]

23 Lapidge, *The Cult of St Swithun*, 590–609, at 590.
24 Lapidge, *Cult of St Swithun*, 236.
25 Ibid., 606.

[We have now related the story of Swithun shortly, and we say truly that the time was blessed and happy among the English people, when King Edgar furthered Christianity and built many monasteries, and his kingdom was dwelling in peace, so that no fleet was heard of, except for those of the people who hold this land. All eight kings of the Cumbrians and the Scots, who live in this land, came to Edgar on a certain day and they bowed to his rule. In addition, there were such miracles accomplished through the holy Swithun, as we said before.]

Here Ælfric attributed the miracles of St Swithun and the relative peace of Edgar's reign to divine approval of his just rule. The passage is filled with longing for the good old days, when Viking armies were not invading England and the whole country profited from the rule of a good king.[26] Although Ælfric's passage praises the virtues of King Edgar much more highly and more specifically than Lantfred's, there is no inflated language or syntax. The difference in style between these two tributes results, in part, from a nuance in genre: Lantfred's *Translatio* was written in a high style that was meant to commemorate and memorialize, while Ælfric's *Life* is part of a hagiographic collection meant for the edification of the Christian reader. The English had to be easily understood or it would not fulfil both its didactic and inspirational purposes; equally, the Latin required an elevated register for celebrating the saint, even though the esoterism of this commemorative register would likely limit its readership to the monastic elite. These observations are not limited to these writers or to the hagiography of St Swithun. Ælfric's collection was one of many collections of homilies and hagiographies produced in the tenth century, all of which exhibit comparatively simple language.[27] Lantfred's *Translatio* was one of many extended works that celebrated saints connected to the reform, most of which affect a style of Latin which equals or exceeds Lantfred's prose in difficulty.[28]

The functional roles of each of these two Swithun narratives parallels a strange dynamic occurring within the circles of Latin and English literacy

26 For Ælfric's description of Viking invasions in his sermons, see Malcolm Godden, "Apocalypse and Invasion in Late Anglo-Saxon England," in *From Anglo-Saxon to Early Middle English: Studies Presented to E.G. Stanley*, ed. M. Godden, D. Gray, and T. Hoad (Oxford, 1994), 130–62.

27 For the homiletic collections, see below, p. 27.

28 For a list of hermeneutic Latin texts, see below, pp. 20–1.

during and after the reform. On the one hand, Lantfred's composition of this narrative in an elevated style performs an important function in memorializing the translation and participates in forming a corporate identity for those who now reside in the monastery, both for the newly imported and the recently reformed monks. Just as the narrative includes all former clerics who wish to accept the new rules of monasticism, the difficult language allows only those readers who have taken on the austerities of monasticism to the extent that they have achieved Latin proficiency, the highest mark of a Benedictine monk. Ælfric's work, by contrast, expands the reading audience to include all those literate in English, lay, clerical, or monastic, thus magnifying the sphere of influence of the reformers. In short, readership and composition of an inflated style of Latin contracts Latin literacy to a small elite, at the same time that literacy in English has expanded.

The contracting circles of Latin literacy juxtaposed against the expanding circles of vernacular literacy constitute the central concern of this book, since this phenomenon implies many conflicting realities. Although I describe the circles of Latin literacy as contracting, there is no question that, as in Lantfred's *Translatio*, the Latin texts were longer, more numerous, and held in higher esteem. And while English literacy can safely be described as expanding for the full length of the tenth century following Alfred's educational program, English works performed different functions and were never regarded as highly as Latin texts. Vernacular writers repeatedly apologized for vernacular composition, as Ælfric does in his preface to the *Lives of Saints*, in which his version of Swithun's *Translatio* is included.[29] In these apologies for vernacular composition, we see a certain kind of identity encoded for readers of each language. Latin is the appropriate language for good and virtuous Benedictine monks, while English is the language for the instruction of the lay population by their appointed ministers, the secular clerics. On the face of it, this easy binary ignores the fact that monks literate in Latin were also literate in English.

29 "Non mihi imputetur quod divinam scripturam nostrae lingue infero, quia arguet me praecatus multorum fidelium, et maxime Æþelwerdi ducis et Æðelmeri nostri, qui ardentissime nostras interpretationes amplectuntur lectitando; sed decrevi modo quiescere post quartum librum a tali studio, ne superfluus iudicer" [Do not blame me that I have translated the divine scripture into our language, since I have been persuaded by the prayers of many of the faithful, especially ealdorman Æthelweard and our Æthelmær, who have embraced our translations for reading enthusiastically]; Jonathan Wilcox, ed., *Ælfric's Prefaces*, Durham Medieval Texts 9 (Durham, 1994), 120.

In fact, many reformers who composed very elaborate Latin texts also wrote English texts with a more didactic or pedagogical goal. The prevalence of English-language educational works brings into focus one of the problems with the inflated Latin style preferred by the reformers, namely, it was very difficult to understand and, in some cases, required an English translation in order to make the text useful to its named audience of Benedictine monks. These conflicting pedagogical and linguistic concerns characterize all the works of the period and not just the hagiography connected to Swithun.

The Hermeneutic Style

Thus far, I have made reference to an "elevated" or "inflated" form of Latin without referring to this style by a name. The elevated Latin style filled with archaisms, Grecisms, and neologisms preferred by the reformers is generally called the "hermeneutic style," a slippery term, which can be difficult to pin down. The word *hermeneutic* itself is misleading, since this style has nothing to do with the modern field of hermeneutics.[30] Lapidge, who wrote the seminal article on the hermeneutic style, suggested that the term "glossematic" might be more appropriate for these texts, since they contain words derived from glossaries; he continued using the word "hermeneutic," however, since it was currently in use.[31] The categorization of texts according to the prevalence of these rare and recherché terms is also a problematic endeavour, because not all hermeneutic texts have the same occurrences of rare vocabulary. The *Life of St Æthelwold*, for instance, has only four Grecisms, no neologisms, and no other archaisms.[32] From the point of view of vocabulary alone, this text can hardly be called hermeneutic, but when compared against Ælfric's abbreviation, its

30 Cf. Michael Lapidge's comments in "The Hermeneutic Style in Tenth-Century Anglo-Latin Literature," in *Anglo-Latin Literature, 900–1066* (London and Rio Grande, OH, 1993), 105–49, at 105 n. 2.

31 Ibid. There is an uneasy distinction between glossaries and *hermeneumata*. W.M. Lindsay suspected that the Épinal-Erfurt glossaries derived from an unknown *hermeneumata*; *The Corpus, Épinal, Erfurt, and Leyden Glossaries*, Publications of the Philological Society 8 (London, 1921).

32 Lapidge and Winterbottom, eds, *Life of St Æthelwold*, cix–cx.

hermeneutic tendencies stand out strongly.[33] Finding a definition of the hermeneutic style that considers more factors than vocabulary is especially important for a text such as Byrhtferth's *Enchiridion*, since this text is filled with rare and exotic words derived from computus,[34] but not every portion that includes these words deserves to be called hermeneutic.

Even in texts that are commonly acknowledged as hermeneutic, like the *Regularis concordia*,[35] the entire text does not maintain an elevated style. The hermeneutic style tends to be connected to prestigious texts that have a ceremonial or memorial function, not workaday texts, like those written by Ælfric.[36] The *Regularis concordia* inhabits a central position between ceremony and utility, because it is both the document that codified the ideals of the Benedictine Reform and a practical customary that outlined the practices to be followed by all religious houses in England.[37] Accordingly, it has a hermeneutic introduction and interruptions in Æthelwold's voice that are also considered to be hermeneutic, but much of the text is not very difficult and intended for functional use.[38] The intermittent hermeneutic style of the *Regularis concordia* provides a more appropriate comparison for a text like Byrhtferth's *Enchiridion*, which has a primarily functional purpose with digressions in this more difficult style that work against its pedagogical goals.[39]

However, despite the realization that hermeneutic texts are uneven in their employment of hermeneutic vocabulary and vary widely in style and

33 See below, chap. 5.

34 For a list of hermeneutic words in the *Enchiridion*, see Lapidge, "Hermeneutic Style," 128.

35 For a discussion of the *prohemium*, see Michael Lapidge, "Æthelwold as Scholar and Teacher," in his *Anglo-Latin Literature, 900–1066*, 192–4.

36 For a discussion and chronology of Ælfric's Latin texts see Christopher A. Jones, "*Meatim Sed et Rustica*: Ælfric of Eynsham as a Medieval Latin Author," *Journal of Medieval Latin* 8 (1998): 1–57 with chronology at p. 18.

37 Notably Ælfric felt compelled to create a redaction of this text for his community that removed hermeneutic vocabulary. For an edition, see Christopher A. Jones, ed., *Ælfric's Letter to the Monks of Eynsham*, Cambridge Studies in Anglo-Saxon England 24 (Cambridge, 1998).

38 Lapidge calls much of the text of the *Regularis concordia* "derivative" since it is compiled from a customary connected to Fleury. "Æthelwold," 193.

39 For an edition see Peter S. Baker and Michael Lapidge, eds, *Byrhtferth's Enchiridion*, EETS, s.s., 15 (Oxford, 1995).

difficulty, no one has concretely discussed and detailed the features of this style's syntax.[40] Michael Winterbottom made an attempt at this when he described this style as "a straining after variatio."[41] This does seem to be the most characteristic feature of hermeneutic Latin: it focuses more on stylistic variations than on precise meanings or correct grammatical forms.[42] In order to show how form prevails over content in a hermeneutic text, I include here an example from Byrhtferth's *Vita Sancti Oswaldi*, a text known for its elevated vocabulary and its tendency to ignore the historical events of Oswald's life in favour of typological interpretations.[43] I have chosen this passage because neither its grammar nor its vocabulary is extraordinary, yet it is still distinctively unlike the Latin of Bede:[44]

> Si genus agnoscere desideras, introducatur unus electus a grege Christi ex plurimis: Oda scilicet archiepiscopus ciuitatis Cantie, qui eius dinoscitur esse patruus. Sic uenerabilis uir grandeuus extitit apostolica dignitate et eadem refulsit gloriosa auctoritate, ut honestatem suorum prenominum eius decoraret vita prelucide, ut non solum a bonis 'ex intimo cordis affectu' diligebatur, uerum etiam a prepotentibus uerebatur.[45]

> [If you wish to know his lineage, let there be introduced one man chosen out of many from the flock of Christ, namely Oda, the Archbishop of Canterbury, who is known to be his uncle. Thus the venerable aged man existed

40 Michael Winterbottom's discussion of Aldhelm's syntax is informative here, but no comparable analysis of the syntax of a tenth-century text exists. See "Aldhelm's Prose Style and Its Origins," *ASE* 6 (1977): 39–76.

41 Michael Winterbottom, "The Style of Æthelweard," *Medium Ævum* 36 (1967): 109–18, at 110.

42 See Winterbottom's many examples of poeticisms and variation in Æthelweard's prose, many of which thwart the rules of Classical Latin grammar. "Style of Æthelweard."

43 Michael Lapidge, "Byrhtferth and Oswald," in *St Oswald of Worcester: Life and Influence*, ed. N. Brooks and C. Cubitt, Studies in the Early History of England 2 (Leicester, 1996), 63–84. An edition of this text is available in Michael Lapidge, ed., *Byrhtferth of Ramsey: The Lives of St Oswald and St Ecgwine*, Oxford Medieval Texts (Oxford, 2009). This edition supersedes the version in the Rolls Series: J. Raine, ed., *The Historians of the Church of York*, vol. 1, Rolls Series 71 (London, 1879), 399–475.

44 The opposition between the Latin of Bede and that of Aldhelm is a common measure in the discussion of hermeneutic Latin. For example, see Alistair Campbell, *The Chronicle of Æthelweard* (London, 1962), xlv.

45 Lapidge, *Byrhtferth of Ramsey*, 8–10.

prominently with the apostolic dignity and shone with this same glorious authority to such an extent that he decorated most splendidly the honorableness of his first names with his life, such that he was not only loved by the good from the innermost affection of their hearts, but he was also feared by the very powerful.]

This text achieves an elevated register in both its syntax and vocabulary, which show the "straining after *variatio*" that Winterbottom describes. Even though none of the words used in this passage are listed in Lapidge's catalogue of hermeneutic vocabulary,[46] many of the words were chosen for their length and their sound, not for nuances of their meaning. For instance, *dinoscitur* (here "is known," but usually meaning "to distinguish or discern") occurs in a context where a form of *scire* [to know] or *cognoscere* [to become acquainted with (i.e., to know)] might have been more appropriate, although these more common words would not have invoked the same elevated register. This higher style is also suggested by compounded forms that imply a superlative meaning. It is not "the powerful" who fear Oda, but "the very powerful" [prepotentibus], and his life is not "bright" or "shining," but "shining greatly" [prelucide]. It is perhaps appropriate that such a superlative saint from a Benedictine point of view should be connected to this elevated register. However, it is also important to point out that this higher style disregards precision of meaning in favour of form. For instance, instead of *nominum* [name], the text reads *prenominum* [first name]. The prefix *prae-* echoes the two examples mentioned above, but in no way changes the meaning of this word here, since Anglo-Saxons use only one name, not a first and a last name as the Normans do.[47]

Traces of superlative diction and an accompanying emphasis on form, not meaning, can be found in individual phrases, such as *a grege … ex*

46 See the list of hermeneutic words in the *Vita Sancti Oswaldi* in Lapidge, "Hermeneutic Style," 131–2. See also the discussion of the style of this text, pp. 129–32.

47 Michael Lapidge suggests the "praenomen" might refer to a common epithet for Oda as "se goda" (ibid., 10 n. 9). Even this interpretation shows Byrhtferth's desire for a poetic similarity in form, rather than precision in meaning, since in Classical Latin this would be a "cognomen," not a "praenomen." Notably, even in Old English, this epithet comes after the name, not before it, as the Latin prefix "prae-" would imply.

plurimis. The idea of "many" communicated in *ex plurimis* is unnecessary since it is already implied by the image of a flock (i.e., many sheep). While the substance of the phrase is redundant, the forms are not – not even the prepositions are repeated. In fact, the use of *a* to indicate a part from a whole shows that the writer is willing to strain good grammar in an effort to avoid repeating the same prepositions, in another kind of "straining after *variatio*."[48] While from a literary point of view there is nothing novel about the images or content, the passage shows a careful attention to affecting an elevated register through diction chosen more for its form than its precision of meaning.

More recently, Lapidge has advanced his ideas about hermeneutic Latin by focusing on the idea of an elevated register, which is not necessarily limited to the hermeneutic vocabulary that he catalogued. While he admitted that when he published his seminal article thirty years ago, he was "naively bedazzled by the display of vocabulary which one encounters there,"[49] and he thought that that the "principal impulse behind the verbal display was that of dazzling the reader with arcane vocabulary,"[50] now he suspects that the style arose from an "attempt to reach in their prose a high stylistic register" through the deployment of vocabulary with poetic resonances.[51] He lists seven classes of such vocabulary: poetic compounds, adjectives terminating in –eus, nouns ending in –men, diminutives, inceptive verbs in –esco, distributive numbers in place of cardinal numbers, and the third-person plural preterite in –ere.[52] Lapidge shows that Bede made a rigorous distinction between poetic and prosaic vocabulary in his writing, eschewing poetic vocabulary when writing prose. Aldhelm, however, did not. Rather, he employed a wider range of poetic vocabulary in his prose than in his poetry. The tenth-century Benedictines followed the Latin of Aldhelm, not that of Bede, in that they adorned their prose with these

48 Another possible scenario is that *a grege* is intended as an ablative of agent; thus, Oda "was elevated by the flock, as one out of many." However, the repetition of *flock* and *many* remains in this cumbersome and awkward phrase. Furthermore, the phrase is neither formulaic nor common, since the database for the *Patrologia Latina* has no occurrences of a form of *elatus* within ten words of *a grege*; http://80-pld.chadwyck.com (proximity search for forms of *elatus* and *grege*; accessed 6 April 2004).

49 Michael Lapidge, "Poeticism in Pre-Conquest Anglo-Latin Prose," *Proceedings of the British Academy* 129 (2005): 321–37, at 336.

50 Ibid., 336.

51 Ibid.

52 Ibid., 324–5.

poeticized words. In some ways, Byrhtferth is the perfect example of this predilection for poetic vocabulary, since his prose saints' lives are adorned with specimens from all seven classifications of poeticisms. Although the *Enchiridion* is not as ornate as Byrhtferth's hagiography, it does exhibit certain poeticisms as well. Perhaps the most prolific one is Byrhtferth's tendency to replace cardinal numbers with distributive numbers, with no difference in meaning, such as in the following phrase, "deinde conscripsimus nomina duodenorum signorum et duodecim mensium"[53] [Next we have written the names of the twelve signs and the twelve months], where *duodenorum*, the distributive number, is used as a variation on the following cardinal number, *duodecim*.

Although the presence of poeticisms might indicate an elevated register, the absence of them does not necessarily indicate a lowered register, nor can presence or absence of one or two classes of poeticisms be used as the only criterion to diagnose a passage as hermeneutic. For instance, many of Byrhtferth's sentences with distributive numbers in place of cardinal numbers show no other signs of poeticism or elevated register. Equally, the above passage from the *Vita Sancti Oswaldi* has only one category of poeticism, two inceptive verbs in –esco (agnoscere and dinosictur), but it has other stylistic features that show concern for the form of words rather than the precision of their meanings, a trait that is more commonly associated with poetry.[54] In light of the latest scholarship on the hermeneutic style and my own work on Byrhtferth, I would like to provisionally define it as a kind of Latin prose that affects an elevated register through importing poetic conventions into prose. I differ slightly from Lapidge's most recent work on this subject in that I will consider connections to poetic texts that extend beyond vocabulary to include hyperbaton (or other instances of irregular syntax), rhyming prose, and other poetic references, especially allusions to Aldhelm.[55] These poetic features stand out in the *Enchiridion*, since it is otherwise a pedagogical work, where one would not expect to find any kind of poeticism.

53 Baker and Lapidge, eds, *Byrhtferth's Enchiridion*, 16–18.

54 Notably, the *Vita Sancti Oswaldi* was the text that Lapidge discussed when writing about poeticisms in Byrhtferth. See "Poeticism," 334–6.

55 For Aldhelm's works, I will not distinguish between poetic and prosaic works, since Lapidge suggests that Aldhelm did not make any such distinction between poetic and prosaic vocabulary. Rather, Aldhelm's prose includes more poeticisms than his poetry.

Literary Context of the Monastic Reform

The conditions that produced the hermeneutic style are firmly rooted in the monastic reform of the late tenth century. Nearly every known Benedictine author during this period attempted hermeneutic prose or verse when composing in Latin, including Wulfstan of Winchester (fl. 996),[56] Lantfred of Winchester (fl. 975),[57] Frithegod of Canterbury (fl. 950),[58] Byrhtferth of Ramsey (c. 970–c. 1020),[59] and Æthelwold, bishop of Winchester (963–84),[60] to name a few. The hermeneutic style was even

56 The hermeneutic works of Wulfstan of Winchester include *The Life of St Æthelwold*, ed. Michael Lapidge and Michael Winterbottom (Oxford, 1991) and *Narratio metrica de S. Swithuno* published in *The Cult of St Swithun*, ed. Lapidge, 372–551. He also composed an epanaleptic poem entitled *Breuiloquium de omnibus sanctis*, published in F. Dolbeau, "Le *Breuiloquium de omnibus sanctis*: Un poème inconnu de Wulfstan, chantre de Winchester," *Analecta Bollandiana* 106 (1988): 35–98. For further discussion of other works attributable to Wulfstan, see Lapidge and Winterbottom, *Life of St Æthelwold*, xv–xxix; and Helmut Gneuss, *Hymnar und Hymnen im englischen Mittelalter*, Buchreihe der Anglia 12 (Tübingen, 1968), 246–8.

57 *Translatio et miracula S. Swithuni*, in Lapidge, ed., *Cult of St Swithun*, 252–333.

58 *Breuiloquium vitae Wilfridi* published in *Frithegodi monachi breuiloquium vitae beati Wilfredi et Wulfstani cantoris narratio metrica de Sancto Swithuno*, ed. Alistair Campbell (Zurich, 1950). For the life of Frithegod, see Michael Lapidge, "A Frankish Scholar in Tenth-Century England: Frithegod of Canterbury / Fredegaud of Brioude," in *Anglo-Latin Literature, 900–1066*, 157–81.

59 Byrhtferth wrote the *Vita S. Oswaldi* and the *Vita S. Ecgwini* in hermeneutic Latin. Editions of both these texts are available in Lapidge, ed. *Byrhtferth of Ramsey*. His *Enchiridion* also contains small sections composed in the hermeneutic style, see Baker and Lapidge, eds, *Byrhtferth's Enchiridion*, with a full discussion of Byrhtferth's works at pp. xxv–xxxiv.

60 The only extant hermeneutic text definitely attributed to Æthelwold is the *Regularis concordia*; for an edition, see Symons, Spath, et al., 61–147. For a discussion of his life and his educational program at Winchester, see Lapidge, "Æthelwold as Scholar" and "Three Latin Poems from Æthelwold's School at Winchester," in his *Anglo-Latin Literature, 900–1066*, 183–211. In addition, Mechthild Gretsch has argued that Æthelwold composed the glosses of the Royal Psalter (the so-called D gloss), those of Aldhelm's *Prosa de virginitate*, and the Old English translation of the Rule of St Benedict; see *The Intellectual Foundations of the English Benedictine Reform*, Cambridge Studies in Anglo-Saxon England 25 (Cambridge, 1999); Gretsch, *Die Regula Sancti Benedicti in England und ihre altenglische Übersetzung*, Texte und Untersuchungen zur englischen Philologie 2 (Munich, 1973); Gretsch, "Æthelwold's Translation of the *Regula Sancti Benedicti* and Its Latin Exemplar," *ASE* 3 (1974): 125–51; and Gretsch, "The Benedictine Rule in Old English: A Document of Bishop

attempted by Æthelweard (d. 998),[61] a layman who supported the reform, and by Dunstan's biographer,[62] a member of the secular clergy. Only Ælfric, who wrote the first Latin grammar in a vernacular language,[63] never attempted the style, preferring to write "non garrula verbositate aut ignotis sermonibus, sed puris et apertis verbis"[64] [not with wordy verbosity or unknown speech, but with clear and open words], although Ælfric here was speaking of vernacular composition, not Latin. His dissension from monastic ranks on this issue is so significant that scholars have spilled much ink attempting to explain this incongruity.[65] Although Ælfric may not have chosen to compose in this elevated style, it seems to have been taught in centres connected to him, as evidenced by his student, Ælfric Bata (fl. s.xi[1]), who composed colloquies including hermeneutic vocabulary for the instruction of monastic students in Latin.[66]

The evidence of Dunstan's clerical biographer might suggest that English church members outside of reformed circles also composed in the hermeneutic style, since he never took monastic orders. The particulars of his history as reconstructed by Michael Lapidge, however, decidedly mitigate that possibility.[67] This cleric, known only as B, seems to have been Dunstan's personal Latin secretary, who served the future archbishop through the reigns of Edmund, Eadred, and Eadwig. After travelling with Dunstan to receive the pallium in 960, he settled in Liège. At some point, presumably

Æthelwold's Reform Politics," in *Words, Texts, and Manuscripts: Studies in Anglo-Saxon Culture Presented to Helmut Gneuss on the Occasion of His Sixty-Fifth Birthday*, ed. Michael Korhammer (Cambridge, 1992), 131–58.

61 Campbell, ed., *Chronicle of Æthelweard.* For a discussion of the style of this text, see Michael Winterbottom, "Style of Æthelweard." For the evidence for the date of Æthelweard's death, see Simon Keynes, *The Diplomas of King Æthelred "The Unready," 978–1016: A Study in Their Use as Historical Evidence* (Cambridge, 1980), 192 n. 139.

62 *Vita S. Dunstani* published in *Memorials of St Dunstan*, ed. W. Stubbs, Rolls Series 63 (London, 1874), 3–52. For a discussion of this Life and its writer, see Michael Lapidge, "*B.* and the *Vita S. Dunstani*," in *Anglo-Latin Literature, 900–1066*, 279–91.

63 J. Zupitza, ed., *Ælfrics Grammatik und Glossar: Text und Varienten.* Sammlung englischer Denkmäler in kritischen Ausgaben 1 (Berlin, 1880; repr. with intro. by Helmut Gneuss, Hildesheim, 2001).

64 Wilcox, ed., *Ælfric's Prefaces*, 111.

65 This hypothesis and Ælfric's education is the subject of chap. 5.

66 For an edition and discussion, see Scott Gwara, ed., and David W. Porter, trans., *Anglo-Saxon Conversations: The Colloquies of Ælfric Bata* (Woodbridge, 1997).

67 His history is reconstructed in "B. and the *Vita S. Dunstani.*" The information in the remainder of this paragraph draws from Lapidge's discussion.

after 971, he became dissatisfied with his life in France and desired to return to England, and he seems to have written Dunstan's *vita*, in part, as a petition to return to his native country. B's status as a secular cleric seems to have been a hindrance to his gainful employment in England's monasticized cathedrals, especially in Winchester and Christ Church, Canterbury, to which he applied in particular. The evidence suggests that B was never permitted to return to England despite his skilful deployment of the hermeneutic style. Given this author's close personal relationship with Dunstan and his desire to be granted the right to return to England by the reformers, this *vita*'s adoption of the hermeneutic style must be seen as further evidence of this style's connection to monastic identity, rather than evidence that secular clerics also composed in hermeneutic Latin.

Furthermore, B's rich depictions of court life as the personal secretary of Dunstan also illustrate the fact that the success of the reform, both ecclesiastically and intellectually, was dependent upon substantial royal support, especially that of Æthelstan and Edgar.[68] The early development of a highly stylized form of Latin is closely connected to the royal court dating as far back as King Alfred. Asser's *Life of King Alfred* was considered by at least one scholar to be so highly stylized that it should (in his opinion) be attributed to the more flamboyant Byrhtferth of Ramsey, who wrote a century later, though this attribution is almost certainly false and this text is not ordinarily considered among those written in the hermeneutic style.[69] The earliest example of a literary work that has legitimately been called hermeneutic by Lapidge, the foremost authority on the hermeneutic style, was also written by a scholar in King Alfred's court, John the Old Saxon, who composed a poem to the future king, Æthelstan, c. 900.[70]

It is Æthelstan's court that produced the early specimens of stylized Latin that are generally included among hermeneutic texts, perhaps most famously in the elaborate Latin charters composed by the scribe known only as "Æthelstan A." These charters celebrate the reign and achievements of Æthelstan in the same elevated style that would later become

68 For an overview of the changes brought about by the reform, and their relationship to the king, see Pauline Stafford, *Unification and Conquest: A Political and Social History of England in the Tenth and Eleventh Centuries* (London, 1989), 184–94.

69 A.P. Smyth, *King Alfred the Great* (Oxford, 1996), 271–367.

70 Michael Lapidge, "Some Latin Poems as Evidence for the Reign of Æthelstan," in *Anglo-Latin Literature, 900–1066*, 60–71.

connected with the reform.[71] Although this scribe cannot be identified, his period of activity (928–35) corresponds with the sojourn of Dunstan and Æthelwold at this court, where they were ordained and remained as part of Æthelstan's retinue.[72] Mechthild Gretsch has suggested that although one boundary clause suggests that this scribe has impeccable Old English, he might be yet another foreigner, Israel the Grammarian,[73] one of the many foreign scholars attracted to Æthelstan's cosmopolitan court. Another poem in the hermeneutic style, "Rex Pius Æthelstan," included on a flyleaf dedication of an ornate gospelbook and given by Æthelstan to Christ Church, Canterbury (London, BL, Cotton Tiberius A.ii), may have been written by yet another foreign scholar who had served in Æthelstan's court, but then resided at Canterbury.[74]

Although attestations of authorship such as those proposed above are only tentative at best, much evidence exists to suggest that many early English specimens of the hermeneutic style were written by foreigners, such as the *Breviloquium vitae Wilfredi* by Frithegod of Canterbury, a scholar whom Lapidge argues should be properly identified as the Frankish Fredegaud of Brioude.[75] This work in many ways exemplifies the ways in which native English and Continental influences coalesce in the hermeneutic style, since it is a metrical redaction of the life of a famous English bishop, St Wilfrid, written by a Frankish scholar with the support of an English monastery and commissioned by an archbishop of Canterbury, Oda (941–58), who once lived in Fleury.[76] The hermeneutic style had a

71 For a discussion of "Æthelstan A," see Simon Keynes, "England, c. 900–1016," in *The New Cambridge Medieval History, vol. 3, 900–1024*, ed. Timothy Reuter (Cambridge, 1999), 456–84, at 470.

72 The ordination is described in Wulfstan of Winchester's *Life of St Æthelwold*, ed. Lapidge and Winterbottom, 10–12. For a discussion of the intellectual exchanges in King Æthelstan's court, see Mechthild Gretsch, "The Junius Psalter Gloss: Its Historical and Cultural Context," *ASE* 29 (2000): 85–121.

73 For the suggestion that "Æthelstan A" could have been Israel the Grammarian, see Mechthild Gretsch, *Intellectual Foundations*, 313–15, esp. 314 n. 162. Her work is based on the prior suggestion by Michael Lapidge in "Schools, Learning and Literature in Tenth-Century England," in *Anglo-Latin Literature, 900–1066*, 21. Also, Lapidge, "Israel the Grammarian in ASE," in *Anglo-Latin Literature*, 95.

74 For a discussion of the dating and circumstances of this poem, see Gretsch, *Intellectual Foundations*, 337–9; and Lapidge, "Poems as Evidence," 81–5.

75 For a reconstruction of Frithegod's career, see Lapidge, "Frankish Scholar."

76 Gretsch, *Intellectual Foundations*, 339–41.

long and venerable tradition on the Continent,[77] the influence of which can most notably be seen in England in the *Occupatio* by Odo of Cluny and the third book of the *Bella Parisicae urbis* by Abbo of St Germain-des-Prés, both of which were heavily studied in English monastic classrooms. Odo's work, though seldom studied by modern scholars, may have been particularly important to the reformers, since he was "the inspirational force behind the Benedictine Reform movement."[78] Dunstan's exile in Ghent and Oswald's study in Fleury (in imitation of his uncle, Archbishop Oda) cannot be overlooked as important channels through which the Continental version of the hermeneutic style travelled into reformed writings in England.[79]

While the hermeneutic style in France was never more than a fashion affected by a few writers, in England this style becomes the dominant mode of high-prestige Latin texts and the personal mark of identification for Benedictine monks.[80] The preference for this style in England is probably related to the curriculum studied in monastic schools, since the English author Aldhelm is among the primary authors studied and imitated by writers affecting the hermeneutic style. Even King Æthelstan seems to have been particularly enamoured of Aldhelm, choosing to be buried at Malmesbury instead of Winchester,[81] and the early flowering of the hermeneutic style in his court may have been related in equal parts to the influence of foreign scholars and the king's own encouragement of Aldhelm scholarship. Since Æthelwold and Dunstan were both members of this court early in their ecclesiastical careers, they probably had their

77 The development of a Continental hermeneutic style has been detailed by Michael Lapidge in "Hermeneutic Style," 107–14. The Continental influences on Aldhelm's style, which contributed greatly to the tenth-century hermeneutic style have been detailed by Michael Winterbottom, "Aldhelm's Prose Style."

78 Lapidge, "Hermeneutic Style," 109.

79 Advisers from these two cities are mentioned in the preface to the *Regularis concordia*; see Symons, Spath, et al., 71–2. For the importance of the Continental influence on the reform, see Antonia Gransden, "Traditionalism and Continuity during the Last Century of Anglo-Saxon Monasticism," *Journal of Ecclesiastical History* 40 (1989): 159–207; and Patrick Wormald, "Æthelwold and His Continental Counterparts: Contact, Comparison, Contrast," in *Bishop Æthelwold*, ed. Yorke, 13–42.

80 According to Lapidge, "In Europe in the early tenth century some few writers affect a hermeneutic style; in England in the later tenth century virtually every Latin author whose works have survived is affected by this stylistic tendency." "Hermeneutic Style," 111.

81 Gretsch, *Intellectual Foundations*, 347–8.

first exposure to Aldhelm here.[82] After leaving the court and moving to Glastonbury, Dunstan and Æthelwold spent the 940s, the period just before the beginning of the Benedictine Reformation, studying Aldhelm and the Benedictine rule, creating extensive glosses to both works. Studying these works together shows the close connection between the tenth-century imitation of Aldhelm present in the hermeneutic style and the reformers' identities as Benedictine monks. The curriculum later established at Æthelwold's school at Winchester further cemented Aldhelm's central place in the English educational curriculum.[83] As this brief survey shows, Benedictine monasticism and an elevated Latin style went hand in hand for Dunstan and Æthelwold, even in the period before the monastic reform began its major work.

When one examines the centres at which the hermeneutic style is practised, it is immediately apparent that the personal pilgrimages of the reformers, Dunstan, Æthelwold, and Oswald, are closely connected to the development of the hermeneutic style in the tenth century. Works written in this distinctive style are connected to Glastonbury, where Dunstan and Æthelwold studied in the 940s, Canterbury, at which Dunstan was appointed archbishop, Ramsey, which was founded by Oswald, and Winchester, where Æthelwold was appointed bishop. When Lapidge described the style, he commented on "differing tendencies (or emphases) in the various monastic centres where it was cultivated: a pronounced penchant for neologism at Canterbury, a predilection principally for the grecism at Winchester, and Byrhtferth's fondness for unusual polysyllabic adverbs at Ramsey (a fondness also remarkable in Bata's works, wherever he may have been)."[84] In addition to these monastic centres, there are other works that cannot be attributed to a specific location, including a certain number of royal charters, especially those of Æthelstan A, the *Chronicon Æthelweardi* written by Ælfric's patron, and B's *Vita S. Dunstani* discussed above. Even these works of uncertain origins have strong connections to either a member of the monastic reform or to the royal court, and possibly both, and thus the circumstances of the texts in the hermeneutic style inscribe the reformers' ideological union of Benedictine monasticism and royal support.

82 Ibid., 348–9.

83 Lapidge claims that hermeneutic texts were not studied so vigorously on the Continent and the reading of Aldhelm had all but ceased outside of England in the late tenth century. "Hermeneutic Style," 114.

84 Ibid., 139.

King Æthelstan was likely instrumental in giving the hermeneutic style a foothold in the English intellectual milieu and offering Dunstan and Æthelwold their first exposure to it, but the full extent of royal support was not experienced until Edgar's reign, since he played a particularly important role in establishing reformed monasticism and thereby cultivating the hermeneutic style.[85] Edgar and Æthelwold had a particularly close connection, since Æthelwold was Edgar's tutor in Abingdon, before the latter's accession to the throne.[86] Edgar also recalled Dunstan, who had been exiled in Ghent during the reign of Eadwig,[87] granting him the bishopric of London (and later of Worcester in plurality),[88] when Edgar became king of the Mercians in 957.[89] Upon the death of King Eadwig in 959, Edgar acceded to the throne of a (soon-to-be) reunited England. With King Edgar in control of England, the reformers had the power and the influence to further the ideals of the monastic life throughout England. Edgar appointed Dunstan archbishop of Canterbury and Æthelwold bishop of Winchester.[90] In addition, Edgar also granted permission for Æthelwold to expel the secular canons that were then in possession of the Old Minster at Winchester and to replace them with Benedictine monks.[91] The connection between the royal and ecclesiastical powers during the reign of Edgar was firmly outlined in the *Regularis concordia*, a customary that established the monarch as the patron of the monasteries and combined regal symbolism with an elevated style of Latin.[92] The relative stability of Edgar's reign, in combination with his strong support of the reformers' activities, created a flowering of intellectual life in the late tenth

---

85 For an overview of the political history of the tenth century, see Pauline Stafford, *Unification and Conquest*.

86 The argument for Æthelwold as the instructor of Edgar, instead of Dunstan, was made by Eric John in "The King and the Monks in the Tenth Century Reformation," in *Orbis Britanniae and Other Studies* (Leicester, 1966), 159–60; see also Lapidge, "Æthelwold as Scholar," 98.

87 The A-text of the Anglo-Saxon Chronicle s.a. 955, "þa feng Eadwig to rice, Eadmundes sunu cinges 7 aflæmde Sancte Dunstan ut of lande," in Janet Bately, ed., *The Anglo-Saxon Chronicle: A Collaborative Edition*, vol. 3, *MS. A* (Cambridge, 1986), 75.

88 Dunstan's appointment to the bishoprics of London and Worcester was recorded in the Anglo-Saxon Chronicle s.a. 959; see Bately, *Anglo-Saxon Chronicle*, 75.

89 Edgar's title was *rex Merciorum*, that is, he controlled all of England north of the Thames.

90 Knowles, *Monastic Order*, 39.

91 This expulsion is described by Wulfstan of Winchester in Lapidge and Winterbottom, *Life of St Æthelwold*, chaps. 30–2.

92 Symons, Spath, et al. "*Regularis concordia*," 75–6.

century.[93] We see this flowering both in the production of several hermeneutic Latin saints' lives, Latin quantitative poetry (also in the hermeneutic style), and several advances in vernacular scholarship as well, including the standardization to late West Saxon.[94]

The Simultaneous Development of English-Language Literature

This same period that cultivated the hermeneutic style also produced a flowering of vernacular literature, accessible to a broad range of people, and not limited to the Latin-educated clergy. Most of the extant homily collections are datable to the second half of the tenth century. In particular, the manuscript of the Blickling homilies dates from the end of the tenth century, but Homily XI is internally dated to 971, and the Vercelli Book is datable to the middle of the second half of the tenth century.[95] Ælfric of Eynsham composed two series of Catholic homilies (990–5) and a collection of saints' lives (992–1002),[96] the latter of which was commissioned by a layman,[97] implying the existence of a literate lay audience.[98] The compilation of the poetic codices is also datable to this period of history. While the possibility of oral transmission makes the dating of individual poems difficult to determine, the composition of each of the four extant poetic manuscripts has been dated on palaeographical grounds to between c. 975 and

93 A sampling of the many contributions of Edgar's reign can be seen in the recent volume arising from the conference dedicated to that king at the University of Manchester. Donald Scragg, ed., *Edgar King of the English, 959–975: New Interpretations*, Publications of Manchester Centre for Anglo-Saxon Studies (Woodbridge, 2008).

94 For an overview of the literary productions of the late tenth century, see Lapidge, "Schools, Learning and Literature," esp. 31–48.

95 N.R. Ker, *Catalogue of Manuscripts Containing Anglo-Saxon* (Oxford, 1957), 451–5 and 460. For an edition of the Blickling homilies, see R. Morris, ed., *The Blickling Homilies*, EETS, o.s., 58, 63, and 73 (London, 1874–80; repr. as 1 vol., London, 1967). For an edition of the Vercelli homilies, see Donald Scragg, ed., *The Vercelli Homilies and Related Texts*, EETS, o.s., 300 (London, 1992).

96 For editions, see Peter Clemoes, ed., *Ælfric's Catholic Homilies: The First Series*, EETS, s.s., 17 (London, 1997); Malcolm Godden, ed., *Ælfric's Catholic Homilies: The Second Series*, EETS, s.s., 5 (London, 1979); and Walter W. Skeat, ed., *Ælfric's Lives of Saints*, EETS, o.s., 76, 82, 94, 114 (London, 1881–1900; repr. as 2 vols, London, 1966).

97 The *Lives of Saints* was written at the request of Æthelweard and his son Æthelmær; see Skeat, *Lives of Saints*, 4.

98 For the chronology of Ælfric's works, see Peter Clemoes, "The Chronology of Ælfric's Works," in *Old English Prose: Basic Readings*, ed. Paul E. Szarmach, Basic Readings in Anglo-Saxon England 5 (London, 2000), 29–72.

the early eleventh century.[99] Although not all of the texts mentioned above can be traced to Benedictine monasteries, their production coincides with the monastic reformation, and they reveal a drastic expansion of literacy throughout the tenth century.

The reformers' work did not begin in a vacuum. Indeed, the translation program connected to King Alfred provided a solid foundation upon which Benedictine teachers like Ælfric, Æthelwold, and Byrhtferth could build their own educational agendas.[100] Alfred's oft-cited translation program of books "most needful for all men to know" and his directive for all free men of means to pursue literacy created a strong precedent for the reformers' creation and cultivation of a simple style of Old English along with a literate audience for their work.[101] The desire for simplicity in the vernacular had both a practical and a historical component, since, as

99 According to Ker, the Vercelli Book and the Exeter Book are the earliest, both of which he dated to the middle of the second half of the tenth century. The Junius manuscript has recently been dated to the same period; see Leslie Lockett, "An Integrated Re-examination of the Dating of Oxford, Bodleian Library, Junius 11," *ASE* 31 (2002): 141–73. And the Beowulf manuscript is dated somewhere at the turn of the eleventh century. Kevin Kiernan has dated the Beowulf manuscript on political grounds to some time after 1016, see *Beowulf and the Beowulf Manuscript* (New Brunswick, NJ, 1981) and "The Eleventh Century Origin of *Beowulf* and the *Beowulf* Manuscript," in *Anglo-Saxon Manuscripts: Basic Readings*, ed. Mary P. Richards, Basic Readings in Anglo-Saxon England 2 (New York, 1994), 277–99, at 280; but Kiernan's dating is rejected on palaeographical grounds by David Dumville, who dates the Nowell Codex c. 1000: see "Beowulf Come Lately: Some Notes on the Paleography of the Nowell Codex," *Archiv für der neueren Sprachen und Literaturen* 225 (1988): 49–63.

100 For the connections between the educational projects of the reform and those of the Alfredian period, see Bullough, "Educational Tradition."

101 The Old English reads, "niedbeðearfosta sien eallum monnum to witonne." *King Alfred's West Saxon Version of Alfred's Pastoral Care*, ed. Henry Sweet, EETS, o.s., 45 and 50 (London, 1871), 6. Nicole Guenther Discenza cautions, however, that this directive for education has often been read too broadly and that Alfred urged those free men with the means to study, not all free men. "Wealth and Wisdom: Symbolic Capital and the Ruler in the Translational Program of Alfred the Great," *Exemplaria* 13 (2001): 433–67, esp. 452–3. For more on Alfred's translation program, see Janet M. Bately, "The Literary Prose of King Alfred's Reign: Translation or Transformation?" in *Old English Prose: Basic Readings*, ed. Paul Szarmach, Basic Readings in Anglo-Saxon Prose 5 (New York, 2000), 3–27. See also Bately, "Old English Prose before and during the Reign of Alfred," *ASE* 17 (1988): 93–138; and "The Alfredian Canon Revisited: One Hundred Years On," in *Alfred the Great: Papers from the Eleventh-Centenary Conferences*, ed. Timothy Reuter, Studies in Early Medieval Britain 3 (Aldershot, 2003), 107–20.

Nicole Discenza argues, "Alfred gives his text distinctiveness not through grammar or dialect ... but through this synthesis of cultural references and modes of discourse."[102] Alfred's translation of Roman material into Anglo-Saxon terms created a model for Ælfric's similar statement that he would not place two rulers in a narrative, but would translate these Roman ideas into Anglo-Saxon terms for the English, who had but one king. In addition, the Latin style of Bede's *Ecclesiastical History*, which was also translated in the ninth century, may have influenced the simple Latin style of Ælfric, the sole Benedictine who preferred the style of Bede to that of Aldhelm.[103] While the writings of the Alfredian court provided ample historical precedent for a simple style of English that translated texts into images relevant to an Anglo-Saxon audience (and may even explain some of the eccentricities of Ælfric's Latin style), the reformers' decision to continue in this simple vernacular style throughout the very different literary and political contexts of the late tenth century has completely different social ramifications from those of Alfred's court just one hundred years previous.

The Benedictine Reformers' role in the creation of vernacular literary texts accessible to a broad audience seems potentially at odds with their cultivation of an elevated Latin style. If the reformers always preferred esoterism and either refused to write in English or composed in a stilted and erudite vernacular style that matched their Latin prose, then their linguistic decisions would perhaps be more straightforward, and modern scholars could surmise that Benedictine literary tastes equated with their preference for very ornate artistic pieces, exemplified in the art of the Winchester school. The explanation is not this simple, however, since some of the same monks who impressed others with their highly rarified Latin wrote in very simple English, such as Æthelwold, who, although he composed the preface to the *Regularis concordia* in the hermeneutic

102 *The King's English: Strategies of Translation in the Old English* Boethius (Albany, NY, 2005), 87.

103 Bede's *Ecclesiastical History* was certainly not translated by Alfred, but is instead a Mercian production; see Dorothy Whitelock, "The Old English Bede," *PBA* 48 (1962): 57–90. The authorship of all Alfredian translations is currently in question; see Paramjit S. Gill, Tim B. Swartz, and Michael Treschow, "A Stylometric Analysis of King Alfred's Literary Works," *Journal of Applied Statistics* 34.10 (2007): 1251–8; Malcolm R. Godden, "Did King Alfred Write Anything?" *Medium Ævum* 76 (2007): 1–23; Janet M. Bately, "Did King Alfred Actually Translate Anything? The Integrity of the Alfredian Canon Revisited," *Medium Ævum* 78 (2009): 189–215.

style, wrote the translation to the Benedictine rule in a very accessible style of English. Æthelwold's school at Winchester seems to have been particularly engaged in vernacular instruction and was responsible for the late West Saxon standard which came to dominate tenth- and eleventh-century Old English prose, regardless of the region in which it was composed.[104] In addition, the reformers developed a specific terminology for discussing religious concepts in English, called Winchester vocabulary or "Winchester Words."[105] These words employed by those connected to Winchester (including Ælfric of Eynsham) are distinguished by the fact that they often translate concepts more specifically than the Latin terms implied, such as *wuldorbeag*, which translates the Latin word *corona*, but only when *corona* refers to the crown of life worn by martyrs (i.e., *corona vitae aeternae*), not when it refers to the crown worn by a king.[106] The evidence of these words combined with Ælfric's extensive collections of homilies suggests that the monastic reformers used the English language in order to offer religious instruction in English to a broad cross-section of society.

Byrhtferth of Ramsey and Ælfric of Eynsham

Two pedagogically minded monastic schoolmasters whose work exemplifies the complicated nature of Anglo-Saxon multilingualism are Byrhtferth of Ramsey (c. 970–c. 1020) and Ælfric of Eynsham. The first of these authors, Byrhtferth of Ramsey, composed prolifically in the highly stylized form of Latin prized by reformers and also wrote a bilingual textbook

104 Mechthild Gretsch, "Winchester Vocabulary and Standard Old English: The Vernacular in Late Anglo-Saxon England," *Bulletin of the John Rylands University Library of Manchester* 83.1 (Spring 2001): 41–87, esp. 82–3.

105 For Winchester vocabulary, see Helmut Gneuss, "The Origin of Standard Old English and Æthelwold's School at Winchester," *ASE* 1 (1972): 63–83; Walter Hofstetter, "Winchester and the Standardization of Old English Vocabulary," *ASE* 17 (1988): 139–61; Hofstetter, *Winchester und der spätaltenglische Sprachgebrauch: Untersuchungen zur geographischen und zeitlichen Verbreitung altenglischer Synonyme*, Münchener Universitäts-Schriften, Philosophische Fakultät, Texte und Untersuchungen zur englischen Philologie 14 (Munich, 1987); Mechthild Gretsch, *Intellectual Foundations*, esp. 89–131; and Gretsch, "Winchester Vocabulary and Standard Old English." For Ælfric's adaptations of Winchester vocabulary, see Malcolm Godden, "Ælfric's Changing Vocabulary," *English Studies* (1980): 206–23.

106 Gretsch, "Winchester Vocabulary and Standard Old English" and *Intellectual Foundations*, 98–104.

on computus, the medieval system of calculating movable feasts such as Easter. This work is crucial for the study of the relationship between languages in late Anglo-Saxon England, because it is a bilingual text that claims to be tailored to two specific audiences in Byrhtferth's classroom, reformed monks and secular clerics. Since this text contains explicit references to audiences and subjects from Byrhtferth's school at Ramsey, it offers valuable insight into how language can serve as an instrument that divides or unites, even among those studying together in a classroom. Byrhtferth is an especially interesting figure to study, since he identified strongly with the monastic reform, but was not educated at the reform centre of Winchester as Ælfric was.[107] Accordingly, he does not employ so-called Winchester vocabulary or affect other standardizations connected to the English-language compositions of Winchester texts. As such, Byrhtferth's work can offer a window into how the reformers' language politics were instituted at Ramsey, a centre known for its scholarship, but not as central to the political fortunes of the reform as the royal see of Winchester. Furthermore, the time is ripe for a major study of the *Enchiridion*. Aside from Michael Lapidge and Peter Baker's scholarly edition, little work has been done on this text because of the difficulty of its language and its subject matter, but this work can offer unparalleled information about the Anglo-Saxon classroom and the language dynamics therein. I argue that careful consideration of Benedictine attitudes towards language has important consequences for the modern interpretation of both vernacular and Latin literature from the late Anglo-Saxon period.

Like Byrhtferth, Ælfric was also a monk, schoolmaster, and prolific writer, who was trained in Æthelwold's school at Winchester.[108] Although Ælfric has been extensively studied, recent work by Christopher A. Jones, Robert Upchurch, and Mary Swan (among others) has caused his role and

107 Biographical information on Byrhtferth is sketchy at best, and is based primarily on his writings. The best summary of this information can be found in the introduction to Baker and Lapidge, eds, *Byrhtferth's Enchiridion*; see also Lapidge, ed., *Byrhtferth of Ramsey*, xxx–xliv; and Peter S. Baker, "The Old English Canon of Byrhtferth of Ramsey," *Speculum* 55 (1980): 22–37.

108 A good introduction to his life can be found in Joyce Hill's "Ælfric: His Life and Works," in *A Companion to Ælfric*, ed. Hugh Magennis and Mary Swan, Brill's Companions to the Christian Tradition 18 (Leiden, 2009), 35–65; a brief overview of scholarship can be found in Hugh Magennis, "Ælfric Scholarship," ibid., 5–34.

relationship to the monastic reform to be reconsidered.[109] Although it would be tempting to closely equate Ælfric's teachings with those of Æthelwold, since Ælfric styles himself as Æthelwold's student and rigorously espouses an ideology in his homilies coloured by a Benedictine vision of the world. However, Ælfric's view of Benedictinism departs in important ways from those of other second-generation reformers like Wulfstan the Cantor and Byrhtferth of Ramsey. My work on Ælfric continues in the direction led by Jones, assuming that while Ælfric is a faithful adherent of the Benedictine Reform, he is sui generis in his implementation of reformed ideals. Therefore, rather than reading Ælfric's many statements about the status of English and Latin as a straightforward unbiased account of Anglo-Saxon linguistic practices, instead I read these opinions against Byrhtferth's more colourful depictions. Accordingly, I find that Ælfric's statements on the use of language also serve important roles in codifying certain kinds of identity by eliding the function of the secular clergy in Anglo-Saxon society.

As faithful adherents of the Benedictine Reform, Byrhtferth and Ælfric represent two very different approaches to the politics of language in the dissemination of reformed ideals. Perhaps because of the great differences in their work, no major study has yet placed these writers side by side. This current book remedies this lack by reading Ælfric and Byrhtferth as representative of the range of possibilities available to reformed writers; across this range, it becomes possible to discern how writing and language were central to the construction of a monastic identity during the Benedictine Reform. This book is divided into two parts. Part One deals with Byrhtferth and examines how various registers of Latin and English would have functioned in a monastic classroom. Part Two considers Ælfric against the backdrop of Byrhtferth's language politics, which more closely represents reformed ideology in his privileging of hermeneutic Latin. Through this examination, the places where Ælfric's linguistic concerns coincided and diverged from the language politics of the Benedictine Reform become more readily apparent. Furthermore, this study illuminates the role and

109 Christopher A. Jones, "Ælfric and the Limits of 'Benedictine Reform,'" in *Companion to Ælfric*, ed. Magennis and Swan, 67–108; Robert K. Upchurch, "Shepherding the Shepherds in the Ways of Pastoral Care: Ælfric and Cambridge University Library, MS Gg.3.28," in *Saints and Scholars: New Perspectives on Anglo-Saxon Literature and Culture in Honour of Hugh Magennis*, ed. Stuart McWilliams (Cambridge, 2012), 54–74; and Mary Swan, "Identity and Ideology in Ælfric's Prefaces" in *Companion to Ælfric*, 247–69.

status of English-language texts in the late Anglo-Saxon period in conversation with the Latin texts that would have been most prized by the Anglo-Saxon monks who wrote them.

The first chapter begins with the only existing manuscript of the *Enchiridion* in order to dismantle many assumptions about its layout and the relationship of languages within the text. Except for those with immediate access to Ashmole 328, the single surviving manuscript, most scholars experience the *Enchiridion* only as mediated by Baker and Lapidge's edition. While that edition is an incredible piece of scholarship on an extraordinarily complicated text, it tends to mislead readers about the layout of the current manuscript and the relationship of Latin and English within it. For instance, Baker and Lapidge present a fully rubricated text, even though the manuscript includes only twenty-eight rubrics, most of which exist in three discrete stints of rubrication. Coloured capitals alone subdivide the remainder of the manuscript. This lack of rubrication and relatively infrequent division of the manuscript suggest that it could not be employed as a reference work to be used in conjunction with a computus in the way that Baker envisions, since it would be difficult to coordinate specific parts of the *Enchiridion* with the computistical material that the book was meant to expound. Furthermore, the text could not be read by a monolingual reader who skipped either the Latin or the English sections, since these portions in each language are not completely interchangeable, nor are language shifts clearly marked. Finally, despite Byrhtferth's protestation that monks can understand very complicated concepts when presented in Latin, the work as a whole belies this premise, since the main language of the *Enchiridion* is English and the majority of the educational and computistical material within its pages is written in English for an audience of Benedictine monks.

The second chapter delves deeper into the complicated language dynamics of the Benedictine Reform as seen in Byrhtferth's famous attacks against the idleness of the secular clerics. Given his frequent comments on the inadequacy of the clerics' education, it seems incongruous that he admonishes them in an elevated style of Latin. This chapter examines in close detail the disjuncture between the stated audience of these harangues, the secular clergy, and the audience implied by their difficulty, monks. Since this inflated style is the prestige dialect of Benedictines, and the monks were the only audience educated enough to read these attacks against the clerics, these portions should be read as epideictic rhetoric, the literature of praise and blame. In these passages, the clerics function not as real students in Byrhtferth's classroom, but as negative exempla of what a good monk ought not to be. The high register of Latin is integral to the form of epideictic rhetoric and codes the material, since an ability to read these very stylized harangues proves that the reader is not subject to their criticism. Thus, this elevated Latin style encodes monastic identity in its emphasis on education as a special feature of monastic life and its exclusion of those without the discipline to master both the rigours of the Benedictine rule and hermeneutic Latin. This chapter accordingly begins to question whether the frequent naming and abuse of the secular clergy may have had motivations beyond Byrhtferth's actual classroom experience, motivations that relate to the language policies of the reform. In the context of the reform, the reference to the secular clergy – not the monastic clergy – had important political connotations, since the secular clerics were the group against whom the monks defined themselves. For Byrhtferth, the naming of a clerical audience authorizes him to translate into English a text that monks should have been able to read in Latin, and thus to provide for his monastic students an English-language text, while claiming that his audience was the all-too-ignorant secular clergy.

The third chapter reconsiders Byrhtferth's statements on the use and utility of English in light of my argument that English was intended to instruct his monastic students in computus, a subject also connected to the self-definition of Benedictine monks. While the study of computus and the correct calculation of Easter have been integral to orthodoxy and proper worship ever since the time of Bede, the Benedictine obsession with computus seems to extend beyond practical considerations of Easter and Lent, since many computistical collections do not even contain current calculations for these feasts. When the *Enchiridion* is considered in the context of other contemporaneous computistical collections also connected to Benedictine centres, it is clear that a Benedictine concern with computus is often connected to a study of hermeneutic Latin vocabulary, suggesting that the study of the more esoteric aspects of computus was yet another facet of monastic self-definition, in a similar manner to their study and acquisition of esoteric Latin vocabulary. The Legend of Pachomius recorded in the *Enchiridion* and in many other computistical texts encodes this connection between monasticism and the study of computus, since this monastic saint receives the correct calculation of Easter from an angelic visitor, as an indication of divine favour for the monastic study of computus. As this legend appears in Byrhtferth's work, however, it is recorded in English and connected to a vernacular translation of a passage from Aldhelm, the inspiration for the tenth-century revival of the hermeneutic style in Latin. In the legend and the Aldhelmian preamble, Byrhtferth explores the relationship between monastic identity, translation, hermeneutic vocabulary, and the study of computus in the vernacular.

Chapter 4 shifts the focus from Byrhtferth to the English writings of Ælfric, who wrote many prefaces in which he explains his translation techniques, his position as an author, and the proper use of the vernacular. Many scholars have already pointed out places where Ælfric does not follow through with goals stated in his prefaces.[110] Rather than reading these works as a program that he failed to follow, this chapter will read these short meditations on language and translation as a constructed position that represents Ælfric's own language politics. Although Ælfric and Byrhtferth differ greatly in their writing styles and choices, their construction of the role and purpose of the vernacular is strikingly similar, especially in their emphasis on English as a language for a non-monastic audience. At these points of intersection between the language politics of two very different authors, a coherent theory of language can be detected, a theory deeply rooted in the reformers' attempts to define, codify, and restrict monasticism to an elite few.

In spite of the impression given by Byrhtferth's work, hermeneutic Latin was not without its detractors. Although Ælfric was a reformed monk educated at the important monastic centre at Winchester, he refused to compose in the hermeneutic style, a choice at odds with his monastic connections. Christopher A. Jones has attempted to explain the disjuncture between Ælfric's writing style and his monastic connections by attributing his simple Latin style to an inadequate education in his youth. According to Jones, Ælfric avoided the hermeneutic style, because he did not feel confident composing such difficult Latin. However, it is hard to believe that a writer as well read as Ælfric was – he wrote the first English-language explanation of Latin grammar – could feel insecure about his Latin ability. The final chapter re-examines Jones's thesis by analysing Ælfric's abbreviation of Wulfstan of Winchester's *Vita S. Æthelwoldi*, a hermeneutic life of the reformed bishop of Winchester. Ælfric shortened this life in an eccentric manner in which he excised the hermeneutic tendencies of Wulfstan's text and copied out the simple text that remained. However, Ælfric changed many words that were neither hermeneutic nor rare. His

110 As an example, Robert Stanton discussed Ælfric's continually broken promises to stop translating. *The Culture of Translation in Anglo-Saxon England* (Cambridge, 2002), 101–71.

changes in these instances show that Ælfric had particular concerns about language, specifically that it presents a univalent and unambiguous text. These concerns are paralleled in his English-language writings. In short, Ælfric attempted to apply the same standards of English-language composition (e.g., Winchester vocabulary) to his Latin texts. Therefore, Ælfric's decision to avoid hermeneutic Latin should not necessarily indicate any distance from the reform movement, since he probably created this abbreviation as a preliminary step to English-language translation.

Studying Byrhtferth and Ælfric together in this way allows a simultaneous exploration of the most prolific English-language author of the period, Ælfric, alongside the most prolific Latin-language author, Byrhtferth. The examination of these two authors and two styles of writing in a single monograph will facilitate a closer investigation of the literary production of the late Anglo-Saxon period by contextualizing vernacular literature in light of contemporary Latin-language production. The late tenth and early eleventh century, the time frame in which the monastic reform occurred, was by far the most productive Anglo-Saxon period for vernacular writing. During this roughly fifty-year period, the vast majority of the extant canon was written. The reasons behind this literary explosion have not yet been accounted for by modern scholars of Anglo-Saxon England. By investigating Ælfric and Byrhtferth, then, this book provides insight into the material conditions that led to the flowering of vernacular literature during and after the monastic reform.

PART ONE

1 Pedagogy of the *Enchiridion*: Layout and Languages

Byrhtferth's *Enchiridion* (written between 1010 and 1012) provides a provocative specimen for studying latent attitudes about language in reformed circles, since it is a bilingual document that provides insight into both the explicit and implicit indoctrination of monks.[1] The *Enchiridion* is not ostensibly a book about language, however. It is instead a bilingual commentary on computus, which is the medieval system of reckoning movable feasts such as Easter.[2] Byrhtferth presumably composed it for the school at Ramsey where he was schoolmaster, and this text may have been a pedagogical tool used as a supplement to Byrhtferth's classroom instruction for either the teacher or the students. As a document that records monastic classroom practices, the *Enchiridion* is an invaluable resource that reveals the formation of Anglo-Saxon monks as multilingual readers and speakers.

1 The standard edition of the *Enchiridion* is Peter S. Baker and Michael Lapidge, eds, *Byrhtferth's Enchiridion*, EETS, s.s., 15 (Oxford, 1995); hereafter Baker and Lapidge's editorial material will be cited as B&L, in order to differentiate it from the text of the *Enchiridion*, which will be cited in the text as *BE*. All translations are my own unless otherwise noted.

2 A brief English introduction to the subject of computus can be found in Beate Günzel, ed., *Ælfwine's Prayerbook: London, British Library, Cotton Titus D. XXVI + XXVII*, Henry Bradshaw Society 108 (London, 1993), 16–30; and Faith Wallis, trans., *Bede: The Reckoning of Time*, Translated Texts for Historians 29 (Liverpool, 1999), xviii–lxiii. An overview of computistical texts in Anglo-Saxon England is available in Stephanie Hollis, "Scientific and Medical Writings," in *A Companion to Anglo-Saxon Literature*, ed. P. Pulsiano and E. Treharne, Blackwell Companions to Literature and Culture 11 (Oxford, 2001), 188–208, at 188–94.

Although the *Enchiridion* could have been used as rudimentary lecture notes for a teacher who was about to embark on computistical esoterica, a classroom setting is not the only possible context for this textbook. Peter Baker suggests that it could have been used in private study to explicate Byrhtferth's own computistical treatise by offering supplementary instruction and English translations for a student who sat with both books open to the corresponding pages.[3] Throughout the *Enchiridion*, however, Byrhtferth did not adhere slavishly to the material in his earlier computistical treatise. Rather, he frequently wandered from this text in order to explain other subjects, including Latin figures of speech and the spiritual meaning of numbers. Partially as a result of Byrhtferth's laxity in adhering to the text of his computus, portions of the *Enchiridion* can be read as a discrete work, especially book 3, which makes no reference to Byrhtferth's earlier computus.[4] In fact, although significant portions of books 1 and 2 offer running commentary on the prior computistical treatise, this information is never cross-referenced to another volume, nor is the reader offered directions to look up material in another work. On the contrary, the *Enchiridion* offers clear prose transitions between sections, allowing a reader without a computus to hand to experience this text as a volume that is complete in itself and that does not require supplementation. The *Enchiridion*, then, has many potential ways in which it could function, either as a reference book to be consulted in private study with a computus, as an independent volume read independently, or as a kind of classroom notebook read by a teacher preparing to teach computistical topics to students.

It is difficult to know which of these three possible scenarios was more common or more plausible, since there is precious little evidence for the circulation of the *Enchiridion*.[5] Furthermore, although this work has been

3 That the *Enchiridion* is a commentary on a computus was first argued by Heinrich Henel in *Studien zum altenglischen Computus*, Beiträge zur englischen Philologie 26 (Leipzig, 1934). Peter S. Baker has since identified the text most closely related to Byrhtferth's computus; see "Byrhtferth's *Enchiridion* and the Computus in Oxford, St John's College 17," *ASE* 10 (1982): 123–42. A reconstructed version of Byrhtferth's computus is now available as the appendix to B&L, 373–427. Faith Wallis has made this manuscript available online, at *The Calendar and the Cloister: Oxford, St John's College MS17*, McGill University Library, Digital Collections Program (2007), http://digital.library.mcgill.ca/ms-17. For a discussion of the relationship between the *Enchiridion* and Byrhtferth's computus, see B&L, xxv–xxvi.

4 Baker, "Byrhtferth's *Enchiridion* and the Computus," 138.

5 For full details on manuscript circulation, see below, pp. 42–3.

called a "commentary" or a "computistical text," it defies typical generic conventions, since in addition to its computistical material, it also includes a wide range of other information useful to the education of ecclesiasts including metrics, grammar, and numerology. Even the word "bilingual" when applied to this text requires much meaningful discussion, since in this case it means that two languages are present, not that the text is identical in both languages, as the modern usage of bilingual would imply. The first two sections (1.1 and 1.2) of the *Enchiridion* present instructional material on computus with a Latin text that is immediately translated into English, just as modern readers would expect in a text denoted as "bilingual." This format may have been the intended structure for the manual, but as the *Enchiridion* continues, the regular alternation of English and Latin breaks down. For instance, section 1.4 opens with a Latin paragraph chastising the laziness of clerics, but this Latin preface is not translated into English; instead, the subsequent English text has no relationship to the preceding Latin passage.[6] Later sections sometimes contain only one language, such as section 2.1, which is only in English, or section 4.1, in which Latin appears without an English translation. Even in portions where the Latin and English texts are the most similar (i.e., sections 1.1 and 1.2), Byrhtferth refused to translate certain topics into English, claiming that it would have been too tedious to translate for the sake of his clerical students who had no Latin. This specific treatment of audience and the idiosyncratic nature of the material included in the *Enchiridion* makes this text perhaps more representative of Anglo-Saxon classroom practices and attitudes than texts that are more regularized for classroom use, such as (say) the colloquies of Ælfric Bata or the pedagogical works of Ælfric of Eynsham.[7]

6 For a discussion of this passage, see chap. 2, pp. 89–91.

7 For an edition of Ælfric Bata's colloquies, see Scott Gwara, ed., and David W. Porter, trans., *Anglo-Saxon Conversations: The Colloquies of Ælfric Bata* (Woodbridge, 1997). Ælfric's of Eynsham's pedagogical work is described by Joyce Hill in "Ælfric's Grammatical Triad," in *Form and Content of Instruction in Anglo-Saxon England in the light of Contemporary Manuscript Evidence*, ed. Patrizia Lendinara, Loredana Lazzari, and Maria Amalia D'Aronco, Fédération Internationale des Instituts d'Études Medièvales, Textes et Études du Moyen Age 39 (Turnhout, 2007), 285–307. Ælfric's grammar is edited by J. Zupitza, *Ælfrics Grammatik und Glossar: Text und Varienten.* Sammlung englischer Denkmäler in kritischen Ausgaben 1 (Berlin, 1880; repr. with intro. by Helmut Gneuss, Hildesheim, 2001).

For these reasons, then, Byrhtferth's *Enchiridion* stands at the crossroads between the reformers' language policies in Latin and English and their formation of the Benedictine identities of novices in a monastic classroom. This intersection makes this text crucially important for studying the hierarchies of language in late Anglo-Saxon England, since the *Enchiridion* includes both the simple English and the stylized Latin forms preferred by reformers. But while these two styles exist separately in most other texts from the period, in the *Enchiridion* they stand together, sometimes even with a single paragraph beginning in one language and ending in another. Not only does this text have an interesting mixture of languages, no other text from the period has quite the same range of registers in each language, since it contains not just the hermeneutic style of Latin connected to memorial occasions, but also simpler forms of Latin that are more useful to the pedagogical circumstances of Byrhtferth's classroom in Ramsey. Equally, the text has passages of English that have been called "hermeneutic," a style avoided by most other reformers when writing in English. In addition to these stylistic issues, Byrhtferth addresses his audience(s) quite specifically at several points throughout the text.[8] The extreme stylistic range and specific attention to imagined audiences makes the *Enchiridion* a fertile field for studying the language politics that underscore the ideology of the Benedictine Reform. In addition to these important social issues, the idiosyncratic nature of the text and its equally bizarre single-surviving manuscript offers an important witness to the experience of the multilingual reader in late Anglo-Saxon England.

The Manuscript of the *Enchiridion*

When a bilingual Anglo-Saxon reader encountered the unique manuscript of the *Enchiridion* (Oxford, Ashmole 328; hereafter A), he or she would have confronted a text with a layout that is unusual both linguistically, in its combination of languages and registers, and visually, in its many diagrams. Whether the *mise en page* was Byrhtferth's intention is nearly impossible to determine because the complete text exists in only one manuscript, which was certainly neither written nor formatted by Byrhtferth's own

8 The presence of these direct addresses of audience once caused René Derolez to call for a study of the relationship between register/language and audience. "Those Things Are Difficult to Express in English ...," *English Studies* 70 (1989), 469–76, at 475. For further discussion of this question, see chap. 2, pp. 83–6.

hand. It is dated to the middle of the eleventh century (s. xi^{med}), and though its origin is unknown, Michael Lapidge and Peter Baker suggest that the most likely centre was Christ Church, Canterbury c. 1050, a scriptorium far from Byrhtferth's monastic classroom in Ramsey and its strong connections to Worcester.[9] The faulty text of the *Enchiridion* can only be corroborated by two other manuscripts: Cambridge, Corpus Christi College 421 (C) and Cambridge University Library, Kk. 5.32 (K). Both of these manuscripts, however, contain only small portions of the *Enchiridion*. K includes only fifty-seven lines of text in the Baker and Lapidge edition running from to 3.3.257–313. The material included in this section is not representative of the rest of the *Enchiridion*, since it does not consist of Easter calculations or diagrams, but of weights and measures and other miscellaneous material. Furthermore, since K seems to have been copied from A, it does not provide independent evidence of a prior manuscript.[10] The other manuscript, C, predates A and is therefore an independent witness to a no-longer-extant exemplar, but C contains only a very minor segment of A, two homilies that have been adapted from book 4 and the "Postscript," also called the "Ammonitio Amici."[11] Just as with K, this homiletic material does not include the mathematical equations or diagrams for which Byrhtferth is famous.

For the vast majority of the *Enchiridion*, therefore, the current editors, Baker and Lapidge, had no other manuscript with which to compare the mistakes of A, a work indisputably riddled with error. As a consequence, Baker and Lapidge strove to "restore authorial readings wherever possible," because "a conservative editor who chose to follow the text of A through thick and thin would provide for students of Anglo-Saxon texts an amusing specimen of scribal ineptitude, but would do little service either to B[yrhtferth] or to the subjects he wrote about."[12] This strong editorial position helps to create a text that is much more coherent than that of the manuscript, but it does not engage with the multilingual layout either of Byrhtferth's inaccessible original or of the manuscript, which represents at least one reader's engagement with this bilingual text. Furthermore, the

9 B&L, cxx.

10 B&L, cxxi–cxxii.

11 B&L, cxxii–cxiv. When these homilies from the *Enchiridion* were added to the Wulfstanian homily collection they were adapted to its format, most notably changing singular addresses of the audience to plural addresses.

12 B&L, cxxiv–cxxv.

layout and format of the text could have been influenced by its creation in Canterbury or another centre likely to have slightly different circumstances than those of Byrhtferth's monastic classroom. Whatever the particulars of its production are, the manuscript can be studied only as one scribe's response to the task of copying the *Enchiridion* rather than an intentional design created by Byrhtferth.

Unfortunately, the one scribe who offers us a dim view of the document designed by Byrhtferth has often been maligned as a careless copyist who knew little and cared less about computus.[13] He clearly bungled many equations, especially in the Latin calculations.[14] For instance, in the midst of a rather simple multiplication by sevens, the scribe became confused enough that he did not notice that the quires were out of order, a mistake repeated by S.J. Crawford in his edition.[15] This mistake indicates that the scribe was not carefully construing sense while copying even relatively basic mathematical formulae. Such mistakes are more understandable in Latin, where one can assume he was mindlessly copying, but it is less forgivable in English, where he also made rather simple mathematical errors. In addition, many of the diagrams are clearly not complete, and even some finished specimens have information in the wrong spaces.[16] Because of

13 Baker and Lapidge offer many examples of this criticism, such as: "Since there is abundant evidence throughout [the] E[nchiridion] of careless, at times mindless, copying by the scribe of A, there is no reason to think that the errors in A originate elsewhere." B&L, cxxii. Such careless and mindless copying is common in computistical manuscripts; cf. the similar comments on the scribe of Cotton Tiberius B.v: "Computistical matter does not inspire, and even a professional scribe might nod over the copying of the text concerning a septuagesimal moon. It is true that many computistical compilations are rambling and carelessly written. Tiberius is particularly careless and sometimes clearly uncomprehending as the following selection of errors shows ..." P. McGurk, "The Computus," in *An Eleventh Century Anglo-Saxon Miscellany*, Early English Manuscripts in Facsimile 21 (Copenhagen, 1983), 53.

14 Such mistakes in calculations are common in computistical manuscripts; cf. the discussion of the computus in Cotton Tiberius B.v in McGurk, "Computus," 53–4.

15 *Byrhtferth's Manual*, EETS, o.s., 177 (London, 1929). The misplaced quire occurs in A at p. 26. The B&L edition has the text in its proper order at p. 28. Despite the deficiencies of the Crawford edition, it is useful since it includes plates of most of the diagrams. Also, after the scribe copied the quires out of order, the unusual jump in material occurred in the middle of a gathering, not at the end of one, making the error harder to detect by Crawford, who was editing a page that suddenly took an unusual turn, a circumstance which is not entirely unprecedented for a medieval manuscript on computus.

16 E.g., p. 94 of A (*BE*, 86, fig. 15), which contains several mistakes, including the incorrect substitution of "aqua" for "terra" among things that are cold and dry, and vice versa among things that are cold and wet.

these relatively obvious mistakes and omissions, it is certain that the scribe has created something in A that does not represent the work of Byrhtferth in some significant ways.

Yet, at the same time, Byrhtferth was not the most reliable of authors, and perhaps not all the mistakes that have been dismissed as scribal should be ignored so readily. Byrhtferth is known in particular for his grammatical irregularities. Baker and Lapidge allowed to stand many Old English grammatical phrasings that Crawford had expunged in the interest of standardization, because these later editors claimed that they did not know enough about Byrhtferth's usage to be sure that these were scribal errors and not Byrhtferth's idiolect.[17] While we can know that Byrhtferth's *Enchiridion* as it exists in A is not exclusively the work of a single author living in Ramsey, it is more difficult to separate with certainty what is scribal from what is authorial. The *Enchiridion* presents a text with very important visual components in the diagrams, the formatting, and the bilingual layout, and therefore the *mise en page* cannot be separated from the body of the text in an examination of the reading experience of this manuscript. Even the diagrams for which Byrhtferth is so famous have been copied, and in many cases altered, by this scribe, which again has blurred the lines between what is scribal and authorial. Equally, paratextual material such as book divisions, rubrications, and glosses have certainly been both deleted and added by this scribe, and it is difficult to separate out Byrhtferth's own hand from that of the scribe in the abrupt beginnings and endings of stints of glossing and rubrication.[18] As a result of these factors, the only surviving manuscript of the *Enchiridion* exists as the unhappy collaboration of Byrhtferth's unrecoverable authorial intent and the layout and design work of a later scribe, who was a rather negligent caretaker of Byrhtferth's creation.

---

17 B&L, cxxvi–cxxvii. In Latin, Byrhtferth's usage is considered a little unusual as well. He is known especially for using the passive infinitive form at times when the active infinitive would be more appropriate. Michael Lapidge, "Textual Criticism and the Literature of Anglo-Saxon England," *Bulletin of the John Rylands University Library of Manchester* 73 (1991): 33; Lapidge, "Byrhtferth and the *Vita S. Ecgwini*," in *Anglo-Latin Literature, 900–1066* (London, 1993), 298–9.

18 Although Baker and Lapidge tend to focus on what the scribe failed to copy, there are several rubrics that were almost certainly added to the manuscript, since they are slightly out of place, or in some cases completely wrong, and it is difficult to imagine them as authorial. E.g., p. 173 of A (*BE*, 156), on which the scribe has written "de LXX," even though this paragraph does not concern Septuagesima.

Such circumstances are not unusual for those working on medieval manuscripts. As James Zetzel's work on medieval scholia has emphasized, the role of the scribe cannot be ignored when examining glossed manuscripts, since the paratextual gloss is unstable and often added to or deleted at the discretion of its copyist.[19] Therefore, while the scribe of A is not an author in the same sense that Byrhtferth is, he does "exercise choice and judgment" in what he copies.[20] Furthermore, in the way that this scribe positions the text on the page, he plays an important role in shaping the manuscript experience that is available to both medieval and modern readers. While it is tempting for those engaged in the study of medieval computus to attempt to erase this scribal interference, acknowledging the role of the scribe in the creation of A is imperative to understanding the language interactions and anxieties that lie behind the multilingual reading experience of the *Enchiridion*. At the same time that A is the work of a single scribe, however, it is also a book that could potentially be read by many possible readers. Therefore, this discussion will now turn to the specific difficulties the current manuscript offered to a multilingual reader in late Anglo-Saxon England.

The Basic Layout and a "Grammar of Legibility"

There is no question that the formatting of the *Enchiridion* would present a reader with decided challenges, especially if that student intended to read this book either as a reference work or as a commentary on another computistical treatise, since the manuscript has few textual or visual markers that provide a "grammar of legibility" or direct readers to specific material.[21] Most importantly, the rubrics that figure so strongly in the Baker and Lapidge edition are not present throughout the majority of the manuscript.[22] Paragraphs are set off on new lines with red or green capitals in the

19 James E.G. Zetzel, *Marginal Scholarship and Textual Deviance: The Commentum Cornuti and the Early Scholia on Persius*, Bulletin of the Institute of Classical Studies Supplement 84 (London, 2005), 144–8.

20 Ibid., 147.

21 The phrase "grammar of legibility" was coined by M.B. Parkes to describe the hierarchy of scripts in seventh- to ninth-century Irish and Anglo-Saxon manuscripts. "The Contribution of Insular Scribes of the Seventh and Eighth Centuries to the 'Grammar of Legibility,'" in *Scribes, Scripts, and Readers: Studies in the Communication and Dissemination of Medieval Texts* (London, 1991), 1–18.

22 The rubrication will be discussed in greater detail below, pp. 55–66.

margins. Some of these paragraph breaks mark a transition in language from Latin to the vernacular, while others simply mark a change in topic. In most cases, therefore, attempts to decipher beginnings or endings must be done with the help of relatively small coloured capitals, and not with rubrics or more prominent visual markings. Although at certain points in the manuscript there are stints of interlinear glossing, and a few sustained stints of rubrication, there is little marginal glossing and, on the whole, there are few other textual pointers that mark specific parts of the manuscript or particular formulae necessary for the calendrical calculations instructed by the *Enchiridion.*

In place of rubrication or other divisions, the endlessly flowing lines of text are broken up by the diagrams for which Byrhtferth is famous. Even these, however, would not necessarily be useful in directing a reader to particular parts of the text, since they are often placed in odd positions far from the relevant textual material and seldom have rubrics that explain or interpret them. Many diagrams have instructions embedded within the long lines of text, but some are not explained at all. Take, for instance, the diagram on p. 18 of A, which shows the correspondence between Roman and decennoval (or Dionysian) cycles.[23] On the manuscript page, this diagram has no headings but consists of two simple rectangular boxes, one down each side of the page filled with a column of Roman numerals. The Roman cycle (*circulus Romanorum*) was an alternative method for reconciling the discrepancy created by the variation in length between the lunar year (354 days) and the solar year (365¼ days). With the addition of an extra lunar month in seven of the years, the lunar and solar cycles repeated every nineteen years in both the Roman and decennoval cycles. Byrhtferth's chart is meant to illuminate the chief difference between the two cycles, namely, that the Roman cycle begins on year four of the decennoval cycle. Baker and Lapidge claim that the copying of this cycle "is indicative of the conservatism of medieval computists," since it "continued to be copied into computi even though it had no practical use. It was, simply, a decennoval cycle similar to the Dionysian cycle used by Bede and B[yrhtferth], but beginning in year four of the Dionysian cycle and ending in year

23 The diagram and its accompanying text is on *BE*, 20. A plate can be found in Crawford's edition. It should be noted that the manuscript of the *Enchiridion* is referred to by a scheme of continuous pagination, not by folio numbers. When referring to specific pages in the manuscript, I will denote these as A + a page number, as in A 205, so as to distinguish these numbers from page numbers in Baker and Lapidge's edition.

three."[24] As Baker and Lapidge point out, there is no conceivable reason that a medieval monk would need this diagram to reconcile these two cycles, since the Roman cycle would never be used in an Anglo-Saxon monastery.

Even if such information were useful, this diagram is almost completely unreadable. The numbers on the left are meant to represent the Roman cycle and begin with seventeen and continue to nineteen before restarting to end at sixteen. In theory, a reader should be able to easily compare these numbers with the decennoval series on the right, which runs in sequence from one to nineteen. In the left column, however, the roman numeral "i" was omitted when the numbers restarted on the left side, and thus the numbers cannot be lined up across the page.[25] Furthermore, since the columns run down opposite sides of the same page interrupted by unrelated lines of text, and there is no rubric offering instructions, it would be physically difficult to line up the two columns in order to find the lunar year in any given decennoval cycle even if all the requisite numbers were present. The diagram would have been far more useful if the two columns were positioned immediately adjacent to one another with a label or rubric explaining the purpose of this tool – that is, assuming such information ever could have been useful.

The instructions included in the lines of the Latin text explain the diagram by stating, "Lunaris annus <primus> incipit decennouenali quarto, et decennouelnalis annus primus incipit lunari .xvii., ueluti luce clara demonstrant margines huius paginule" (*BE*, 20) [The first year of the lunar cycle begins on the fourth year of the decennoval cycle, and the first decennoval year begins on the seventeenth year of the lunar cycle, just as the margin of this little page demonstrates with a clear light]. While these instructions embedded within the Latin passage are fairly clear, the diagram does not enclose these words, but instead encloses the English text that summarizes other earlier Latin material. The equivalent English passage is not an exact translation, and it never mentions the diagram in the margins. Instead, the English text merely explains, "Se circul ongynð on þam feorðan geare decennouenali and geendað on þam þriddan" (*BE*, 20) [The cycle begins in the fourth year of the decennoval cycle and ends in its third]. None of this information, however, is immediately relevant to the diagram at hand, since this English explanation appears on p. 19 of the manuscript, one page after the chart. In short, the diagram included no

24 B&L, 260.

25 This is a problem for many of the diagrams.

explanatory rubrics whatsoever, just two defective lists of Roman numerals down each side of the page. The instructions for the diagram were on the previous page (but not distinguished by rubrics or other textual pointers), and the English material that concerns it will not occur again until the following page. Thus, this diagram exists both out of context and out of place.

It is not the only diagram to exist in such limbo. The table of concurrents is misplaced and in its current position lacks instructions or explanatory rubrics.[26] In the Baker and Lapidge edition, the editors explain their repositioning and reformatting of this chart with the following comments: "The table of concurrents is actually found not here, in A p. 23, but on the facing page, 22, where it is arranged in a single column in the left margin. Since it belongs with the discussion of concurrents ([lines] 43–134), however, we have reproduced it at this place in the text."[27] In addition to moving the chart to a more appropriate position, Baker and Lapidge also reformatted the chart so that rather than running in a single column down the leftmost margin, it was listed in a horizontal format (4 rows and 7 columns) across the top of a section division. This horizontal arrangement of the concurrents is common in computistical texts from the period, and would have been much easier to place on the page in the appropriate position, but the scribe apparently did not know he could reformat the text in this way. The original chart in Oxford, St John's College 17 (the manuscript which may most closely represent the form of Byrhtferth's original computus) is also presented in a vertical (and not horizontal) format, and the vertical format here works against the usability of this diagram. Therefore, it is likely that the scribe merely copied out the layout of Byrhtferth's original, which was aligned vertically. The misplacement of the diagram in A may have had practical considerations for the scribe, because the other side of the page had been ruled for a similarly sized chart. While these two charts are not identical in form, since on the previous page, two charts with more elaborate outlines filled this space instead of one, the similarity

26 Just as the decennoval cycle reconciled the solar and lunar years, the concurrents relate the solar year to the days of the week, since the 365¼ days of the solar year exceed the total days of fifty-two weeks by 1¼ days (as in 52 × 7 = 364). Consequently, the same date in the following year will occur on the following day of the week, until the leap year, when it will occur two days later. A full cycle of concurrents occurs every twenty-eight years, since 7 (days of the week) × 4 (leap years) = 28.

27 B&L, 263.

in width may have encouraged the placement on this page instead of the more appropriate page that followed. Just as in the previous example, the strange placement and misalignment of this diagram interferes with the readability both of the diagram and of the text as a whole.

In summation, the diagrams, which offer a visual cue that could link the reader to specific points of computistical material potentially of interest, are so often misplaced that they cannot serve as effective textual pointers that direct readers to specific parts of this manuscript. The lack of particular textual cues in the current manuscript works against its pedagogical purpose,[28] assuming it was intended, as Baker claimed, as a kind of commentary on Byrhtferth's own computus with both books open simultaneously to the same page.[29] Such visual and textual cues that allow the reader to reference specific material easily would be particularly important in the *Enchiridion*, because the contents of this manuscript do not follow the same order as those of J, which Baker argues is a copy of Byrhtferth's original computus.[30]

Furthermore, in addition to these formatting problems, the scribe of A did not aid the reader in finding Latin or English sections by distinguishing between the languages through different scripts, as was common among many late Anglo-Saxon monastic manuscripts. The fact that the languages are not differentiated by script is somewhat obscured for those scholars who have not physically held A in their hands, since Baker and Lapidge's description of the manuscript is misleading on this point. They write: "Ashmole 328 was written by one scribe writing, for the Latin text of [the] E[nchiridion], a late style of Anglo-Caroline miniscule (Dumville's Style IV) and, for the Old English text, Anglo-Saxon set miniscule."[31] While this statement is not unequivocally false, since the scribe did at times use Anglo-Caroline for the Latin text, the *Enchiridion* was not formatted consistently like many other late-tenth-century manuscripts with

---

28 The issue of the missing rubrics of the manuscript will be dealt with below, pp. 55–66.

29 Baker, "Byrhtferth's *Enchiridion* and the Computus," 124.

30 Ibid., 123–42. The relationships are laid out again in B&L, liii–lv, though the authors caution: "The presence of matter manifestly composed after B[yrhtferth]'s death (41^{v}–58^{r}) warns us that J cannot be considered an exact copy of the collection assembled by him" (lv). Faith Wallis expresses scepticism that all the material in this manuscript can be attributed to a single predecessor compiled by Byrhtferth of Ramsey. "Background Essay: St John's College 17 as a Computus Manuscript," in *The Calendar and the Cloister: Oxford, St. John's College MS17* (Montreal, 2007), http://digital.library.mcgill.ca/ms-17.

31 B&L, cxv.

a clearly delineated difference between Latin and English sections based on a rigorous segregation of script, such as Cotton Tiberius A.iii, which employs Anglo-Caroline for the Latin text of the manuscript and Anglo-Saxon set minuscule for the interlinear gloss and for the exclusively English sections of the manuscript. On the contrary, the *Enchiridion* is written in "a characteristically eleventh-century form of Anglo-Saxon miniscule"[32] for both English and Latin text for the first 205 pages.[33] The next thirty-eight pages consist of Latin text in Anglo-Caroline. When the text returns to a bilingual arrangement on A 244, the scribe alternates between Old English set minuscule for the English text and Anglo-Caroline for the Latin. It seems strange that a scribe familiar with Anglo-Caroline and accustomed to using it for a Latin script would copy this manuscript in such a haphazard way using an English script for Latin but later carefully differentiating languages based on script. This quirk seems particularly unusual since Dumville argues that the history of Anglo-Caroline script is strongly connected to monastic centres, and thus the tendency to differentiate between languages through script is closely connected to monastic identity.[34] Baker and Lapidge explain this discrepancy between the script and language by asserting that the first part of the Enchiridion is "predominantly vernacular" and the final part is "predominantly in Latin."[35]

While ultimately I agree with Baker and Lapidge's assessment about the predominance of these two languages in the *Enchiridion*, I do not think that this reasoning necessarily explains the issues of script at this point. A mistake in the manuscript at A 35 suggests that in the exemplar some Latin sections were written in Anglo-Caroline, since the scribe has written "derci" when the correct word is "clerici." In Anglo-Caroline, a "cl" could easily be mistaken for a "d," but cannot be in Insular minuscule, since the back of the "d" is at an approximately forty-five degree angle to its circle in this vernacular script. Furthermore, in the Byrhtferthian homilies in C, the Latin words embedded in the Old English text are written in Anglo-Caroline, although Insular minuscule is used for the English text. These two facts taken together and added to the sudden appearance of the bilingual alternation of script in book 4 suggest that Byrhtferth's original

32 B&L, cxvi.

33 This number refers to manuscript pages.

34 David Dumville, *English Caroline Script and Monastic History: Studies in Benedictinism, A.D. 950–1030*, Studies in Anglo-Saxon History 6 (Woodbridge, 1993).

35 B&L, cxvi.

probably differentiated between Latin and English through script, as would have been common for other early-eleventh-century manuscripts, though the scribe failed to copy this aspect of the manuscript's layout.

The lack of script differentiation could imply that this scribe was more at home in Insular minuscule rather than in Anglo-Caroline, which Bishop describes as "the most difficult of scripts." He continues: "Caroline minuscule is peculiarly unsuitable for calligraphic treatment by common scribes like those whose heavy strokes, bad proportions, mannerisms, and perverse forms appear in many English MSS. from the middle and second half of the eleventh century."[36] The Insular minuscule of this scribe belies these conclusions, however, since the form of his "h" is influenced by his prior training in Anglo-Caroline.[37] Furthermore, neither a preference for Insular minuscule nor the prevalence of the vernacular would necessarily explain the choice of script in the *Enchiridion*, since both explanations presuppose or imply that the text begins in English with Insular minuscule, and after this vernacular opening, the transition to Latin was not marked by a change in script. On the contrary, the work begins in Latin, and the evidence suggests that these words were written in Anglo-Caroline in Byrhtferth's original. A scribe who sat down to copy the *Enchiridion* and flipped through the first book would have seen a Latin text intermixed with shorter English translations, particularly in the first two bilingual sections (1.1 and 1.2). It is only much further into the manuscript, sometime after the start of 1.3, that the volume of English text noticeably outstrips that of Latin.

Even though I have argued elsewhere that English is the dominant language of most portions of the *Enchiridion*,[38] excepting sections 4.1 and (possibly) 4.2, the manuscript does not give this impression at first glance. The very earliest sections of the *Enchiridion* privilege the Latin language both textually and visually. The first page has sixteen lines of Latin compared with four lines of English, even though this section is often described as bilingual. The following two pages of text show similar ratios. The second page of text has twelve lines of Latin and eight lines of English. The third page has 11.5 lines of Latin and 8.5 lines of English. In sum, the

36 T.A.M. Bishop, *English Caroline Minuscule*, Oxford Paleographical Handbooks (Oxford, 1971), xxiii.

37 B&L, cxvi.

38 "Byrhtferth's Enchiridion: The Effectiveness of Hermeneutic Latin," in *Conceptualizing Multilingualism in England, 800–1250*, ed. Elizabeth Tyler, Studies in the Early Middle Ages (Turnhout, 2011), 121–44.

first three pages of the *Enchiridion* have sixty lines of text, of which the 39.5 lines of Latin dwarf the 20.5 lines of English. In the first three pages of copying the manuscript, when the scribe was establishing the form that the rest of the text would follow, the scribe had written only 20.5 lines of English. And it is therefore difficult to see how he could have decided that English was the more important language in this text at this early point. In fact, the dominance of the Latin text continues through the end of p. 20, with Latin still slightly outpacing English, 203.5 lines to 189.5, respectively, as the two languages continue to alternate in a bilingual format.[39]

The complicated relationship between Latin and English goes beyond the physical layout on the page and can be seen in the opening lines of the *Enchiridion*, "Incipit compotus Latinorum ac Grecorum Hebreorumque et Egiptiorum, necnon et Anglorum" (*BE*, 2) [Here begins the computus of the Latins, the Greeks, the Hebrews, the Egyptians, and also the English]. By beginning the treatise in Latin and then listing this language first in a list of great languages/peoples, Byrhtferth asserts the traditional dominance of Latin.[40] And it comes as no surprise that when the manuscript is described as bilingual, readers probably assume that the text will begin in Latin followed by an English translation. Therefore, it follows that by listing the English people last, he suggests that the vernacular is inferior to the ancient languages of the great civilizations of the Romans, Greeks, Hebrews, and Egyptians. The inferiority of English is emphasized visually on the page even in this opening paragraph, since the vernacular section is greatly abbreviated, a fact that cannot be missed by even the least Latinate reader, since the English section is decidedly shorter. Elsewhere, however, I have argued that despite the fact that the English section has many fewer words, the relevant portions have been translated into English, and the sentences that were not translated add to the elevated register of the Latin style, though not to the content on the page.[41] This is an important conflict that keeps recurring throughout the *Enchiridion*: although the Latin language has higher prestige, the English language is

39 In order to reach these numbers, I counted two lines of text on A 8, which have been torn out, but were certainly Latin, and a full page of text (20 lines) on A 12[bis], on which only eight partial lines of Latin text are visible. According to the alternation of languages here, this missing text was almost certainly Latin. If these lines were not counted, the ratio of Latin to English would be even closer.

40 But note that this is a common formula to begin computistical treatises. Henel, *Studien*, 10–12.

41 "Byrhtferth's Enchiridion," 127–9.

more *useful*, and in some contexts, things that are more practical are also more valuable.

The English language presents a certain danger to Latin precisely in its utility, since a reader might skip the Latin, reading only the English, and thereby master material connected to a monastic classroom without also mastering the Latin language and specific styles appropriate to the discourse community.[42] In this circumstance, the English translation begins not just to complement the Latin original, but instead to supplement and even supplant it.[43] One could interpret the first line of the *Enchiridion* to allude to this process by which the English language could supplant Latin in the emphatic phrasing "necnon et Anglorum" [and yet even of the English]. Thus, by listing the English last, Byrhtferth implies that the language of the English people is capable of articulating the same computistical material previously available only in the great languages of Latin, Greek, Hebrew, and Egyptian. In this latter reading, the English language is more powerful than Latin, because it has subsumed the material of the Latin text, reinterpreted it, and thus superseded the original. Although allowing these two readings to stand next to each other and suggesting that English could be both inferior to and greater than Latin at the same time is perhaps the scholarly equivalent of having one's cake and eating it too, the vernacular did inhabit both of these positions in the conflict between the textual practices most clearly connected to the *Enchiridion* and the ideology that lingers throughout it.

The scribe's failure to distinguish between scripts for Latin and English may be related to the conflicted position of English both in the *Enchiridion* and in late Anglo-Saxon monastic culture. Although it is not clear why the scribe replaced the Anglo-Caroline that he – in all probability – saw on the opening page of the *Enchiridion* with Insular minuscule, since he clearly was capable and comfortable in both scripts, this change had important implications for the "grammar of legibility" and the hierarchy of languages throughout the *Enchiridion*. In using an English-language script for the Latin material, he subsumes and supplants the Latin text, in that the manuscript might appear to be "predominantly vernacular" to a multilingual reader who has read other bilingual books that divide languages by script.

42 Brian Stock, *The Implications of Literacy: Written Language and Models of Interpretation in the Eleventh and Twelfth Centuries* (Princeton, NJ, 1983).

43 For more on how these ideas are similar to those of Rita Copeland, see chap. 3, p. 118n39, and chap. 4, p. 183n100.

Yet at the same time, putting both languages into the same script undermines the utility of the English translations, since a reader could not easily flip to vernacular sections, but instead would have to labour to find the end of the Latin text, especially in the manuscript's current form, which lacks an effective scheme of rubrication. Although the response of the multilingual reader/scribe of A potentially indicates that he was so comfortable in both English and Latin that he did not feel compelled to distinguish between them, he created a manuscript that required a reader to be as skilled in both languages as he was. In addition, in its use of an English script, rather than a Latin one, the manuscript's utility is further limited, since this script would be most useful for a native English reader, not an imported French monk. And while that distinction may not have been politically powerful when the manuscript was produced, c. 1050, the vernacular script could have limited its later circulation since it would have appeared to a post-Conquest reader to be a heavily English manuscript. This issue of script may provide a partial explanation to the limited circulation of this copy of the *Enchiridion*. Whatever the status of the *Enchiridion* after the Conquest, it is certain that in its current form it presented decided challenges to an Anglo-Saxon multilingual reader who wished to reference specific material due to its lack of an effective "grammar of legibility" either in hierarchies of script or other textual pointers, like rubrication.

The Rubrication of the Enchiridion

The sporadic rubrication of the *Enchiridion*'s manuscript also reflects the conflicted relationship between Latin and English in Anglo-Saxon monastic culture. Those encountering this material in an edition will see a hierarchically ordered text broken up by clear Latin rubrics that number each book and section, just as should be expected from Latinate monks educated in Benedictine schoolrooms. Such clear and orderly divisions would allow quick consultation of specific sections and paragraphs, but as the previous section has explained, the *Enchiridion* is not laid out in such a user-friendly and easily referenced format. In the manuscript, there is no indication that any of the books or sections were numbered, other than the rubric which marks the third book. Furthermore, since the rubrics do not appear evenly throughout, the fact that the majority of them are in Latin but designate English-language text is much more visually arresting in the manuscript. The sporadic presence of these Latin rubrics for English sections suggests a very different language dynamic than that implied by the printed edition with its regular rubrication and numbering. Furthermore, the sudden appearance of the rubrics is often closely keyed to changing language dynamics and linguistic anxieties embedded in the text. Rubrics appear when the bilingual format is disrupted, and they also tend to appear in close proximity to the sections most disparaging of the secular clergy.[44] Although I do not claim that the current sporadic state of the rubrics is authorial, I do suggest that an investigation of their rather haphazard placement offers an interesting commentary on the linguistic anxieties that underpin the manuscript in its present form.

Rather than a fully rubricated text with book, chapter, section, and paragraph divisions clearly delineated, the current manuscript consistently indicates only paragraph divisions, which have been marked on new lines with coloured capitals in red and green, but without rubrics or titles in most cases. In addition, there are approximately twenty-eight rubrics scattered throughout the manuscript. If Byrhtferth's original were as fully rubricated as Baker and Lapidge conclude, very few of these have survived in the *Enchiridion*'s current form. The examination of rubrics in this text is important, because the Baker and Lapidge edition significantly misleads the reader not only about the number of rubrics, but also about their importance and usefulness in laying out a hierarchically ordered book, with sections subordinated to chapters, which in turn constitute parts of books. Aside from book 3, there are no rubrics that specifically mark the separation between books. Even in places where a stint of rubrication passes beyond the introduction of a new book, the ensuing rubric is not more prominent than any other and does not indicate any kind of division or subdivision. Also, when a string of rubrics appears, they do not begin at the inception of sections or books, where one might expect the beginning of a new formatting choice; rather, the beginning of successive stints of rubrication usually starts in the middle of sections or books, usually with the first paragraph or two (as indicated by Baker and Lapidge) unmarked. These continuous series of rubrics usually end just as abruptly as they begin.

Since the carelessness of this scribe is well documented throughout the *Enchiridion*, it is easy to attribute the loss of the majority of the rubrics to this scribe's negligent copying practices. Baker and Lapidge insist "there can be little doubt that [the] *E*[*nchiridion*] once contained an extensive

44 For more on the treatment of the secular clergy, see chapter 2.

system of rubrication, including headings and subheadings." Their evidence for the division into books lies in the fact that book 3 is marked as "Incipit tertia Pars,"[45] thus "suggesting that the text once contained headings for Parts One, Two and Four."[46] In addition, in section 2.2, "both existing headings and the source suggest that each of the seven readings on the embolisms had a heading, but only four of them survive."[47] As an indication that these rubrics were created by Byrhtferth and are not the accidental addition of a capricious scribe, Baker and Lapidge show how the *Enchiridion* resembles Byrhtferth's practice in other texts, since he "supplied similar headings for the numbered Parts, four and five respectively, of [*Vita S. Ecgwini*] and [*Vita S. Oswaldi*]."[48] Baker and Lapidge, however, must ultimately admit that their placement of rubrics and their division of the text on the whole should "be regarded as conjectural."[49] Byrhtferth's original plan in rubricating this manuscript, whatever it may have been, is wholly lost to modern scholarship.

In postulating that the *Enchiridion* was once a fully rubricated manuscript, Baker and Lapidge are following the example of many Latin computistical treatises that often contain complete tables of contents and headings for every chapter. However, even individual manuscripts of texts that are known to be fully rubricated do not contain all the relevant rubrications, if the scribe fails to copy them. The Parker Library manuscript CCCC 291 shows a certain irregularity of rubrication that is perhaps typical of contemporaneous manuscripts. This computistical miscellany begins with Bede's *De temporum ratione*. Before the treatise begins, the scribe has neatly copied a table of contents in two columns. Then, with each chapter, a number is given along with the name of the chapter in red rubrics. Although all chapter divisions in this text are marked, the marks are not consistent. Beginning on f. 37v, the chapter names have disappeared and only the chapter numbers remain, but the chapter names reappear on f. 88r, only to disappear just as quickly. While a variety of manuscripts exist to reconstruct an idea of which rubrics are authorial for Bede's text, as a unique manuscript A offers no way to know how many rubrics appeared in Byrhtferth's no-longer-extant original or what form they might have taken.

45 A 134.
46 B&L, cxxvi.
47 Ibid.
48 Ibid.
49 Ibid.

Another problem with determining a possible layout of Byrhtferth's original rubrics lies in the difference between the rubrication of Latin and English manuscripts. Although extensive rubrication is common in Latin computus manuscripts, such as those of Bede's *De temporum ratione*, it is less common in vernacular manuscripts, or in vernacular portions of bilingual computistical collections, such as Tiberius A.iii. The arrangement of the many versions of Wulfstan's Commonplace book, while not a computistical collection, shows a similar tendency, in that the Latin texts often have far more extensive rubrication than the comparable English sections. The trend in the *Enchiridion*, however, is quite the opposite, since, with the exception of a short string of bilingual glossing in section 4.1, the extant rubrics appear in the Old English text, not the Latin. Although adding Latin rubrics to a computus manuscript may not seem odd, especially in a manuscript designed to be a commentary on a Latin computus, it does suggest a very specific idea about the hierarchy of Latin and English as languages. In such a context, Latin is clearly the dominant language that visually subjects and controls the Old English text. It is interesting that this subjection of the English to the Latin language occurs only after the initial bilingual layout breaks down. No rubrics at all occur in sections 1.1 or 1.2, which are fully bilingual.[50] In fact, the majority of extant rubrics appear in a stint spanning from sections 1.3 to the beginning of book 3.

The environment of the first rubric shows the complicated language dynamics that occur when a primarily vernacular text is rubricated with Latin. This first rubric appears on A 38, in the section that Baker and Lapidge distinguish as 1.3. Although the previous two sections, 1.1 and 1.2, alternated relatively faithfully between Latin and English, this section begins with a Latin diatribe against the idleness of the secular clergy and is followed by three sets of Latin computistical verses, each of which are explicated in English. The first rubric of the manuscript appears to introduce the second set of verses with "De regularibus feriarum dicamus" (*BE*, 48; A 38) [Let us speak concerning the ferial regulars]. At the moment that this first rubric occurs, the language dynamics of the text have shifted slightly, since the verses to which the rubric refers are introduced with the English sentence "Heræfter uton þa regulares feriarum mid leoðe geglengan" (*BE*, 48; A 38) [Hereafter let us adorn the ferial regulars with song]. Whereas the previous set of verses were introduced in Latin and

50 There is, however, a stint of rubrics in the bilingual portion of 4.2.

then translated into English, these verses are couched on both sides with an English-language introduction and an English-language explication. Since this rapid switch between English and Latin is not marked with a coloured capital and a new paragraph, the Latin text appears to stand as a quotation in an otherwise English paragraph. In other words, the first Latin rubric in A appears in the English-language text at a point when the language dynamics are unstable and English is unseating Latin visually on the page as the dominant language.

Furthermore, in as far as Byrhtferth offers to adorn the ferial regulars with song, he suggests that this Latin mnemonic verse was created as a kind of decorative supplement to his English-language instruction. Of course, these verses were not created for the *Enchiridion* in particular, but rather appear in many computistical manuscripts.[51] The introduction to this set of verses in both format and wording greatly upsets the language hierarchies in the text, because for this immediate section, Latin is not the dominant language. On the contrary, it is a supplemental language, a kind of footnote to the predominantly vernacular text. The introduction to the third set of verses makes the supplementary status of Latin even more clear, reading, "Hyt gerist borlice wel þæt we æfter þæs foresprecenan weres dihte þa regulares <lunares> mid leoðe gegretun" (*BE*, 50) [It accords exceedingly well that we should address the lunar regulars with song, after the composition of the aforesaid man]. At this point, the English-language is announcing transitions in subject matter, and thus enclosing the Latin verses of this section within an English-language text. As the unruly vernacular text begins to supplant the dominance of the Latin text, the rubric attempts to restore the expected linguistic order in which the ecclesiastically approved language maintains primacy. The highly stylized Latin critique of the secular clergy that occurs at the beginning of this section confirms the higher prestige of Latin-language texts,[52] even if the immediate context of this passage shows the greater utility of English-language instruction.

After the first rubric appears on A 38, there are no more rubrics until A 57. After this point there are one or two rubrics a page until A 62, for a total of ten continuous rubrics, at which point the rubrics abruptly stop. The gap between A 38 and A 57 is not as large as it appears, since this is the

51 B&L, 276.

52 For the passage, see chap. 2, p. 96.

section that copies the misplaced quire from the exemplar.[53] If these rubrics were original to the exemplar, and if the text is read continuously, as it is in the Baker and Lapidge edition, there are only five manuscript pages without rubrics, on which Baker and Lapidge have supplied three missing rubrics.[54] Therefore, in as far as this stint of rubrication can be interpreted to reflect that of its lost exemplar, this first rubric may well be connected to those that follow. In the current manuscript, however, it occupies a space by itself on pages that have no other rubrication or divisions other than the coloured capitals that mark individual paragraphs.

The next ten rubrics occur together as part of a sustained stint of rubrication encompassing sections 1.4 and the beginning of 2.1. There is no rubric to mark the section break, nor to mark the first topic of 1.4, but the rubrics begin with the second paragraph, and each paragraph is then marked with a red rubric in space that has been left either on the right-hand side of the text or in a skipped line. The beginning of 1.4 marks a point in the text that displays a dynamic shift in language hierarchies. Just like section 1.3, this section also begins with a diatribe against the secular clergy in hermeneutic Latin, which is never translated, and then continues throughout in English. Although section 1.3 intersperses Latin verses within its primarily English framework, this is the first section to be almost completely in English. The following section, 2.1, continues in the vernacular as well, and the rubrication continues beyond this particular section break without any indication of a new book. Since the format of the rubric beginning 2.1 is identical to all the others rubrics in this section, there is nothing to indicate that this rubric served to mark anything more than the paragraph to which it is attached.

Each of these Latin rubrics marks a division of sense between Old English paragraphs. Thus, as English becomes the dominant language of the text, these rubrics intrude to reassert a Latinate identity. The desire to add rubrics to mark each paragraph division in this part of the text is so

53 For a discussion of the misplaced quire, see B&L, 264.

54 The scribe appears to have copied an exemplar with the quires out of order. On p. 40 line 16, the text breaks off, as the scribe follows the misplaced quire, with the continuous line of thought to be resumed again on p. 54 line 5. The problems with the misplaced quire are discussed thoroughly in B&L, 264. The explanation of the misplaced quire was first published in Henel, *Studien*, 5–7; and in N.R. Ker, "Two Notes on Ashmole 328 (Byrhtferth's Manual)," *Medium Aevum* 4 (1935): 16–19.

strong that the same rubric "De bissexto" [about the leap year] is repeated three times in a row. The final paragraph marked thus is one of Byrhtferth's characteristic asides: "Ymbe þises bissextus upasprungnysse oððe gefyllednysse we wyllað rumlicor iungum cnihtum geopenian, þæt hig cyrtenlice his fandunga understandon and þæt hig syððan his sydunge oðrum gecyðon þe his gerena ne cunnon" (*BE*, 58) [We wish to disclose to young boys more liberally about the derivation or completion of the bissextile day, so that they may more intelligently understand its proofs and so that they afterwards may make known its growth to others who do not know its mysteries]. The rubric "De bissexto" is strange here, because this paragraph has little to do with the bissextile day, but instead explains the transition from the previous paragraph to the next paragraph. Since this sentence serves as a textual transition that renders rubrics unnecessary or even extraneous, it seems strange that the impulse to have a rubric was so strong that it was added regardless of its relevance. Notably after the next rubric, "De augmentatione bisexxti" [Concerning the growth of the bissextile day], the rubrics stop just as abruptly as they began. From this point on, the text continues uninterrupted in English. Just as the rubrics stop, there is again a concern for what young men do not know. Thus, this stretch of English text with Latin rubrics is sandwiched on each side by concerns for the inferior education of Byrhtferth's audience, particularly his clerical audience. There is no indication of why the rubrication stopped, or why a more formal rubric marking the beginning of book 2 might be absent. What is apparent, however, is that this set of ten rubrics appears as this manuscript turns to a completely vernacular layout. Thus, the individual paragraphs are set off and enclosed in Latin headings, even though Latin is no longer used for the main body of the text.

To move to another example, the rubrication of the seven embolisms in 2.2 was one of the main pieces of evidence that Baker and Lapidge used to postulate that the whole of the *Enchiridion* had an extensive system of rubrication. Of the rubrics for these seven embolisms, only three red rubrics survive: those for the second, third, and fourth years in the hendecad, or the eleven-year part of the decennoval cycle. In addition, the rubric for the third year of the ogdoad is written in the manuscript, but it is written in the same ink as the main text, and is therefore not set apart in red as a rubric, but instead appears to be interpolated into the text. Like the previous stints of rubrication, this group of rubrics also occurs in the midst of an unstable hierarchy of languages, but this time the instability is present in the rubrics themselves, rather than the surrounding text. This set of rubrics begins on A 108 with an Old English rubric written in red that reads, "Be þam oðrum embolismum" (*BE*, 98) [Concerning the second embolism]. This rubric is glossed in Latin with "scilicet in endecade" (*BE*, 98) [namely in the hendecad]. As the first Old English rubric in the manuscript, it unseats the privileged place of Latin and supplants the prestige of Latin further by glossing this Old English rubric with Latin, rather than vice versa. What makes this rubric even more unsettling is the fact that it is translated into Latin in the first few words of this paragraph as "De secundo anno embolismi" (*BE*, 98; A 108) [Concerning the second embolismic year]. In J, the computus most closely connected to the one Byrhtferth is following at this point, this Latin phrase is the rubric for the relevant section,[55] and it seems that the rubric and the first line of the paragraph have become switched somehow, either by this scribe or in the original manuscript.

The presence of the Latin gloss is perhaps the easiest piece of this puzzle to explain, since a similar gloss in red appears in J that reads, "in endecadem." In the context, it is not actually a gloss, but part of the rubric that has been omitted, and a mark indicates where it should be added after the rubric for the first year. In A, however, this is decidedly a gloss written in brown, and appears with the rubric for the second year and not the first. After this first rubric for the second embolism, rubrics also appear in A for each of the remaining three embolisms, followed by a final rubric that gives the title for what Lapidge and Baker distinguish as section 2.3. All the following rubrics are in Latin, however, not English, and none have glosses. Although this stray Old English rubric could be seen as an error by a careless scribe who sloppily swapped the rubric and the first line of the paragraph, at the same time the presence of this vernacular rubric with its Latin gloss reflects what is happening in the text of *Enchiridion* at this point, in that the Latin text has been completely replaced by the vernacular, which has become the dominant language. The Latin text remains only as quotations and individual words, a kind of gloss on what effectively becomes a predominantly vernacular text. When the rubrics are next re-established later in book 2, they gradually shift from Latin to English, and it is not immediately apparent why some rubrics are in the vernacular, while others remain in Latin. Perhaps the gradual transition to English-language rubrication towards the end of book 2 indicates a giving up of the project of rubricating entirely and a kind of victory for the English-language text.

---

55 The rubric appears in J (considered by some to be Byrhtferth's computus: see above, p. 40n3) in an abbreviated form (f. 15^{r}).

While this investigation heretofore has studied short stints of rubrics individually, the rubrics that span from 1.3 to the end of book 2 perhaps deserve to be grouped together and examined as a cohesive unit. The sporadic presence of these rubrics throughout this section indicates that this text may have once been as fully rubricated as Baker and Lapidge envision. There is no evidence, however, that the first two bilingual sections of the *Enchiridion* were ever rubricated. At least, the current scribe felt no cause to rubricate these sections when he created his copy. The whole of book 3 has only one stray rubric that reads, "De LXX" (*BE*, 156; A 173) [Concerning Septuagesima], which Baker and Lapidge have corrected to read "De rationibus ad compotvm spectandis" (*BE*, 156) [Concerning calculations appropriate to computus]. It is difficult to surmise why a rubric would appear unexpectedly at this point, since it is not correct, and the paragraph that discussed Septuagesima occurred three pages previously. There is also a single stray rubric in section 4.1, which reads, "De dvodenarii nvmeri"[56] (*BE*, 220; A 230) [Concerning the number twelve]. None of the previous eleven numbers were distinguished with a rubric, and it is difficult to form any coherent argument about why this one may have been added, since the following page is missing. The manuscript additionally includes six rubrics in the bilingual portion of 4.2. The bulk of the rubrics, therefore, occurs between sections 1.3 to the end of book 2, specifically the stretch spanning from the disintegration of the initial bilingual layout to the inception of book 3, which is clearly indicated as a book for monks.[57]

It is also interesting to note that where successive strings of rubrics trespass the bounds of books or sections as indicated by Baker and Lapidge, they are not treated any differently by the scribe than those that divide individual paragraphs. The only exception to this rule is the break for the beginning of book 3. This is the only book division marked in the entire manuscript. On the page before the book divide, the scribe has written five lines of Latin in red rustic capitals, the script normally reserved for rubrics. These few lines serve as an *explicit* of sorts for book 2, reading, "Valete, patres dignissimi et filii ecclesie karissimi. / Spiritus alme, ueni, <sine> quo non diceris umquam; / Munera da lingue, <qui das in munere linguas>"[58] (*BE*, 120) [Farewell, most worthy fathers and dearest sons of the church. Come, nurturing spirit, without your presence, your name

56 B&L correct this to "numero."

57 For a discussion of book 3 as designed specifically for monks, see below, pp. 64 and 84.

58 Notably, the manuscript omits the final half-line at this point.

cannot even be said. Give the gift of tongues, you who give tongues as a gift]. The final two lines from the curriculum poet Arator are classified by Baker and Lapidge as "one of B[yrhtferth]'s favourite quotations,"[59] and occur after an announced shift in audiences. The text claims that the next chapter contains items too complicated for an uneducated clerical audience:

> Manega þing we mihton of þeodwitena gesetnysse herto geicean, ac forþan þe we witon þæt þas þing þincað clericum and uplendiscum preostum genoh mænigfealde, nu wille we ure spræce awendan to þam iungum munecum þe heora cildhad habbað abisgod on cræftigum bocum, swylce ic of manegum feawa hrepige: Hig habbað ascrutnod Serium and Priscianum and þurhsmogun Catus cwydas þæs calwan esnes and Bedan gesetnysse þæs arwurðan boceres. (*BE*, 120)

> [We could add many things from the writings of learned men, but because we know that these things seem complicated enough to clerks and rustic priests, we will now turn our speech to the young monks who have been occupied since their childhoods with learned books. I mention a few of many: They have scrutinized Sergius and Priscian, and have read through the sayings of Cato the bald man and the compositions of Bede the venerable writer.][60]

This shift to an exclusively monastic audience, one that is well versed in many Latin curriculum authors, seems to create some linguistic anxiety at this point in the manuscript, as reflected in the rubrication of the lines from Arator and the sudden appearance of a marker for book 3, although no other books have such a distinction. Despite Byrhtferth's assertion about the wide reading of his monastic students, the book directed to them is in English, not Latin.[61] The transition to book 3, however, is marked in Latin by an author among those fairly advanced in the Anglo-Saxon curriculum on a "graded sequence of difficulty."[62] Although these poetic lines do not

59 B&L, 313.

60 Translation by Baker and Lapidge.

61 For a more complete discussion of the audience of book 3, see my "Byrhtferth's Enchiridion," 138–41.

62 Lapidge lists Arator last on his scale of difficulty after the *Disticha Catonis*, Prosper of Aquitaine's *Epigrammata*, Juvencus's *Evangelia*, and Sedulius's *Carmen Paschale*. "Schools," in *The Blackwell Encyclopaedia of Anglo-Saxon England*, ed. Michael Lapidge, John Blair, Simon Keynes, and Donald Scragg (Oxford, 1999), 409.

necessarily merit rubrication – and Baker and Lapidge offer them no such distinction in their edition – the sudden shift into Latin may have precipitated a desire to distinguish them in colour and script, especially since books 2 and 3 are almost wholly in English. Furthermore, the scheme of rubrication is resuscitated in close proximity to a reference to the tension between the monks and the clerics in Byrhtferth's classroom, a tension which is nearly always encoded in linguistic terms.[63]

The final set of rubrics also comes immediately after a passage referencing the discrepancy in education between monks and clerics. Byrhtferth claims that he will explain the six ages of the world:

> ut habeant minus indocti clerici horum mysteriorum ueritatem quam sequi ualeant absque fuco mendacii. Hęc uero monasterialibus uiris cognita sunt perfecta ratione, qui ab ipso pubertatis tyrocinio cum lacte carnis genetricis eorum lac sugxerunt aecclesię catholicę qui student amminiculatione summe trinitatis et indiuidue unitatis non solum binas uel ternas metretas uehere Domino sanctorum regi, uerum etiam tricenarii fructum et sexagenarii gratum holocaustum afferre, necnon centenarii millenis dignitatibus sertis decoratum lacteis cordibus gestare. (*BE*, 232)
>
> [So that the less-educated clerics may have the truth of these mysteries and may be strong enough to follow them without the deception of lies. However, the monks know with complete understanding, because from the time of their youthful training they have sucked the milk of the catholic church at the same time as their mother's milk, and attempt with the support of the high trinity and the undivided unity to carry to the Lord, King of the saints, not only two or three measures, but to bring even the thirty-fold and the sixty-fold fruits as a pleasing sacrifice, and still to offer the sacrifice of one hundred-fold fruits with their milk-drinking hearts adorned with a thousand garlands.]

The rubrics, however, do not begin after this passage, but after its English translation, "We witon þæt iunge clericas þas þing ne cunnon, þeah þa scolieras þe on mynstre synd getydde þisra þinga gymon and gelomlice heom betwux wealcun" (*BE*, 232) [We know that young clerics do not

63 For the distinction between monks and clerics, see chap 2, pp. 73–5.

know these things, though the students who were instructed in the minster take notice of these things and often discuss it among themselves]. These rubrics are distinctive, since this is the only bilingual part of the manuscript that is rubricated, and thus these are the only Latin passages in the entire manuscript to have rubrics. Notably, these rubrics appear, not when the manuscript switches to a monolingual Latin format for section 4.1,[64] but when the text returns to a bilingual format, which is carefully presented on the page with a clear delineation in script between Anglo-Caroline for Latin text and OE minuscule for vernacular. Once again, however, the rubrics disappear before the end of the section. In the sixth age, the rubric for the English section is missing, and the seventh age lacks rubrics entirely. The text then turns to a homiletic English-only format without any rubrics to distinguish this part of the text from that on the ages of the world. While it is difficult to discern why the rubrics begin and end as capriciously as they do, it is clear that the tension on the page between the Latin and English text marked by the sudden intrusion of rubrics coincides with a rearticulation of the conflict in Byrhtferth's classroom between the monks and the secular clerics.

To summarize the findings of this section, most rubrics in the *Enchiridion* are in Latin but mark sense divisions in an English-language text. Each running stint of rubrication occurs within close proximity of a reference to the inferior Latin education of secular clerics, thus suggesting that the language dynamics on the page may be related to conflicts among Byrhtferth's students. The rubrics speak to the vexed language hierarchy of the *Enchiridion* because they occur when the alternation of languages is changing and when the text has made direct references to the superiority of Latin. Thus, they attempt to reinstate Latin's superiority over an unruly vernacular text, but their sporadic presence marks the futility of this gesture. English is indisputably the dominant language in the *Enchiridion*, despite the presence of Latin peppered throughout the text. However, the battle is not over in the *Enchiridion*. Rather this text as a work in progress shows the conflict in Byrhtferth's classroom – and in Byrhtferth's copyist – between Latin, the major identifying language of the Benedictine monk, and English, which is the predominant language of pedagogy, even for Benedictine monks who should know Latin well.

64 With the exception of the inexplicable rubric for the number 12 (*BE*, 220; A 230).

Conclusion

While many idiosyncratic features of A cannot be explained fully, it is possible that the ever-present unstable language dynamics may in some ways account for many peculiarities of the manuscript, including the abrupt change in script at the beginning of book 4, when the scribe was suddenly faced with a monolingual Latin text. Furthermore, a certain insecurity about the propriety of a text that relies so heavily on English may also account for the intermittent appearance of rubrics. Their equally sudden appearances and disappearances coupled with the gradual transition into an English-language format may show the futility of attempting to control and regulate the native language with Latin. Even the use of an English script, rather than a Latin script, for the majority of the manuscript may be attributed to the scribe's comfort with a vernacular alphabet rather than the Latinate Anglo-Caroline, which is regarded by palaeographers as extremely difficult.

Despite the fact that the *Enchiridion* is a predominantly vernacular text, in many ways, it visually privileges Latin by offering Latin first, with the occasional use of Latin rubrics. The real work of this treatise, though, is in English, not in Latin. The text and the manuscript, however, seem not to be wholly comfortable with the privileged position that English holds throughout most of the *Enchiridion*, as can be seen in the frequent references to the superior education of monks, an education that is always implied to be Latinate. Despite the Latin training of these monks, Byrhtferth instructs them in English, their native tongue, even when discussing Latin tropes and other material relevant to Latin texts. This battle between the cultural supremacy of Latin among ecclesiastics and the utility of the mother tongue plays out on every page of the extant manuscript of the *Enchiridion*. The language conflicts throughout the *Enchiridion* hinge on a specific construction of monastic identity, one that is Latinate and knowledgeable about computus. The next chapter will investigate how this Benedictine identity is constructed through the creation of a caricatured other: the ignorant, unsophisticated, and unLatinate secular cleric.

2 Scapegoating the Secular Clergy: The Hermeneutic Style as a Form of Monastic Self-Definition

Byrhtferth's rather derogatory depiction of the undisciplined and unLatinate secular clergy is connected to a widespread tendency among tenth-century English monastic writers, who enthusiastically describe the moral laxity of those clerics who would not accept the rigour of Benedictine discipline.[1] Sins condemned in the Rule of St Benedict figure prominently among lists of vices to which secular clerics are disposed, as in Wulfstan's

1 See, for instance, the description in Michael Lapidge and Michael Winterbottom, eds, *Wulfstan of Winchester: The Life of St Æthelwold*, Oxford Medieval Texts (Oxford, 1991), 31–3. For the date for the expulsion of the canons, see the discussion in the same volume, xlvi–xlvii. As an example of the denigration of the secular clergy in a text designed to praise the monastic reform, see the *Regularis concordia*, in which Æthelwold wrote that Edgar, "eiectisque neglegentium clericorum spurcitiis non solum monach[os] uerum etiam sanctimonial[es], patribus matribusque constitutis ad dei famulatum ubique per tantam sui regni amplitudinem deuotissime constituit" [after ejecting the filth of the negligent clerics, established faithfully not only monks but also nuns, with fathers and mothers appointed to them, for the service of God everywhere throughout the whole breadth of his kingdom]. T. Symons, S. Spath et al., ed., "Regularis concordia Anglicae nationis," in *Consuetudinum saeculi X/XI/XII monumenta non-Cluniacensia*, ed. K. Hallinger, Corpus Consuetudinum Monasticarum 7.3 (Siegburg, 1984), 61–147, at 70. I have emended my citation to read *monachos* and *sanctimoniales* instead of this edition's *monachus* and *sanctimonialis*, since the text in this instance calls for an accusative plural, not a nominative singular. The editors of this edition of the *Regularis concordia* have faithfully reproduced the readings (and grammatical errors) of London, British Library, Cotton Faustina B.iii. The other manuscript of the *Regularis concordia* (London, British Library, Cotton Tiberius A.iii) has the correct reading here, namely, *monachos* and *sanctimoniales*. The earlier edition of the *Regularis concordia* follows the Tiberius manuscript here; see T. Symons, ed., *The Monastic Agreement of the Monks and Nuns of the English Nation* (London, 1953), 2. All translations are mine unless otherwise noted.

Vita S. Æthelwoldi, which describes canons "hindered by pride, insolence and extravagance," and "given perpetually to drunkenness and gluttony."[2] The secular canons were so lascivious and lazy, Wulfstan claimed, that they failed to celebrate the mass properly and failed to honour their marriage vows, divorcing their wives and taking others.[3] This last criticism of the secular clergy is perhaps the easiest to understand, since clerical marriage presented a problem for the reformers, because it implied the possession of personal property, something strictly forbidden under the Rule of Benedict.[4] In the *Vita S. Oswaldi*, Byrhtferth of Ramsey quite clearly connected

---

2 A secular cleric is an ecclesiastic who is not a monk; the term secular canon is more specific, describing a cleric who serves in the bishop's *familia*. Technically speaking, the clergy evicted from Winchester were canons (since this was a cathedral), and are so named in texts closely associated with the Winchester reform, such as Lantfred's *Translatio et miracula Sancti Swithuni* (c. 975) and Wulfstan's *Narratio de Sancto Swithuno* (992 X 996). Editions of both are available in Michael Lapidge, ed., *The Cult of St Swithun*, Winchester Studies 4.2 (Oxford: Clarendon Press, 2003), 252–333 (Lantfred) and 372–5 (Wulfstan). However, in the writings of Byrhtferth of Ramsey and Ælfric of Eynsham, the word *canon* is replaced by the more general word *cleric*, even when the clergy in question were members of the bishop's *familia* and indisputably canons. For a discussion of this see R. Stephenson, "Deliberate Obfuscation: The Purpose of Hard Words and Difficult Syntax in the Literature of Anglo-Saxon England," PhD diss., University of Notre Dame (2004), 176. See also below n. 5, for an instance in which Byrhtferth described Oswald's companions at Winchester as clerics, even though they would have been identified more correctly as canons. For the debate on the dating of the word *canonicus* in monastic texts, see Lapidge and Winterbottom, eds, *Life of St Æthelwold*, clv.

3 "Erant autem tunc in Veteri Monasterio, ubi cathedra pontificalis habetur, canonici nefandis scelerum moribus implicati, elatione et insolentia atque luxuria praeuenti, adeo ut nonnulli illorum dedignarentur missas suo ordine celebrare, repudiantes uxores quas inlicite duxerant et alias accipientes, gulae et ebrietati iugiter dediti. Quod minime ferens sanctus uir Æthelwuoldus, data licentia a rege Eadgaro, expulit citissime detestandos blasphematores Dei de monasterio." [There were then in the Old Minster, where the seat of the bishop is located, canons engaged in abominable practices of wickedness. They were hindered by pride, insolence, and extravagance, to such an extent that many of them refused to celebrate masses according to their order. They divorced wives whom they had married unlawfully, and then took others in their place. They were given habitually to drunkenness and gluttony. Since the holy man Æthelwold would not bear it, he expelled the detestable blasphemers of God from the monastery with the utmost haste and with the permission of King Edgar.] Lapidge and Winterbottom, eds, *Life of St Æthelwold*, 30.

4 For the problems presented by clerical marriage, see Catherine Cubitt, "Images of St Peter: The Clergy and the Religious Life in Anglo-Saxon England," in *The Christian Tradition in Anglo-Saxon England: Approaches to Current Scholarship and Teaching*, ed. P. Cavill, Christianity and Culture: Issues in Teaching and Research (Cambridge, 2004), 41–54, at 50–4.

clerical marriage to avarice, since the clerics gave their treasures to their wives (and presumably their children) rather than the church.[5] Thus, clerical marriage presented a threat not only to celibacy, but also to the treatment of property that the Rule of St Benedict required.[6] As Eric John has shown, the echo of major changes in land tenurial practices and the communal holding of property brought by the reform can be heard in the depiction of lascivious clerics in reformed texts.[7]

These criticisms of the secular clergy have been read with a healthy amount of scepticism by modern scholars, who understand that the secular clerics' immorality is probably overstated and the clerics are guilty merely of a lack of appropriate observances measured by Benedictine standards.[8] However, the same scepticism has not been accorded to the depictions of the secular clergy in the *Enchiridion* of Byrhtferth of Ramsey.

---

5 "In diebus illis non monastici uiri nec ipsius sancte institutionis regule erant in regione Anglorum; sed erant religiosi et dignissimi clerici qui tamen thesauros suos quos auidis adquirebant cordibus, non ad ecclesie honorem, sed suis dare solebant uxoribus. Cum his mansitabat pius adolescens, uelut Loth in Sodomis." [In those days, there were not monastic men nor the holy rules of this institution (i.e., monasticism) in the region of the English, but instead there were high-born and religious clerics, who nevertheless did not give to the honour of the church the treasures which they acquired with eager hearts, but were accustomed to giving these to their wives. When the pious youth was dwelling among them, as Lot in Sodom.] Michael Lapidge, ed., *Byrhtferth of Ramsey: The Lives of St Oswald and St Ecgwine*, Oxford Medieval Texts (Oxford, 2009), 34.

6 J. McCann, ed. and trans., *The Rule of St Benedict* (Westminster, MD, 1952), 84–6 (chap. 33).

7 As John has noted, the communal holding of land with permission of the king stipulated by the Benedictine Reform marked an important change in land tenure. Before the monastic reform, prebends and abbacies were inherited within certain powerful families. However, the *Regularis concordia* called for the end of *secularium prioratus* and replaced it with royal dominion. Thus, all land for monasteries and all appointments proceeded directly from the king, subtly removing land and influence from the powerful families from which the secular clergy had arisen. Eric John, "The King and the Monks in the Tenth-Century Reformation," in *Orbis Britanniae and Other Studies* (Leicester, 1966), 154–80. As Byrhtferth tells us, the clerks evicted from Winchester were "*dignissimi*" [of high birth]. For a discussion of this term implying nobility, see ibid., 170. For a discussion of descriptions of married clerics in Winchester charters, see Alexander R. Rumble, *Property and Piety in Early Medieval Winchester: Documents Relating to the Topography of the Anglo-Saxon and Norman City and Its Minsters*, Winchester Studies 4.3 (Oxford, 2002), 18.

8 Cf. the comments of Lapidge and Winterbottom, "Æthelwold's programme, referred to more generally as the 'Benedictine Reform movement,' is known to us chiefly through the writings of Benedictine monks such as Wulfstan, and it is inevitable that their

Throughout this text, Byrhtferth repeatedly claimed that he was compelled to write the *Enchiridion* for the remediation of the secular clergy who required supplemental instruction in English, since these same clerics were too busy playing dice to study their Latin computistical texts.[9] Scholars have accepted Byrhtferth's description of his audience rather uncritically, intimating directly or indirectly that Byrhtferth's depictions of the secular clergy, although exaggerated, are more or less accurate representations of the realistic needs of students in Byrhtferth's classroom. Cyril Hart suggested that the structure of the manual reflected the inadequate education of clerics: "By the time [Byrhtferth] had reached halfway through Part III, he had dealt with as much of the *computus* as his clerks were capable of absorbing – indeed he had gone too far for most of them; they neither needed all these obscure computations for the practice of their calling, nor could they comprehend them. *So he left them to their dice-playing.*"[10] Ironically, this allegation of dice-playing, one of Byrhtferth's more preposterous charges, is repeated in other scholarship, such as that by Reginald Berry, who wrote: "Byrhtferth considered the manifold knowledge of the *computus* to be an effective remedy against *the dice-playing … of his students.*"[11] These scholarly comments overlook the fact that Byrhtferth could have had a motivation for presenting the secular clergy as lazy and uneducated besides his actual classroom experience.

---

perspective should have been biased in favour of the monks at the expense of the secular clergy who staffed cathedrals and parish minster churches; recent scholarly work has begun to focus more clearly on the secular clergy and to redress somewhat the monkish bias which informs tenth-century accounts of the movement and has inevitably influenced modern treatment of the political and institutional aspects of that movement." *Life of St Æthelwold*, xlv.

9 "Cum quodam tempore silens residerem in loco oportuno et perscrutatus essem multiplicem computandi prudentiam, cepi cordetenus ruminare pauca ex plurimis, quali medicamine possem clericis proficere ut *alee ludos relaxarent* et huius artis notitiam haberent." [When, at a certain time, I was sitting silently in an opportune place and I was thinking about the manifold knowledge of computus, I began inwardly to ruminate on a few things (out of many), about what sort of medicine I could apply to the clerics so that they would lay off the games of dice and have knowledge of this science.] Peter S. Baker and Michael Lapidge, eds, *Byrhtferth's Enchiridion*, EETS, s.s., 15 (Oxford, 1995), 52 (italics mine). As in the previous chapter, the text of the *Enchiridion* will be cited as *BE* and the editorial material written by Baker and Lapidge will be abbreviated as B&L.

10 Cyril Hart, "Byrhtferth and His Manual," *Medium Ævum* 41 (1972), 95–109, at 97–8 (emphasis mine).

11 "'*Ealle þing wundorlice gesceapen*': The Structure of the *Computus* in Byrhtferth's Manual," *Revue de l'Université d'Ottawa* 52 (1982), 130–41, at 138 (emphasis mine).

Although both monks and clerics were students at Byrhtferth's school, no one has questioned why Byrhtferth rarely addressed his audience as monks, but usually addressed an audience of secular clergy,[12] even in sections containing hermeneutic Latin too complicated for the proposed audience of poorly educated clerics.[13] Since the sources are thin about the lives and education of the secular clergy,[14] my research focuses not on their actual lives, but on the caricature of the secular clergy in the text of the *Enchiridion*.[15] This chapter will undertake to answer two questions: (1) Why does Byrhtferth emphasize his clerical audience to such a degree, virtually ignoring his monastic audience in many parts of the treatise, and (2) Why does he chastise the secular clergy in hermeneutic Latin, a style characteristic of the reform, but far too difficult for the lazy clerics that Byrhtferth described. These highly stylized harangues against the secular clergy are central to understanding their position in the *Enchiridion*,

---

12 The audience for books 1 and 2 is almost always addressed as clerical, but in book 3 the text switches to a monastic audience. For a thorough discussion of Byrhtferth's naming of his audience see below, pp. 75–93. For one example in which book 3 departs from the subject of computus, see below, pp. 81–3. The passage where Byrhtferth indicates that he will now write book 3 for monks, not clerics, is discussed, pp. 64 and 84.

13 For a description of the hermeneutic style, see the Introduction, pp. 14–19.

14 For the sources and the problems in researching secular clergy in the tenth and eleventh centuries, see Julia Barrow, "The Clergy in English Dioceses c.900–c.1066," in *Pastoral Care in Late Anglo-Saxon England*, ed. Francesca Tinti, Anglo-Saxon Studies 6 (Woodbridge, UK, 2005), 17–26; see also John Blair, "Secular Minster Churches in Domesday Book," in *Domesday Book: A Reassessment*, ed. P. Sawyer (London, 1985), 114–25; and Blair, *The Church in Anglo-Saxon England* (Oxford, 2005), 341–67.

15 The reformers translated into Old English the "Enlarged Version" of the Rule of Chrodegang, a text that would have imposed a rule similar to that of Benedict on the secular clergy, further extending the influence of the reform. This translation has recently been dated 950 X 970 based on its vocabulary. However, it is difficult to know where and when these practices were truly adopted. So, while this rule can offer clues about how the reformers wanted the clerics to behave, it is unclear whether or not it was followed. For an edition of the Rule and its dating, see Brigitte Langefeld, ed., *The Old English Version of the Enlarged Rule of Chrodegang: Edited together with the Latin Text and an English Translation*, Münchner Universitätsschriften, Texte und Untersuchungen zur Englischen Philologie 26 (Frankfurt, 2004), with a discussion of dating at 125–44. For a discussion of evidence for its use, see ibid., 15–20; and Langefeld, "*Regula canonicorum* or *Regula monasterialis uitae*? The Rule of Chrodegang and Archbishop Wulfred's Reforms at Canterbury," *ASE* 25 (1996), 21–36. Michael Drout has also weighed in on the question of dating the Rule of Chrodegang, suggesting a date as early as 940 X 950 based on stylistic evidence within the text; see "Re-Dating the Old English Translation of the Enlarged Rule of Chrodegang: The Evidence of the Prose Style," *JEGP* 103 (2004): 341–68.

because the difficulty of the text and the strong connection of the hermeneutic style to the monastic reform suggest that these sections were intended for the eyes of a Latin-literate monastic audience. In the same way that descriptions of *lascivious* clerics reflect the threat that clerical marriage presented to the land tenurial changes of the reform, Byrhtferth's depictions of lazy and uneducated clerics reflect the importance of hermeneutic Latin in monastic self-definition.

The Historical Background

The importance of an attempt at monastic self-definition may be lost on a modern audience, for whom Benedictines constitute a clear and definite class. However, prior to the tenth-century reform, the lines between monk and cleric were blurred in Anglo-Saxon England.[16] Sarah Foot has argued that the Latin word *monasterium* and the Old English word *minster* applied to dwellings of both monks and secular clergy without any effort being made to distinguish between the two groups in the period before the reform.[17] In charters, the distinctions between monks and clerics are also unclear. In a ninth-century will, a canon of Christ Church Canterbury named Werhard referred to the members of his community as "brother monks," when, by the standards of the Benedictine Reform, this was a secular community, not monastic.[18] The division of labour between monks and clerics was not rigid before the reform either. In theory, secular clergy were responsible for the *cura animarum*, the pastoral care for a region. Monks, by contrast, performed the *opus dei*, the rigid schedule of monastic prayers emphasized in the Rule of St Benedict and the *Regularis concordia*. The non-cloistered clergy were pastors, while the monks were responsible for praying for the kingdom. However, Giles Constable has shown that monks had been performing the *cura animarum* since the sixth century.[19] Furthermore, records show that, in England, communities

16 See the discussion of early monasteries in Patrick Sims-Williams, *Religion and Literature in Western England, 600–800*, Cambridge Studies in Anglo-Saxon England 3 (Cambridge, 1990), 115–17. See also Blair, "Secular Minster Churches," 115.

17 Sarah Foot, "Anglo-Saxon Minsters: A Review of Terminology," in *Pastoral Care before the Parish*, ed. John Blair and Richard Sharpe (Leicester, 1992), 212–25, at 222–4.

18 John, "King and Monks," 166.

19 Giles Constable, "Monasteries, Rural Churches, and the *cura animarum* in the Early Middle Ages," *Settimane di stuidio del Centro italiano di Studi sull'alto medioevo* 28 (1982), 349–89, at 358–9.

of monks were established to provide pastoral care, a role which in theory should have been restricted to the secular clergy.[20] However, we also have records that suggest that communities of secular clergy were abiding by a rule and living in common.[21] The confusion between the roles of secular clerics and monks can be traced back to Gregory's sixth-century mission, which established both Christianity and monasticism in England. Gregory sent monks from his own monastery as missionaries, monks who were joined in their mission of converting England by Frankish priests. Legend holds that the two houses founded at Canterbury (one monastic, one clerical) were intended to resolve the dispute between the clerics and monks of this original delegation.[22] Theoretically, this mission should have been the sole province of clerics, not of monks. The later Anglo-Saxon missions to the Continent showed the same ambiguity, since these too were led by monks, rather than the secular clergy.[23]

The Benedictine Reform of the tenth century attempted to make a firm distinction between clerics and monks by establishing universal standards for monasticism as outlined in the Rule of St Benedict and the *Regularis concordia*, the customary intended for all regular monastic houses in England. Monks were now required to abide by strict rules governing communal property and obedience to the abbot as dictated in the Rule. Any ecclesiastic not in compliance with these strict standards could not be considered a monk. Furthermore, the Rule also stipulated that monks spend certain hours of the day in study and speaks disparagingly of those who are unable or too undisciplined to meditate on the holy scriptures.[24] An echo of this criticism can be heard in Byrhtferth's derogatory descriptions of the secular clergy, whom he claimed were too lazy to master certain aspects of their Latin computistical training. The important role of education in the self-definition of Benedictine monks has been discussed by Wilhelm Busse, who wrote that the reformers "considered themselves as the *boceras* [scholars] of their age; as monks and teachers of the people whom all others have to obey and to follow; as successors of famous,

20 Foot, "Anglo-Saxon Minsters," 224.

21 John, "King and Monks," 165–6.

22 Nicholas Brooks, *The Early History of the Church of Canterbury: Christ Church from 597–1066* (Leicester, 1984), 89.

23 Ibid., 87.

24 "Si quis vero ita *negligens* et *desidiosus* fuerit, ut non velit aut non possit meditare aut legere ..." [If anyone were so negligent or lazy, that he does not wish or is not able to meditate or read ...]. McCann, *Rule of St Benedict*, 112 (italics mine). The hours of the day stipulated for study are described in chap. 48 of the Rule; see ibid., 110–12.

erudite men and teachers of the Church."[25] Any educational divide between monks and secular clergy would have been exacerbated by the privileging of a highly stylized Latin in monastic centres, since this more complicated register required more training than simpler styles of Latin. Thus, the difficulty of hermeneutic Latin may have encoded in linguistic terms the division between monks and clerics articulated by the ideology of the Benedictine Reform.

The Audience of Byrhtferth's *Enchiridion*

A prima facie reading of Byrhtferth's comments about English and Latin in this text suggests that the Latin portions were written for monks, while the English portions were written for the secular clergy, especially in sections 1.1 and 1.2, in which Byrhtferth occasionally indicated a transition from Latin to English with the claim that he would now write in English for secular clerics, who could not read Latin, as in this sentence: "Iam alio modo dicamus qualiter sint clericis nota que monachis sint perspicue cognita"[26] (*BE*, 12) [Now let us speak in another manner, so that these things that are thoroughly known to monks may be made known to clerics]. A careful study of Byrhtferth's actual addresses to his audience reveals different conclusions, however, since he addressed his monastic audience when writing only in English and often addressed a clerical audience when writing in Latin. Determining the exact composition of Byrhtferth's audience is further complicated by the inconsistent vocabulary for these potential audiences. Byrhtferth uses the Latin word *clericus* or its OE loan *cleric* twenty-four times. He also uses the OE word *preost* on forty-nine occasions to refer to a similar non-monastic audience.[27] While it is tempting to refer to this second audience with the modern English word "priest," the context in which the words "cleric" and "preost" appear suggests that the Modern English loan word is not the most appropriate and that these audiences are not necessarily distinct from one another.[28] In the portions

25 "*Sua gað ða lareowas beforan ðæm folce, & ðæt folc æfter*: The Self-Understanding of the Reformers as Teachers in Late Tenth-Century England," in *Schriftlichkeit im frühen Mittelalter*, ed. Ursula Schaefer, ScriptOralia 53 (Tubingen, 1993), 58–106, at 83.

26 See also similar statements that indicate that Latin is a language for the "boceras" and English translation is necessary for the unlearned, 1.1.214, 2.2.7, 2.3.21.

27 I have excluded the occasion in which Byrhtferth uses the word *mæssepreost* to refer to his own status as an ordained priest (3.2.199).

28 For a different view, see Phillipa Semper, who maintains that the *Enchiridion* had a tripartite audience, whom she ennumerates as "clerics, 'rustic' priests, and *iunge*

of the *Enchiridion* that are most closely bilingual, the Latin word *clericus* is sometimes translated as OE *cleric* and sometimes as OE *preost* without any distinction between the two terms. For instance, the Latin "Originem uero istarum libet demonstrare *clericis* concurrentium"[29] (*BE*, 28) [It is fitting to demonstrate to clerics the origin of these concurrents] is translated as "Vs gelustfullað þissera rynela (concurrentium) angin *preostum* ætywan"[30] (*BE*, 30) [We desire to show to the clerics the beginning of these runners, that is the concurrents]. In this case *preostum* is clearly an exact equivalent for *clericis*. At other times, the case is less clear. The Latin "Nouimus pro certo quod plurimi sub<ur>bani ignorant *clerici*"[31] (*BE*, 18) [We know for certain that many country clerics do not know] has no exact equivalent in the Old English text, but the English section begins with the phrase "Vs þingð to langsum þæt we ealne þisne cwide on Englisc *clericum* geswutelion"[32] (*BE*, 20) [It seems too tedious to explain this whole passage in English for the clerics]. It seems clear from context that the OE *clericum* is referring to the same group as the Latin *clerici*. At other times in English passages that have no Latin equivalent, Byrhtferth seems to alternate between *preost* and *cleric* for simple variation. For instance in this passage in book 3, Byrhtferth writes, "Nim, la *preost* se wynsuma, þa twelf of þam getæle"[33] (*BE*, 184) [Delightful cleric take a twelfth from that number]. The passage continues by asking *þu* (presumably this *preost*) to divide in diminishing numerical quantities until he finally divides by half. At this point, Byrhtferth interjects, "Gy<t> ic wylle ymbe þis getæle wið þe, la *cleric*, spræce habban"[34] (*BE*, 184) [I wish to speak more with you about this number, O cleric]. In this case, Byrhtferth does not appear to have changed his audience, but rather has used a different word in continuing to address the same audience.

There are two points, however, at which Byrhtferth might be suggesting a distinction between a *cleric* and a *preost*. The first is the following sentence where OE *cleric* is used in a doublet with *uplendiscum preostum*:

---

mynstermen"; "Doctrine and Diagrams: Maintaining the Order of the World in *Byrhtferth's Enchiridion*," in *The Christian Tradition in Anglo-Saxon England: Approaches to Current Scholarship and Teaching*, ed. Paul Cavill (Cambridge, 2004), 121–37, at 127.

29 Emphasis added.

30 Emphasis added.

31 Emphasis added.

32 Emphasis added.

33 Emphasis added.

34 Emphasis added.

"Manega þing we mihton of þeodwitena gesetnysse herto geicean, ac forþan þe we witon þæt þas þing þincað clericum and uplendiscum preostum genoh mænigfealde, nu wille we ure spræce awendan to þam iungum munecum þe heora cildhad habbað abisgod on cræftigum bocum" (*BE*, 120) [We could add many things to this work from the writings of learned men, but since we know that these things seem to be too complicated to clerics and country priests, we wish now to turn our speech to the young monks who have kept themselves busy with learned books since their childhood]. Placing both terms together in this line might indicate an attempt to distinguish between these two groups or to indicate a difference between the rural and urban clergy. What is more strongly emphasized in this passage, however, is not the marked difference between these two groups of people, but their collective identification as antithetical to the monastic audience. Strong contrasts, such as these, between virtuous monks and the insufficiently educated secular clergy appear throughout the *Enchiridion*.

The second passage that makes a distinction between *preost* and *cleric* is more problematic. It reads, "Ymbe þa feower timan we wyllað cyðan *iungum preostum* ma þinga, þæt hig magon þe ranclicor þas þing heora *clericum* geswutelian"[35] (*BE*, 82) [We wish to make known to the young priests more things about the four seasons so that they may more boldly explain these things to their clerics]. This passage implies a hierarchical situation with the priest in a position above the clerics who serve him. In this context, Byrhtferth may be contrasting those in major orders of priesthood (here: *preostum*) with those in minor orders (here: *clericum*), but it is difficult to speak with any assurance on this issue since in most other passages Byrhtferth uses these terms interchangeably. Furthermore, Ælfric, a contemporary of Byrhtferth, used the word *preost* to refer to the secular clergy, not as an English equivalent of *presbyter*, which Ælfric translated as *mæssepreost* (i.e., one in the sixth order of the priesthood and able to perform the sacraments).[36] Byrhtferth seems to follow this usage when he

35 Emphasis added.

36 Malcolm Godden makes this point in *Ælfric's Catholic Homilies: Introduction, Commentary, and Glossary*, EETS, s.s., 18 (London, 2000), 239. Sarah Foot makes a similar argument in more general terms in "Language and Method: The Dictionary of Old English and the Historian," in *The Dictionary of Old English: Retrospects and Prospects*, ed. M.J. Toswell, Old English Newsletter Subsidia 26 (Kalamazoo, MI, 1998), 73–87. In J. Bosworth and T. Northcote Toller, *An Anglo-Saxon Dictionary* (Oxford, 1898), the first example given of *preost* used in an Anglo-Saxon text is as a gloss on *clericus*.

refers to himself as "mæssepreost," not simply as *preost*.[37] This distinction is important, because monks can be ordained into the orders of the priesthood, as Byrhtferth and Ælfric both were, but they are still distinct from the members of the secular clergy.

Despite the seventy-three references to the clerical audience of the *Enchiridion*, the monastic audience is mentioned only twelve times.[38] Four of these are in direct address of a specific student in class, such as "La mynsterman, wylt þu witan hwæt þis tacnað?"[39] (*BE*, 126) [O monk, do you wish to know what this means?]. Two refer to the practice of good monks, who pray at the appointed hours, such as "þæt ys hancred, þonne sceolon gode munecas arisan and Gode singan" (*BE*, 114) [that is cockcrow, when good monks should rise and sing to God]. The remaining four emphasize the divide between the monastic and secular audiences, in every instance suggesting that monks have more education than clerics.[40] The wealth of references to the secular clergy, when contrasted with the dearth of direct references to the monastic audience, might suggest that the majority of the *Enchiridion* was directed to an audience of secular clergy, but this does not accord with what we know about monastic classrooms in the early eleventh century. If this text were meant for Byrhtferth's classroom at Ramsey, then the core of his students would likely have been monks raised in the monastery. Although the secular clergy were present, they were interlopers who did not belong and would not remain once their training was complete.

Although the contextual evidence indicates that Byrhtferth usually did not bother to make distinctions among the various grades of the secular clergy, the salient identification in Byrhtferth's classroom seems to have been the distinction between his secular and his monastic pupils. The contrast between these two groups is frequently reiterated, as in this passage:

---

37 3.2.199.

38 There are a further two instances where monks are mentioned, but not in the context of an audience, such as this example in which Byrhtferth illustrated polysyndeton with an English sentence: "God me geunne þæt ic mote his willan gewyrcan and ealra his halgena and mines kynehlafordes and ealra minra broðra" (*BE*, 168) [God grant that I may do his will and the will of his saints, my king, and all my brothers], where *gebroðra* seems to refer to Byrhtferth's monastic brothers, but not necessarily to the audience. The other example is *munucheape* at 3.2.37.

39 One of these is plural, "la arwurðan gebroðro" [O, noble brothers], 3.1.28. Cf. the eight times he used OE *cleric* in this manner, and a further eight for OE *preost*.

40 The four quotations are above on pp. 75 and 77, and below on pp. 79–80.

> ut habeant minus indocti clerici horum mysteriorum ueritatem quam sequi ualeant absque fuco mendacii. Hęc uero monasterialibus uiris cognita sunt perfecta ratione, qui ab ipso pubertatis tyrocinio cum lacte carnis genetricis eorum lac sugxerunt aecclesię catholicę qui student amminiculatione summe trinitatis et indiuidue unitatis non solum binas uel ternas metretas uehere Domino sanctorum regi, uerum etiam tricenarii fructum et sexagenarii gratum holocaustum afferre, necnon centenarii millenis dignitatibus sertis decoratum lacteis cordibus gestare. (*BE*, 232)

> [so that the less-educated clerics may have the truth of these mysteries and may be strong enough to follow them without the deception of lies. However, the monks know with complete understanding, because from the time of their youthful training they have sucked the milk of the catholic church at the same time as their mother's milk, and attempt with the support of the high trinity and the undivided unity to carry to the Lord, King of the saints, not only two or three measures, but to bring even the thirty-fold and the sixty-fold fruits as a pleasing sacrifice, and still to offer the sacrifice of one hundred-fold fruits with their milk-drinking hearts adorned with a thousand garlands.]

In this passage, the clerics are presented as *minus indocti* [less uneducated], suggesting that they have some modicum of education, but are still prone to being led astray by deception and liars. In contrast, the monks are presented as knowing these issues perfectly, because they have imbibed the teaching of the Catholic Church from a young age, when they were given them as oblates. The emphasis on mother's milk (both the church's and the natural mother's) throughout the passage emphasizes the practice of oblation, the dedicating of children to religious service, which the Benedictine Reform encouraged.[41] The hundred-fold gift that the monks

41 For a discussion of child oblation in minsters in early Anglo-Saxon England, see Sarah Foot, *Monastic Life in Anglo-Saxon England, c. 600–900* (Cambridge, 2006), 140–5. For a thorough discussion of child oblation centred on Carolingian Europe, see Mayke de Jong, *In Samuel's Image: Child Oblation in the Early Medieval West*, Brill's Studies in Intellectual History 12 (Leiden, 1996). See also Janet L. Nelson, "Parents, Children and the Church in the Earlier Middle Ages," in *The Church and Childhood: Papers Read at the 1993 Summer Meeting and the 1994 Winter Meeting of the Ecclesiastical History Society*, ed. Diana Wood, Studies in Church History 31 (Oxford, 1994), 81–114, with discussion of rituals concerning oblation at 107–12.

present to their lord is virginity,[42] which is represented as being nurtured from the inside by their milk-drinking hearts.[43] Since this purity begins on the inside, it is not so much a battle or a struggle to contain lust, but rather something that is nurtured or developed among oblates. This passage is presented rather more concisely in English as "We witon þæt iunge clericas þas þing ne cunnon, þeah þa scolieras þe on mynstre synd getydde þisra þinga gymon and gelomlice heom betwux wealcun" (*BE*, 232) [We know that young clerics do not know these things, though the students who were instructed in the minster have noted these things and often discuss it among themselves]. The connection between virginity and oblation is omitted from the English text, but the salient division between a monastic and a clerical audience is maintained, even to the extent of suggesting that the monastic students have conversations to which the clerical students are not privy.

Notably, the Latin passage that outlines the differences between monks and secular clerics also contains some hints of the hermeneutic style. The reference to the youth of the monks includes a line from Aldhelm, "ab ipso pubertatis tyrocinio."[44] In this case, *puerilitatis* [childhood] might have been the more appropriate time to drink mother's milk than *pubertatis* [the beginning of manhood],[45] but invoking a higher register through an Aldhelmian quotation is more important than the precise age difference between childhood and puberty. A higher register is also invoked by other poeticisms, the rare word *amminiculatione* [support], and the distributive numbers *binas* [two], *ternas* [three], *tricenarii* [thirty], *sexagenarii* [sixty], *centenarii* [one hundred], and *millenis* [one thousand]. Although this diction is not nearly as inflated as some parts of Byrhtferth's saints' lives, it is

42 The thirty-fold, sixty-fold, and hundred-fold returns comes from the biblical parable of the sower and his field (Matt. 13:8). Aldhelm in the *Prosa de virginitate* follows Ambrose, Jerome, and Augustine in interpreting the hundred-fold return as virginity. For Aldhelm's text, see *Aldhelmi Opera*, ed. R. Ehwald, Monumenta Germaniae historica, Auctores antiquissimi 15 (Berlin, 1919), 226–323, at 249; see discussion of this passage in Michael Lapidge and Michael Herren, trans., *Aldhelm: The Prose Works* (Cambridge, 1979), 55–7.

43 Baker and Lapidge translate this as "milk-white" (*BE*, 233).

44 Cf. Aldhelm's "sub ipso pubertatis tirocinio." Ehwald, ed., *Prosa de virginitate*, 311.

45 Notably in Aldhelm, this line refers to King David, who is said to have maintained his virginity "sub ipso pubertatis tyrocinio." Aldhelm maintains that the early deeds of David's life are directly attributable to his virginity.

interesting that when describing the difference between monks and clerics, he used a style that modern scholars have shown to be strongly connected to those who identify with the Benedictine Reform.

Furthermore, even though secular clerics are the most frequently named audience in the English sections, and their lack of Latinity is emphasized, the difficulty of some English sections requires that the reader be literate in Latin and some passages even require knowledge of Aldhelm, a notoriously difficult author.[46] Some sections of book 3, even though they are in the vernacular, require an extensive knowledge of Latin in their reader, especially section 3.3. In this portion, Byrhtferth undertook the explanation of literary figures, a topic that is normally applicable only to Latin texts.[47] The examples explicating these figures appear in Latin without translations or explanations of Latin grammatical constructions. The discussion of the first figure shows the linguistic difficulty of this section:

> Prolemsis hatte þæt forme, þæt ys on Lyden anticipatio uel preocupatio uel presumptio, þæt ys on Englisc forestæppung oððe dyrstynnys, þonne se nama byð beforan þe sceolde beon bæftan. Þæt ylce we cweðað be þam worde, and þis uers we doð to trumre bisne: "Fundamenta eius in montibus sanctis, diligit Dominus portas Sion." Ær he cwæð "eius" ær "Dominus." (*BE*, 162)

> [The first (figure) is called *prolepsis*, that is, in Latin *anticipatio*, *preocupatio*, or *presumptio*, and anticipation or presumption in English, when the noun comes before, but ought to come after. This applies equally to the verb, and we offer this verse as a trustworthy example, "*Fundamenta eius in montibus sanctis, diligit Dominus portas Sion.*" This says "*eius*" before "*Dominus.*"]

46 See chap. 3, pp. 123–9.

47 This section presents material translated from Bede's *Liber de schematibus et tropis*. For a discussion of these figures in Byrhtferth, see Gabriele Knappe, "Classical Rhetoric in Anglo-Saxon England," *ASE* 27 (1998): 5–29, at 18. Notably this is the first discussion of literary figures in the English language; Knappe, *Traditionen der klassischen Rhetorik im angelsächsischen England*, Anglistische Forschungen 236 (Heidelberg, 1996), 271. For the dissemination of rhetorical figures in Anglo-Saxon England, see also Janie Steen, *Verse and Virtuousity: The Adaptation of Latin Rhetoric in Old English Poetry* (Toronto, 2008).

Although the English vocabulary does not appear to be very difficult, it does require knowledge of the technical vocabulary of grammar.[48] The words *nama* and *worde* here have specific grammatical meanings: noun (*nama*) and verb (*worde*),[49] rather than *name* and *word*, which would be their more usual meanings. These two Old English words directly translate the Latin words for the parts of speech: *nomen* (noun, literally "name") and *verbum* (verb, literally "word"). While this technical use of grammatical terminology would not be difficult for anyone who had studied Latin grammar, it would have been a stretch for a reader who was literate only in English and did not understand the double meaning of the Latin words. Furthermore, the noun *forestæppung* [anticipation] has no attestation in Old English outside of Byrhtferth, although the related verb appears in some works of Ælfric.[50] This word appears to be the closest Old English approximation possible for the Latin word *anticipatio*,[51] but is probably not common enough to provide assistance in rendering the Latin form. The untranslated Latin in the passage presents linguistic difficulties as well, especially since Byrhtferth expected his audience to parse the Latin sentence successfully and comprehend that *Dominus* is

48 For the importance of grammatical instruction in Anglo-Saxon England, see Knappe, "Classical Rhetoric," 16–20. See also Helmut Gneuss, "The Study of Language in Anglo-Saxon England," in *Textual and Material Culture in Anglo-Saxon England: Thomas Northcote Toller and Toller Memorial Lectures*, ed. Donald Scragg, Publications for the Manchester Centre for Anglo-Saxon Studies 1 (Cambridge, 2003), 78–88.

49 Ælfric uses these words in the same way in his *Grammar*, see *Ælfrics Grammatik und Glossar: Text und Varianten*, ed. J. Zupitza, Sammlung englischer Denkmäler in kritischen Ausgaben 1 (Berlin, 1880; repr. with an intro. by Helmut Gneuss, Hildesheim, 2001), 8–9. For a discussion of the possibility of grammatical instruction in English, see Gneuss, "Study of Language," 81–2. For a comparison of grammatical terminology of Ælfric and Wulfstan, see Gneuss, ibid., 87.

50 B&L, cxiii. A form of the verb *forestæppan* appears earlier in *BE* at p. 160. Forms of *forestæppan* also occur in glosses, most frequently glossing forms of the Latin, *praecedere*, but also glossing other verbs that combine the Latin prefix *prae-* with a verb implying forward motion, such as *praevenire* and *praeire*. However, *forestæppan* never glosses *anticipo*, the Latin verb related to *anticipatio*. *Dictionary of Old English, Old English Corpus* [electronic resource], ed. Antonette diPaolo Healey (Ann Arbor, 1998).

51 The word *anticipatio* is not in Bede's *Liber de schematibus et tropis*, but arises from glosses to Bede derived from a commentary by Remigius of Auxerre; for a discussion of *anticipatio* see Knappe, *Traditionen*, 275–9 and 292 n. 1; for a discussion of the likelihood that it was a gloss and not the whole commentary, see ibid., 281–4.

the antecedent of *eius*.[52] Both the untranslated Latin and the technical vocabulary of grammar indicate that this passage was written in English for a reader with a fairly extensive knowledge of Latin, but one who could understand some concepts better when explicated in English. Furthermore, since this Latin figure does not have any relevance for the interpretation of vernacular literature, it probably would not be useful to someone literate only in English.[53]

Perhaps the most conclusive examination of the audience of the *Enchiridion* would be to correlate the difficulty of the text with its implied audience, as suggested by René Derolez, who claimed,

> Our understanding of [Byrhtferth's] method as demonstrated in the *Enchiridion* is complicated by various parts of the work being apparently addressed to different audiences, to judge by the way a number of readers ... or auditors ... are addressed individually ... Only a detailed analysis of the text could tell us whether, and how far, there is any relation between the sort of addressee a paragraph is aimed at, and the degree of difficulty of that paragraph.[54]

Accordingly, Derolez listed a number of different readers of the text as Byrhtferth addressed them: iunge men, scolierum, la arwurða cleric, la broðer etc.[55] The problem, however, with understanding the audience for each section separately is that Byrhtferth frequently addressed his audience in several different ways within the space of a few paragraphs, or sometimes even a few sentences. For instance in this passage, Byrhtferth stated his reasons for writing this book: "We gesetton on þissum enchiridion (þæt ys manualis on Lyden and handboc on Englisc) manega þing ymbe gerimcræft forþon we woldon þæt *iunge men* mihton þe leohtlicor þæt Lyden ongitan and wið ealde preostas ymbe þas þing þe rumlicor

52 Admittedly, the Latin example comes from the psalms, which both a monk and a cleric should know by heart, but rote memorization of the psalms does not imply a thorough knowledge of their grammatical constructions. For the study of the psalms in a monastic classroom, see Pierre Riché, *Éducation et culture dans l'occident barbare*, Patristica sorbonensia 4 (Paris, 1962), 156–7.

53 For a discussion of the relevance of Latin figures to vernacular literature, see Knappe, "Classical Rhetoric," 20–5.

54 "Those Things Are Difficult to Express in English ...," *English Studies* 70 (1989): 469–76, at 475.

55 Ibid.

sprecan"[56] (*BE*, 120) [We have placed many things in this enchiridion (that is manual in Latin and handbook in English) about computus, because we wanted young men to be able to understand the Latin text more easily and speak with old clerics about these things in greater detail].

Derolez cited this passage as an example in which Byrhtferth showed concern for "the young whose command of Latin was still limited."[57] These young men, who apparently could be either monastic or clerical, are contrasted with old clerics with whom they must speak, perhaps to prove their knowledge to their older colleagues. However, when this passage is read in conjunction with the preceding paragraph, a very different picture of the audience emerges: "Manega þing we mihton of þeodwitena gesetnysse herto geicean, ac forþan þe we witon þæt þas þing þincað clericum and uplendiscum preostum genoh mænigfealde, nu wille we ure spræce awendan to þam iungum munecum þe heora cildhad habbað abisgod on cræftigum bocum" (*BE*, 120) [We could add many things to this work from the writings of learned men, but since we know that these things seem to be too complicated to clerics and country priests, we wish now to turn our speech to the young monks who have kept themselves busy with learned books since their childhood].

In this paragraph, it is clear that the young men mentioned earlier are in fact not clerics, but monks, to whom Byrhtferth has turned his attention. Byrhtferth tells us that these young monks can read Latin – they have already read Sergius, Priscian, Cato, and Bede – but still they understand explanations in English more easily than in Latin. These monks are specifically contrasted in both paragraphs with *clericum and uplendiscum preostum* and *ealde preostas*. Thus, Byrhtferth implied that the young monks needed to discuss computus with the old clerics in order to instruct them, not the other way around.

This passage, like many we have discussed thus far, presents a distinct contrast between studious monastic students and insufficiently educated clerics, despite the many names used to address the audience. The passage also contains an explanation of the reasons for the difference in the intellectual abilities of the two groups. The monks know more Latin because they were given as oblates and have studied in a monastic classroom since

56 Emphasis added.
57 Ibid., 474.

childhood,[58] an advantage that Byrhtferth's clerical students apparently did not have. However, despite the monastic students' knowledge of Latin, Byrhtferth will address book 3, which is mostly in English, to them, because the difficult concepts contained within it will be easier for them to read in their vernacular language.

As this section has shown, English sections of the *Enchiridion* were not necessarily intended for the secular clergy. Some portions of the text explicitly intended for a monastic audience were written in English, and some vernacular passages required an extensive knowledge of Latin. I suggest that the frequency with which the secular clergy are named in the *Enchiridion* has less to do with their relative importance to the text or Byrhtferth's classroom, but rather that attention is called to them so frequently to reinforce the difference between monks and clerics and to emphasize the divide between the monks, who will remain at Ramsey under the strictures of the Benedictine rule, and the clerics, who will not. The next section will look in greater detail at the portions of the *Enchiridion* that are the most critical of the secular clergy, focusing especially on those passages that have affinities with the hermeneutic style that is so closely connected to monastic identity.

Secular Clergy in the *Enchiridion* and the Difficulty of Hermeneutic Latin

Since the secular clergy left no narratives of their own, it is unclear to what level of learning they routinely aspired. Nor is it easy to determine what they would have considered difficult reading.[59] There is reason to believe that monks and clerics were educated together in the same classroom in Ramsey as Byrhtferth described it, since this practice was common at Worcester.[60] Turning to Ælfric's and Wulfstan's handling of the secular clerics, it is clear that the clergy were expected to be able to read and to

58 See above pp. 70–81.

59 For a discussion of difficulty in Latin prose, see Carin Ruff, "The Perception of Difficulty in Aldhelm's Prose," in *Insignis Sophiae Arcator: Essays in Honour of Michael W. Herren on His 65th Birthday*, ed. Gernot Wieland, Carin Ruff, and Ross G. Arthur, Publications of the Journal of Medieval Latin 6 (Turnhout, 2006), 165–77.

60 Worcester seems not to have made the rigid distinctions between monk and cleric that are seen in Winchester, as is evidenced by the Worcester charters. For a discussion see Julia Barrow, "The Community of Worcester, 961–c.1100," in *St Oswald of Worcester: Life and Influence*, ed. Nicholas Brooks and Catherine Cubitt, Studies in the Early History of England 2 (Leicester, 1996), 84–99, with discussion of Worcester charters at 86–8.

own a selection of books including a computus.[61] However, Ælfric also expressed concerns about the education of clerics, especially their mastery of Latin.[62] Although Byrhtferth expressed reservations about the inadequate training of the secular clergy at some times, at other times he treated them with respect. This section will first review in what circumstances Byrhtferth referred to the secular clergy and then examine how he described them differently in Latin and in English.

Byrhtferth's numerous references to the secular clergy throughout the *Enchiridion* suggest that they are a very important audience of this text, or at least the audience who needs extra explanations and vernacular translations. The most common use of the word *preost* occurs on the seventeen occasions when Byrhtferth claimed he would show something to the *preostas* or make something known to them, as in "Vs gelustfullað þissera rynela (concurrentium) angin preostum ætywan" (*BE*, 30) [We desire to show to priests the origin of the runners, that is the concurrents]. Seven of these occurrences introduce a diagram immediately following or immediately preceding, as in "Her we hig wyllað amearkian, þa epactas and eac þa regulares lunares, þæt hig openlicre and orpedlice standun beforan þæs preostes gesyhðe"[63] (*BE*, 44) [Here we wish to write out the epacts and also the lunar regulars, so that they may stand more openly and clearly before the cleric's sight]. In these cases, Byrhtferth visually illustrates to his audience what he has previously explained with words. On one other occasion, the statement that he will show the *preostas* something occurs in close proximity to a diagram, but not in the sentence immediately before it.[64] Examples such as these suggest that the *preostas* are set apart for extra attention, since the studious monastic students should have been able to read the Latin computus without the supplementary instruction contained in the *Enchiridion*. Comments such as "Ic wene, la uplendisca preost, þæt þu nyte hwæt beo a<tom>os, ac ic wylle þe þises wordes gescead gecyðan" (*BE*, 110) [Oh rustic cleric, I think that you do not know what an atom is

61 *Die Hirtenbriefe Ælfrics in altenglischer und lateinischer Fassung*, ed. B. Fehr, with suppl. by P. Clemoes, Bibliothek der angelsächsischen Prosa 9 (Darmstadt, 1966), 1.52, 2.137, and 2.157–8. The lists are discussed in Christopher A. Jones, "Ælfric's Pastoral Letters and the Episcopal Capitula of Radulf of Bourges," *Notes and Queries* 42.2 (June 1995): 149–55.

62 See below, chap. 4.

63 This is one of the seven instances that precede a diagram.

64 2.3.43–4.

and I will make known this word to you] support the widespread view that these clerics needed extra education and are perhaps the primary audience for the *Enchiridion*. A sense of resentment about this extra time spent on remediation occasionally surfaces in comments like "Vs þingð to langsum þæt we ealne þisne cwide on Englisc clericum geswutelion" (*BE*, 20) [It seems too tedious for us to explain all these words in English for the clerics].

However, Byrhtferth's view of the secular clergy is not unequivocally negative. Rather he suggests that the realm of computus is something belonging to or owned by *preostas*. There are six instances in which Byrhtferth defines a computistical term by saying that *preostas* call it that, as in "preostas cigeað feriarum" (*BE*, 52) [clerics call *feriarum*]. Sometimes these *preostas* are qualified by an adjective such as *rimcræftige* [skilled in computus],[65] but at other times they are simply *preostas*. There are eight references to things *preostas* should know, such as "Eac ys þam preoste to witanne þæt þes middaneard stent on feower gesceaftum" (*BE*, 84) [Clerics should also know that the world stands on four elements]. Similarly, on three other occasions Byrhtferth suggests that there are things that *preostas* do know or are part of knowledge owned by them, such as "we willað þa stafas onsundron gewriðan þe þa estfulla preostas on heora getæle habbað" (*BE*, 184) [we wish to fasten on separately the letters, which the gracious clerics have in their reckoning]. Notably, the glossary of the current edition defines the word *preost* as "one skilled (or expected to be skilled) in computus."[66] The fact that priests should own the knowledge of computus is sometimes turned against them: there are two references to things a *preost* does not know, but should. There are a further two examples warning priests to guard themselves lest they be deceived, and one assuring them that using this knowledge they may calculate without fear. This accumulation of examples suggests that the knowledge of computus belongs or should belong to the clerical sphere.

The numerous direct addresses of clerical audience members also suggest that the secular clergy is the primary audience. There are eight direct addresses to a specific *preost* who might be either reading or sitting in Byrhtferth's class. Most of these look something like, "Rim, la wynsuma

65 1.2.256 and 3.3.307.

66 B&L, 457, s.v. "preost."

preost, swa fela daga" (*BE*, 142) [O delightful priest, count how many days]. In these cases, Byrhtferth gives specific instructions to a particular priest, usually in the singular,[67] to count or to manipulate the mathematical equations. There are a further eight addresses of his audience with OE *cleric*, as in "Nu þu, la cleric, fundist þæs embolismaris monan" (*BE*, 94) [Now, cleric, you have found the embolismic moon]. Sometimes these have modifying adjectives, such as *orpeda*[68] [bold] and arwurða[69] [honourable], and many include the second-person pronoun *þu*.

When writing in Latin, by contrast, Byrhtferth always addresses the clerics in the third person, and never with a vocative. In Latin, the clerics also do not receive complimentary adjectives to describe them; rather Byrhtferth calls them *indocti* [unlearned],[70] *imperiti* [unskilled],[71] *desides* [lazy],[72] and *suburbani* [rustic].[73] Of the nine occurrences of the Latin *clericus*, only one can be described as neutral: "Originem uero istarum libet demonstrare clericis concurrentium"[74] (*BE*, 28) [It is fitting to demonstrate to clerics the origins of the concurrents]. The other eight tend to suggest the inadequate knowledge of the clerics, such as "Nouimus pro certo quod plurimi sub<ur>bani ignorant clerici quo<t> sunt genera annorum, sed eorum ignauiis consulere placet suffult<us> patrum patrocinio, cum quorum canibus indignus sum recumbere" (*BE*, 18) [We know for certain that a great number of rustic clerics do not know what the types of years are, but supported by the protection of the fathers, with whose dogs I am unworthy to lie down, it is pleasing to tend to their laziness]. Two references directly contrast the knowledge that clerics lack with that possessed by monks, as in "Iam alio modo dicamus qualiter sint clericis nota que monachis sint perspicue cognita"[75] (*BE*, 12) [Now let us speak in another manner, so that these things that are thoroughly known to monks may be made known to clerics]. Although Byrhtferth's treatment of the clerics is uneven in

67 But 3.2.264 addresses a plural "arwurðan preostas," and 3.2.230 similarly addresses a plural audience, "wynsume preostas."

68 3.1.183. This is a rare word connected to glosses.

69 1.2.172.

70 4.2.12.

71 1.3.2.

72 1.4.3.

73 1.1.172.

74 Notably Byrhtferth translates this into English as *preost*.

75 The other example is cited above, p. 79.

English, sometimes flattering, sometimes accusing, his treatment of them in Latin is almost universally negative. It is important to note that they are never addressed in the second person, but only in the third person, as if Byrhtferth is talking about them, not speaking directly to them.

Furthermore, the passages most critical of the secular clergy tend to occur in the hermeneutic style, an elevated register that calls attention to the disjunction between the stated goal of improving the clerics' Latinity and the difficulty of the text. The passage in which Byrhtferth accuses the clerics of over-indulgence in games of dice, mentioned in the introduction, provides a good example of an extended harangue against the secular clerics in Latin seemingly too difficult for them:

> Quoniam sermo iste ad desides congruit clericos, ammonemus, pacis reuerentia, eos ut discant que ignorant et postmodum doceant ceteris que didicerint. Simul erunt rei in conspectu iusti arbitris: qui nolunt scire et qui nolunt docere. Ambo igitur una pena puniuntur. Sufficiat hoc in loco nostre seueritatis obiurgatio. Cum quodam tempore silens residerem in loco oportuno et perscrutatus essem multiplicem computandi prudentiam, cepi cordetenus ruminare pauca ex plurimis, quali medicamine possem clericis proficere ut alee ludos relaxarent et huius artis notitiam haberent. Superius eis pulmentarium aduexi non modicum; nunc libet eis et poculum propinare. Plurima affati sumus que iterum placet renouari nostro eloquio, ut qui Latinitatis elogium non potuerint sumere accipiant saltim uulgarem nostrum sermonem. (*BE*, 52)

> [Since this discussion is appropriate for lazy clerics, we admonish them – with a reverence for peace – to learn those things that they do not know and afterwards to teach to others the things that they have learned. At the same time, they both will be guilty in the sight of the just judge: those who do not wish to know and those who do not wish to teach. Therefore, both will receive the same punishment. Let this rebuke from our severity suffice in this place. When, at a certain time, I was sitting silently in an opportune place and I was thinking about the manifold knowledge of computus, I began inwardly to ruminate on a few things (out of many), about what sort of medicine I could apply to the clerics so that they would lay off the games of dice and have knowledge of this science. Above, we have conveyed a large meal to them; now it is pleasing also to offer them a drink. We have said many things which it is pleasing again to repeat here in our language, so that those who are not able to receive an utterance of Latinity may at least receive our instruction in the vernacular.]

Notably, this exhortation to better Latinity and better behaviour is in a more stylized Latin than that which Byrhtferth normally employs for the teaching of computus. For example, in the first line of this passage, two instances of hyperbaton, or irregular word order, occur in the statements, "ad *desides* congruit *clericos*" and "*ammonemus*, pacis reverentia, *eos*."[76] In both instances, a simple envelope patterning occurs:[77] in the first, the adjective is separated from the noun it is meant to modify by a finite verb, and in the second, the verb is separated from its object by an ablative interjection, a verbal aside inserted into the text. While neither of these constructions is particularly unusual in medieval Latin (and the syntax here does not reach the virtuosity of Aldhelm's style), this word order contrasts distinctly with Byrhtferth's more didactic prose, in which words that modify each other (especially adjectives that modify nouns) are adjacent to one other.[78] Furthermore, the hyperbaton seems to have been chosen so that words with similar endings will occur at the end of phrases; thus *clericos* now mirrors *eos*. In this case, the homoeoteleuton caused by the identical declensional ending creates a deliberately stylized rhymed prose.[79] Such adornment continues in the following lists of verbs: *discant*, *ignorant*, and *doceant*.[80] Two of these three verbs are subjunctive, and while these forms are not grammatically inappropriate, the selection of mood (i.e., indicative vs. subjunctive) seems to have been based more on a desire to make verbs from different conjugations have the same endings than a sense of grammatical precision. Equally, in the phrase "Cum quodam tempore silens *residerem* in loco oportuno et *perscrutatus essem*," one might

76 I have italicized the words that are related to each other and would normally appear together in sequence. In the first instance, a verb intrudes between an adjective and a noun, and in the second, a noun phrase separates a verb from its object.

77 For a discussion of separating adjectives from nouns as a means of providing variety in the writings of Aldhelm, see Michael Winterbottom, "Aldhelm's Prose Style and Its Origins," *ASE* 6 (1977): 39–76 at 41.

78 The following sentence is an example of Byrhtferth's more didactic and grammatically simple prose: "Est annus lunaris qui habet dies trecentos quinquaginta quattuor, quem solaris exsuperat <undecim> diebus" (*BE*, 18) [The lunar year is one which has 354 days; the solar year exceeds (the lunar year) by 11 days].

79 I thank Daniel Sheerin for pointing this out to me. For the magisterial text on rhymed Latin prose, see K. Polheim, *Die Lateinische Reimprosa* (Berlin, 1925). For a discussion of rhyme in texts connected to the reform, see Lapidge, ed., *Cult of St Swithun*, 228–9.

80 Notice also the near-rhyme on *didicerint*. There is a recurring pattern throughout this passage of one or two phrases with homoeoteleuton, and then with a following phrase that diverges only slightly from the pattern.

expect both verbs of the temporal clause to have the same tense. The imperfect tense would have been the most grammatically precise for both verbs, since they both express continuing action.[81] However, since the latter verb (*perscrutor*) is deponent and takes passive forms, only the pluperfect would produce an ending similar to *residerem*.[82] All these grammatical and syntactical choices show more concern for affecting an elevated poetic register connected to the hermeneutic style, rather than instructing those whose Latin is poor.

While the vocabulary of this section is not that unusual, there are some traces of stylization. Note the repetition of "p" and "c" in the phrase "perscrutatus essem multiplicem computandi prudentiam, cepi cordetenus ruminare pauca ex plurimis, quali medicamine possem clericis proficere." While this goes beyond alliteration to a broader sound repetition, it does suggest a more stylized prose form. In addition, this phrase contains the word "medicamine" [medicine], a noun ending in –men, which can be categorized according to Lapidge's terms as a poeticism. This passage also contains an additional two items characteristic of Byrhtferth's hermeneutic saints' lives: *in conspectu iusti arbitris* and *cordetenus*.[83] The accumulation of all these poetic features within eleven lines suggests that this stylized passage might be called "hermeneutic" when compared to other sections of the *Enchiridion*, even though it does not reach the virtuosity of which Byrhtferth is capable.

It seems strange, however, to affect a higher register of Latin through poetic ornamentation, when the stated goal is to remediate an audience whose Latin is poor. Interestingly enough, Byrhtferth did not translate any of this passage into English even though this section is bilingual. Furthermore, no attack of the secular clergy in English is quite as critical of their laziness. For instance, in this passage from section 1.2, Byrhtferth admonished the clerics in much gentler tones than above: "Nu wolde ic þæt þa æðela clericas asceocon fram heora andgites orðance ælce sleacnysse, þæt hig þe borlicor mihton beforan arwurðum biscopum gecyðan þæra epactana gescead" (*BE*, 42) [Now I want the noble clerics to shake from their

81 It is also possible that Byrhtferth thought *perscrutatus essem* was imperfect, since *essem* is the imperfect form of the verb "to be."

82 Following these two verbs occurs a kind of off-rhyme with the following *prudentiam*.

83 See discussion of this passage, B&L, 278. The full phrase *in conspectu iusti arbitris* occurs in the *Vita S. Oswaldi* 3.4 and *iusti arbitris* occurs at 2.2 and 4.2. The word *cordetenus* occurs commonly in the *Vita S. Oswaldi*, the *Vita S. Ecgwini*, and the *Historia regum*.

intellect's comprehension any slowness/laziness, so that they might more excellently recite the calculation of the epacts before worthy bishops]. This passage has no corresponding Latin section, although this portion of the text alternates between Latin and English, which could potentially suggest that it was meant as a direct address to an English-speaking audience. There is little derision here. The clerics are called *æðela* [noble], and they are told to comport themselves *borlicor* [more excellently]. Even the most critical word in the passage, *sleacnysse*, is not unequivocally negative. Although *sleacnys* can be translated "laziness," it also can mean "slowness," as it does in Ælfric's *De temporibus anni*, where the *sleacnys* of the sun is contrasted with the *swyftnys* [swiftness] of the moon.[84] Thus, the clerics were told to "shake the slowness from their intelligent perception." On the whole, Byrhtferth was relatively kind to clerics in this English section; he addressed them with respect and suggested that they were capable of learning, a very different tone than the one he had taken in the Latin passage discussed above.

Although Byrhtferth addresses the secular clergy in both flattering and unflattering terms in English, it is interesting that almost all occurrences of the Latin *clericus* are accompanied by a criticism of the laxity of the secular clergy. Notably these harangues also tend to be associated with a more stylized form of Latin, one that approaches a version of the hermeneutic style. Although there were probably some clerics who attained that level of Latinity,[85] on the whole the hermeneutic style is strongly connected to monastic identity. I suggest that the Latin harangues against the secular clergy in the *Enchiridion* are not intended for the clerics whom they chastise, but for monks, as an encouragement for them to act like Benedictines, and not like these rustic priests. Furthermore, the assumption that English-language sections are for the secular clergy is an equally dubious one, since Byrhtferth

84 The full quotation is "Swa swa þære sunnan sleacnys acenð ænne dæg & ane niht æfre ymbe feower gear, swa eac þæs monan swyftnys awyrpð ut ænne dæg, & ane niht of ðam getele his rynes æfre embe nigontyne gear, & se dæg is gehaten Saltus lune, þæt is ðæs monan hlyp, forðan ðe he oferhlypð ænne dæg, & swa near þam nigonteoðan geare swa bið se <niwa> mona braddra gesewen." *Ælfric's De temporibus anni*, ed. H. Henel, EETS, o.s. 213 (London, 1942), 58. The passage is not substantively different in the new edition: Martin Blake, ed., *Ælfric's De temporibus anni*, Anglo-Saxon Texts 6 (Cambridge, 2009), 90.

85 The *Vita S. Dunstani* was written by a secular cleric known as B. For a discussion of this Life and its writer, see Michael Lapidge, "*B.* and the *Vita S. Dunstani*," in *Anglo-Latin Literature, 900–1066* (London, 1993), 279–91.

writes substantial sections of book 3 in English for an audience that he defines as monastic.[86] I suggest that the frequent naming of the secular clergy as the audience of the *Enchiridion* has less to do with the realities of Byrhtferth's classroom (which almost certainly held as many monks as clerics), but with his construction of monasticism as centrally defined by Latinity, and as strongly connected to a stylized form of Latin. Thus, throughout the *Enchiridion* he claims to translate for the sake of the less-educated clerics, not for the monks, who need no such remediation. In these statements, the presence of the secular clergy gives Byrhtferth permission to translate into English for all the students in his classroom, while still maintaining a monastic identity that privileges Latinity. The next section will further examine how Byrhtferth's negative depictions of the secular clergy encode specific features of a reformed Benedictine identity.

Monastic Self-Definition and Epideictic Literature

While it is easy to see how Byrhtferth's stylized diatribes excluded the secular clergy and made them the brunt of the joke for his Latin-literate monks, what is happening in these stylized passages is even more complicated than that. Since these caricatures of the secular clergy were intended for the eyes of monks, and not the clerics themselves, then we are in the realm of epideictic literature, the literature of praise and blame. This genre is described in Aristotle's *Rhetoric* as a highly stylized literary form intended to prove that someone is worthy of praise or blame. By extension, the hearer/reader is also praised because of a connection to the object praised, just as a funeral oration for a dead soldier tends to celebrate all members of that nation, not just the deceased. The study of epideictic literature is appropriate to our discussion of the *Enchiridion*, because it allows us to examine Byrhtferth's harangues of the secular clergy in light of the hearer/reader, the monastic audience, who are being encouraged to better behaviour so that they may not fall prey to the sins of the secular clergy.

Applying the theories of classical rhetoric to the literature of Anglo-Saxon England is problematic, however, because knowledge of rhetoric

86 The use of English to educate monks is discussed in greater detail in my article "Byrhtferth's Enchiridion: The Effectiveness of Hermeneutic Latin," in *Conceptualizing Multilingualism in England, 800–1250*, ed. Elizabeth Tyler, Studies in the Early Middle Ages (Turnhout, 2011), 121–44.

was transmitted to the Anglo-Saxons via the study of grammar, not rhetorical treatises.[87] Therefore, it seems unlikely that Byrhtferth would have known what the word "epideictic" meant,[88] nor would he have understood the theory behind this kind of literature. Furthermore, epideictic works handling blame, as the *Enchiridion* does, are far less common than those dealing with praise. Aristotle's *Rhetoric* discusses speeches of praise in great detail, but says of blame only, "No special treatment of censure and vituperation is needed. Knowing the above facts, we know their contraries; and it is out of these that speeches of censure are made."[89] Epideictic literature of the early Middle Ages is similarly focused on praise not blame, as is shown by many extant panegyric poems praising rulers among others,[90] especially the writings of Venantius Fortunatus, whose works were known in Anglo-Saxon England.[91] It is possible that Byrhtferth could have had an idea of epideictic literature from these texts, since some understanding of the classical rhetorical tradition was passed through the practice of imitation, rather than instruction in rhetoric, per se.[92] Blame, however, did serve an important role in the stigmatization of minority groups, such as the Jews, who often appeared as a caricatured other against which the majority group defined itself.[93]

87 Knappe, "Classical Rhetoric," 15 and 28. Janie Steen argues that the knowledge of rhetoric was transferred through the study of Christian Latin poets; see *Verse and Virtuosity*, 7–20. For evidence of Byrhtferth's knowledge of rhetorical figures, see above, pp. 81–3.

88 In fact, Byrhtferth was confused by other words with the Greek prefix "epi-," as is evidenced by his use of the word *epilogus* to mean *pre*face, rather than epilogue. For a discussion of this see Michael Lapidge, "Byrhtferth and the *Vita S. Ecgwini*," in *Anglo-Latin Literature: 900–1066* (London, 1993), 293–315, at 299 n. 32.

89 Aristotle, *Rhetoric and Poetics*, trans. Rhys Roberts (New York, 1954), 63 (1.9).

90 For a discussion of the late antique panegyric, see Sabine G. MacCormack, *Art and Ceremony in Late Antiquity*, The Transformation of the Classical Heritage 1 (Berkeley and Los Angeles, 1981).

91 For a discussion of Fortunatus's panegyrics, see J. George, *Venantius Fortunatus: A Latin Poet in Merovingian Gaul* (Oxford, 1992), 35–61. For evidence of knowledge of Venantius Fortunatus, see Michael Lapidge, "Knowledge of the Poems of Venantius Fortunatus in Early Anglo-Saxon England," in *Anglo-Latin Literature, 600–899* (London, 1996), 399–407.

92 Knappe, "Classical Rhetoric," 25 and 28.

93 For the stigmatization of minority groups in medieval Europe, see R.I. Moore, *The Formation of Persecuting Society: Power and Deviance in Western Europe, 950–1250* (Oxford, 1987). For the depictions of Jews in Anglo-Saxon England, see Andrew P. Scheil, *The Footsteps of Israel: Understanding Jews in Anglo-Saxon England* (Ann

Although a direct line cannot be established between (say) Aristotle's *Rhetoric* and Byrhtferth's *Enchiridion*, it is useful to discuss Byrhtferth's writing within the context of epideictic literature, because his work reserves elevated and highly stylized discourse, the purpose of which was not to narrate or to educate,[94] for the chastisement of a clerical audience. Classical rhetoricians, such as Aristotle, declared that a work's style should be appropriate to its content, and a high style was most suitable to speeches of praise and blame, because of the position of the hearer, whose job in epideictic rhetoric was not to determine a verdict (as in legal speeches), but only to act as an observer, who must "decide on the orator's skill" in praising or blaming.[95] The success of the argument in convincing the hearer of the need for praise or blame is more closely connected to a speech's rhetorical sophistication in epideictic rhetoric than in any other form. The close connection of style and argument in epideictic literature perhaps explains why Byrhtferth's most elaborate style in the *Enchiridion* is reserved for the vituperation of the secular clergy, not the explication of computus.

Since Byrhtferth repeatedly indicated that his criticisms did not apply to his monastic audience, he flatters the monks by implying that they studiously avoid these vices committed by the clerics. The role of flattery in positioning the reader of epideictic literature has been described by John Lockwood:

> Flattery operates by putting what is supposedly the referent ... at a distance, which is easily done since neither the speaker nor speech knows, represents, the referent. Instead, the referent is used merely as a pretext for constructing a praising representation in which the listener is included. The praise flatters by collapsing together the listener and the referent, the object of praise,

Arbor, MI, 2004). For medieval Jews more generally, see Kenneth R. Stow, *Alienated Minority: The Jews of Medieval Europe* (Cambridge, MA, 1992); Jacob Katz, *Exclusiveness and Tolerance: Studies in Jewish–Gentile Relations in Medieval and Modern Times* (Oxford, 1961). For the tradition of polemical writings against the Jews, see Gilbert Dahan, *The Christian Polemic against the Jews*, trans. Jody Gladding (Notre Dame, IN, 1998). Anti-Jewish polemics were written by such writers as Augustine, John Chrysostom, Peter Damian, Petrus Alfonsi, and Peter the Venerable, to name a few.

94 Cf. the comments of MacCormak, who described the late antique panegyric, "even when written in prose," as a genre that tended "towards description rather than narrative and analysis." *Art and Ceremony*, 7.

95 Aristotle, *Rhetoric*, 32 (1.3).

> through an operation of inclusion, transporting the praise from its ostensible object onto the listener.[96]

The referent in this case is the secular clergy, whom Byrhtferth is not really addressing. Rather, the secular clergy are a *pretext* for encoding an institutional identity for Benedictine monasticism. However, what Byrhtferth wrote is not praise, the subject of Lockwood's comments, but blame; thus, he used flattery in exactly the reverse manner to what is described above. Rather than "constructing a praising representation" that includes the reader, the rhetoric of blame operates by separating the listener/reader from the object of blame, and thus proving that the listener is to be praised, not blamed. In other words, Byrhtferth's hermeneutic diatribes define what a good monk is by defining what he is not: a secular cleric.

In order to explain how the *Enchiridion*'s depictions of the secular clergy represent the inverse standard expected of reformed monks, let us to turn to the following passage, which criticizes Byrhtferth's clerical students for their rejection of the study of computus:

> Extermina<n>t huiusmodi mensuras nonnulli <clerici> imperiti (heu, pro dolor!) qui non habere desiderant philacteria sua; uerbi gratia, ordinem quem susceperunt in gremio matris ecclesie non seruant, nec in doctrina sancte meditationis persistunt. Intuend<a> est soller<ter> uia phariseorum et saduceorum, et respuenda uelut peripsima doctrina eorum. Procurator clericus anime sue fieri debet, et sicut primas subicit pullum subiugalem, animum suum debet seruituti subicere, implendo alabastrum pretioso unguento, hoc est intus esse diatim debet, diuinis legibus obtemperando <et> monitis redemptoris. His dictis, redeamus uenusto animo unde discesseramus mediocri alloquio. (*BE*, 46)

> [Some ignorant clerics reject calculations of this kind (for shame!) and do not wish to keep their phylacteries, that is, they do not preserve the order, which they have received in the bosom of mother church, nor do they persist in the holy teaching of meditation. They should consider carefully the way of the Pharisees and the Sadducees, and they should spit out their doctrine like filth. A cleric ought to be the keeper of his own soul, just as a noble man subjects

96 R. Lockwood, *The Reader's Figure: Epideictic Rhetoric in Plato, Aristotle, Bossuet, Racine and Pascal*, Histoire des idées et critique littéraire 351 (Geneva, 1996), 125.

a young foal to the yoke, so he ought to subject his own soul to service, by filling the alabaster box with precious oil, that is, he ought to be inwardly subjected daily, by obeying the divine laws and admonitions of the Redeemer. Having said these things, let us return with a graceful soul from whence we have digressed with our mediocre speech.]

As occurs elsewhere in the *Enchiridion*, this attack against the laziness and lack of education of clerics appears in a stylized form of Latin laced with Aldhelmian phrases and hermeneutic vocabulary. Even the number of clerics who are subject to this critique is unclear, since Byrhtferth employs the rhetorical device of litotes. He names the number of negligent clerics as "nonnulli," which literally means "not none" and is often translated as "some," but since litotes is predicated on understatement, Byrhtferth might actually be implying that this criticism could be assigned to "many" or "most" clerics. The words *philacteria* and *peripsima* are on Lapidge's catalogue of hermeneutic vocabulary.[97] Furthermore, the phrase "in gremio matris ecclesie" is reminiscent of the Aldhelmian "ad maternum sanctae ecclesiae gremium."[98] Equally, the connection of *peripsima* with the verb *respuo* in the phrase "respuenda uelut peripsima doctrina eorum" seems also to have been derived from Aldhelm.[99] The elaborate images and esoteric vocabulary in this passage situate the speaker as an authority, since hermeneutic vocabulary proves that Byrhtferth has the intellectual credentials to chastise the ignorance of the clerics. Proof of the speaker's *bona fides* are crucial to the construction of praise in epideictic literature,[100] because the success of the praise and blame of epideictic rhetoric is predicated upon the ethical position of the speaker, who must show that he knows the thing he praises.[101] In this case, Byrhtferth proved his own educational prowess in his complex biblical allusions, Aldhelmian phrasing, and use of poetic vocabulary.

In this passage, Byrhtferth attributed three undesirable qualities to these unskilled clerics: laziness, lack of education, and an inner soul that fails to maintain the piety of its outside appearance. In each case, Byrhtferth blamed the clerics through the use of grammatically negative constructions.

97 Lapidge, "Hermeneutic Style," 128.

98 Aldhelm, *Prosa de virginitate*, chap. 44. Passage is discussed in B&L, 274.

99 *Prosa de virginitate*, chap. 10. B&L, 274.

100 Lockwood, *Reader's Figure*, 45–9.

101 Ibid.

For instance, he described the clerics as *imperiti* (literally "not-skilled," and here referring to their lack of education) rather than using a word such as *rudis*, which would also suggest an insufficient education but lack the negating prefix "*in.*" Furthermore, he alleges that they do not preserve proper order (*non* seruant),[102] and do not persist in meditation (*nec* ... persistunt). By expressing each of these criticisms in a negative form, Byrhtferth implied that the corresponding positive statement could apply to a good cleric or monk, who deserved to be praised, not blamed. In order to delve deeper into the rhetoric of blame in this text, let us examine three dichotomies suggested by Byrhtferth's criticisms of the secular clergy listed above: interior/exterior, laziness/discipline, and *imperiti/periti* [uneducated/educated].

First, the passage suggests a conflict between the inner soul and outward appearance in the reference to Matthew 23:6: "Woe unto you scribes and Pharisees, hypocrites! for ye are like unto whited sepulchres which indeed appear beautiful outward, but are within full of dead men's bones, and of all uncleanness. Even so ye also outwardly appear righteous unto men, but within ye are full of hypocrisy and iniquity."[103] That Byrhtferth was alluding to this verse can be confirmed by his injunction to spit out the doctrines of the Pharisees and Sadducees as filth. The concern that external piety may not align with the inward soul is a common theme of reformed texts.[104] The Rule itself describes Sarabaites, as those whose "tonsures mark them as liars,"[105] because their private behaviour does not comport with the piety suggested by their outward signifying marks. Strict observance of the Rule serves, in part, to force the inward spirit to conform through outward disciplines, by providing the rule as a fire in which to try the monks.[106]

---

102 The Latin word *ordo* could refer to "order" in general terms or more specifically to ecclesiastical rank, especially to a clerical rank.

103 Matt. 23:27–8 (KJV); cf. the Vulgate, which reads, "Vae vobis scribae et Pharisaei hypocritae, quia similes estis sephulchris dealbatis, quae a foris parent hominibus speciosa, intus vero plena sunt ossibus mortuorum et omni spurcitia. Sic et vos a foris quidem paretis hominibus iusti, intus autem pleni estis hyposcrisi et iniquitate." (I have added modern punctuation.)

104 Cf. especially the comments by Wulfstan of Winchester that connect the clerics' lack of morality with their inability to celebrate the mass properly; see above p. 69n3.

105 McCann, *Rule of St Benedict*, 14–15; cf. the Latin, which reads, "mentiri Deo per tonsuram noscuntur."

106 The iniquity of the Sarabaites is attributed to the lack of a rule that will test them: "qui nulla regula approbati experientia magistra sicut aurum fornacis, sed in plumbi natura milliti"; McCann, *Rule of St Benedict*, 14.

Second, discipline is implied in this passage by the simile in which Byrhtferth suggested that the clerics subjugate their own soul, just as a noble man subjects a foal to the yoke. The Rule of Benedict is commonly depicted in late Anglo-Saxon art as a kind of yoke that both binds the monks together and subjugates each individually. For instance, in the frontispiece to the *Regularis concordia*,[107] the same scroll connects King Edgar, Dunstan, Æthelwold, and an anonymous monk, who wraps it around his waist as a gesture of his acceptance of its observances.[108] The lost frontispiece for the OE translation of the Rule preserved in the Arundel Psalter also depicts a monk (thought to be Æthelwold) wrapping himself in a similar scroll on which the words "*zona humilitatis*" [belt of humility] are written.[109] While Byrhtferth's passage does not refer to the discipline of the Rule specifically, nor does it directly call the clerics lazy,[110] these things are insinuated when Byrhtferth claimed that the clerics refused to persist in meditation and failed to preserve order,[111] perhaps an oblique reference to the Rule itself.[112]

Third, the inability to accept discipline makes the clerics *imperiti*, unskilled through laziness. The difficult language of the text encodes the connection between education and discipline in its elevated register, which requires a certain level of discipline to master. In fact, the ability to read this passage of Latin inherently implies that the reader is not undisciplined and therefore not subject to its criticism The Rule also connects education to discipline by attributing a monk's inability to read to laziness: "Si quis vero ita *negligens* et *desidiosus* fuerit, ut non velit aut non possit meditare aut legere, injungatur ei opus quod faciat, ut non vacet"[113] [If anyone is so negligent and lazy that he does not wish to read or study, or is not able, let a job be imposed upon him, so that he may work and not be idle].

107 The original frontispiece is lost, but a copy of it is preserved in London, British Library, Cotton Tiberius A.iii, fol. 2v.

108 Robert Deshman, *The Benedictional of Æthelwold*, Studies in Manuscript Illumination 9 (Princeton, NJ, 1995), 180.

109 Ibid. See also Deshman, "*Benedictus Monarcha et Monarchus*: Early Medieval Ruler Theology and the Anglo-Saxon Reform," *Frühmittelalterliche Studien* 10 (1976): 204–40, at 205 and 215.

110 However, the clerics are specifically called "lazy" elsewhere, see above, pp. 89–90.

111 See the discussion of grammatically negative statements above, pp. 97–8.

112 Or this could refer to the clerics' own ecclesiastical rank, which they failed to uphold.

113 McCann, *Rule of St. Benedict*, 11, italics mine. The word *negligens* may be a play on words made up of *nego* [to refuse] and *lego* [to read]. Therefore, a negligent monk is one who refuses to read.

Furthermore, the Rule also stipulated that monks spend certain hours of the day in study,[114] which may have been another factor that separated them from their secular counterparts.

In each of these negative criticisms of the secular clergy, the corresponding positive represented the goal towards which a reformed monk should strive. Thus, a careful reading of these harangues against the secular clergy reveals the elements of monasticism especially valued by Byrhtferth, who placed a special emphasis on education, discipline, and an observance of the Rule strict enough to mark the monk's inner soul, as well as his outward appearance. Notably, the text complains that clerics are uneducated, because they will not persist in the practice of meditation [*meditationis*], a word linked in the Rule specifically to study.[115] Thus, the education of Benedictine monks is connected to their ability to follow the discipline of the Rule, which stipulates the hours of the day that a monk must spend reading. In their exclusion from the blame reserved for the secular clergy, the monks are praised for their discipline, which can be seen in their ability to read Latin, especially the hermeneutic style, the difficulty of which limits its audience to only those who persist with their study.

Conclusion

Despite the frequent naming of the secular clergy, their importance as an audience of the *Enchiridion* has probably been overstated. Although there seem to have been secular clerics in Byrhtferth's classroom, there were at least as many monastic students, even though these pupils are much less

---

114 For a discussion of the central place of writing and *grammatica* in the *Rule of St Benedict*, see Martin Irvine, *The Making of Textual Culture: "Grammatica" and Literary Theory, 350–1100*, Cambridge Studies in Medieval Literature 19 (Cambridge, 1994), 191–2. Michael Lapidge suggests that after mastering the psalms, students in an Anglo-Saxon classroom might have then begun studying important Latin poetic works in "perhaps a graded sequence of difficulty, beginning with the anonymous *Disticha Catonis* and/or the *Epigrammata* of Prosper of Aquitaine, then the *Evangelia* of Juvencus, the *Carmen Paschale* of Caelius Sedulius, and the *Historia apostolica* (or *De actibus apostolorum*) of Arator. This sequence could be amplified so as to include other Christian Latin poets: Avitus, Dracontius, Venantius Fortunatus, Prudentius (especially the Psychomachia)." "Schools," in *The Blackwell Encyclopaedia of Anglo-Saxon England*, ed. M. Lapidge, J. Blair, S. Keynes, and D. Scragg (Oxford, 1999), 407–9, at 409. See also Lapidge, "The Study of Latin Texts in Late Anglo-Saxon England," in *Anglo-Latin Literature, 600–899* (London, 1993), 455–98.

115 See above, p. 99, in which the word "meditare" in the doublet "meditare aut legere" clearly refers to concentration on a book.

frequently mentioned. The disparaging treatment that secular clerics receive in Latin suggest that these more difficult sections were intended for monastic students, but the reverse is not true, that is, the English sections were not intended solely for a clerical audience. The figure of the lazy secular cleric throughout the *Enchiridion* is something of a bogeyman, a scapegoat. The presence of this insufficiently educated audience permitted Byrhtferth to translate the text into English. Once translated, this text could be read even by those monks who should be fully literate in Latin. Thus, by frequently reiterating the need for a vernacular translation specifically for the secular clergy, Byrhtferth authorized a translation for his monastic students, while reminding them of the importance of Latinity in monastic identification.

Therefore, the descriptions of secular clerics in the *Enchiridion* should not be read as accurate depictions of real members of the secular clergy. Instead, this caricature of clerical laziness should be read for what it reveals about how the Benedictines are constructing and defining themselves during this period of reform. The monks are identifying themselves as Latinate and *boceras*, specifically distinguishing themselves from a certain kind of secular cleric, like the one who only knew Latin "be dæle" [in part], made famous by Ælfric in his preface to the Old English translation of Genesis.[116] The development and cultivation of hermeneutic Latin plays an important role in this act of self-definition, since the audience of a hermeneutic text is limited by the hours of study and discipline required to learn it. Just as the Benedictine rule and the *Regularis concordia* draw firm lines of division between monks and clerics, the practice of writing hermeneutic Latin reinforces and reinscribes those boundaries, by creating a discourse accessible only to a monastic elite. Byrhtferth's work also provides an important caution about taking the explicit linguistic commentary of Benedictine writers at face value. Since issues of language were closely tied to constructions of monastic identity, modern scholars must read through the identity politics of the period if they hope to unearth the roles of, and hierarchies between, Latin and English during the late Anglo-Saxon period. The next chapter will attempt to elucidate the politics surrounding English-language texts by further examining the vernacular sections of the *Enchiridion*, which present a further complication, since their subject, computus, is also closely tied to monastic identity.

116 Jonathan Wilcox, ed., *Ælfric's Prefaces*, Durham Medieval Texts 9 (Durham, 1994), 116. There is a sustained discussion of this preface in chapter 4 below.

3 The Politics of English: Computus, Translation, and Monastic Self-Definition

The previous two chapters examined the reading experience of the *Enchiridion* and the role of the hermeneutic style in defining monks. Now that we have seen that the secular clerics are not so much an accurately depicted real audience, but rather an elaborate excuse for English-language translation for a monastic audience, then it is time to re-examine the English sections of the *Enchiridion* in order to elucidate the role and status of English in a monastic classroom. This issue bears on most Anglo-Saxon literature because monks educated in Benedictine classrooms throughout England are the same authors and scribes who produced or copied the majority of extant Old English manuscripts. Furthermore, the private affairs of Byrhtferth's classroom may well reflect attitudes and mentalities similar to those in other monastic classrooms throughout England.

In order to understand fully the status of the English-language text in the *Enchiridion*, we must now turn to its central content: computus. Many ecclesiasts considered this knowledge to be a vital component of any clerical training.[1] Byrhtferth claims that secular clerics need to know computus in order to pass an examination in front of their bishop.[2] Both Ælfric's pastoral letter and the Rule of Chrodegang list a computus among the

1 For an introduction to computistical material in Anglo-Saxon England, see chap. 1, p. 39n2. For a handlist of prognostical manuscripts, many of which also include computistical materials, see Roy Liuzza, "Anglo-Saxon Prognostics in Context: A Survey and Handlist of Manuscripts," *ASE* 30 (2001): 181–230.

2 Peter S. Baker and Michael Lapidge, eds, *Byrhtferth's Enchiridion*, EETS, s.s., 15 (Oxford, 1995), 42; this chapter will continue the practice of citing the text of the *Enchiridion* as "*BE*" and the editorial matter of Baker and Lapidge as "B&L." All translations are mine unless otherwise noted.

books that a secular cleric is required to own.[3] While this evidence would suggest that knowledge of computus might have been expected among the secular clergy, much more evidence suggests that it was closely tied to a sense of monastic identity. Byrhtferth explains that the computistical training of his monks began "ab ipso pubertatis tyrocinio cum lacte carnis genetricis eorum lac sugxerunt aecclesię catholicę"[4] (*BE*, 232) [from the time of their youthful training they have sucked the milk of the catholic church at the same time as their mother's milk]. Here Byrhtferth makes a fairly profound argument for the foundational place of computistical training in monastic identity formation, when he calls it the *milk* of the church's teaching that is imbibed at a young age. Byrhtferth himself presumably learned his computus from the great Benedictine Abbo of Fleury, who was exiled at Ramsey from 985 to 987.[5] At the same time that Abbo was encouraging computistical exploration at Byrhtferth's home in Ramsey, the important reformed centre of Winchester developed a standard computus, a fact that suggests that Byrhtferth was not alone in his obsession with this line of enquiry.[6] The reformers' deep-seated interest in computistical topics can also be seen in Ælfric of Eynsham's *De temporibus anni*, which introduces scientific aspects related to computus in an English-language format.[7]

3 *Die Hirtenbriefe Ælfrics in altenglischer und latinischer Fassung*, ed. B. Fehr, with suppl. by P. Clemoes, Bibliothek der angelsächsenischen Prosa 9 (Darmstadt, 1966), 1.52, 2.137 and 157–8. *The Old English Version of the Enlarged Rule of Chrodegang: Edited together with the Latin Text and an English Translation*, ed. Brigitte Langefeld, Münchner Universitätsschriften, Texte und Untersuchungen zur Englischen Philologie 26 (Frankfurt, 2004), 317.

4 For the full quotation in context, see chapter 2, p. 79.

5 B&L, xx–xxiii.

6 For a history of the evolution of computus in Anglo-Saxon England, see R.M. Liuzza, "In Measure, Number, and Weight: Writing Science," in *The Cambridge History of Early Medieval English Literature*, ed. Clare A. Lees (Cambridge, 2013). The Winchester computus is reflected in the Cotton Titus D.xxvi and xxvii (the *Prayerbook of Ælfwine*), Cambridge Trinity College R. 15. 32, pp. 15–36; British Library Cotton Vitellius E.xviii, BL Arundel 60 and BL, Cotton Tiberius C.vi, fols. 2r–7r. For a discussion of the Winchester computus and its relationship to Byrhtferth's computus, see Faith Wallis, "Background Essay: St John's College 17 as a Computus Manuscript," in *The Calendar and the Cloister: Oxford, St John's College MS17* (McGill University Library, Digital Collections Program, 2007), http://digital.library.mcgill.ca/ms-17.

7 Ælfric's *De temporibus* has been released in a new edition by Martin Blake, *Ælfric's De temporibus anni*, Anglo-Saxon Texts 6 (Woodbridge, UK, 2009).

Although computus cannot claim to be an exclusively Benedictine practice in the same way that hermeneutic Latin is, there does seem to be a strong connection between monastic identity and the study of the more esoteric aspects of computus (as will be argued in more detail below). The creation of English-language works that deal with computistical topics by both Ælfric and Byrhtferth, however, creates a problem in our understanding of the use of English in the period. If computistical knowledge were an important facet of monastic identity, then we would expect this study to be encoded in Latin, thus restricting the knowledge to monks with the leisure to study. The presence of these two English-language works might suggest the opposite, namely, that this practice was meant to be disseminated more broadly, especially among the secular clergy. This chapter first examines the manuscript context of some contemporary computistical material, since computus was a discipline that, while not limited to monks, was an important part of their construction of a Benedictine identity. The functions these texts serve sometimes diverge significantly from our modern expectations of scientific inquiry or education. Furthermore, since the predominant use of English for a largely monastic enterprise presents a great contrast to Byrhtferth's explicit statements about the worth of the vernacular, the chapter then turns to his explicit comments about the purpose and utility of English, focusing especially on those statements that are contradicted by the visible practices of the text. Finally, the chapter ends by considering Byrhtferth's "hermeneutic English," a section in book 3 that adapts an Aldhelmian passage into a rather flamboyant style of English. This particular section also relates the Legend of St Pachomius, a monastic saint known for receiving instructions for calculating Easter through divine inspiration. In this moment in the *Enchiridion*, Byrhtferth brings together the strong monastic identification and ownership of computus along with an English version of the hermeneutic style in a manner unlike anything else produced in the vernacular literature of the reform. This passage shows the strongest example of how Byrhtferth's (and Ælfric's) explicit statements about the worth and utility of English diverge from Byrhtferth's practical use of English in the training of his novices.[8]

8 For more on Ælfric's comments on the vernacular, see chap. 4.

The Functions of Computistical Material

It is now time to turn beyond the *Enchiridion* to look more broadly at the context of computistical material in a few representative manuscripts from the late Anglo-Saxon period that illustrate some of the functions that this scientific material can have. Manuscripts with computistical matter often hold other texts that are also connected to monastic identity, but, in each of these collections, the Easter tables and related material perform functions that are often quite unscientific, ranging from the devotional to the decorative. These manuscript contexts suggest that the eleventh-century practice of computistical inquiry is about much more than the calculation of Easter.

The connection between computistical study and specifically monastic devotion is encoded in the British Library's Cotton Titus D.xxvi and xxvii, which originally constituted a single manuscript commonly called *Ælfwine's Prayerbook*.[9] This manuscript belonged to Ælfwine when he was deacon of Newminster in Winchester,[10] and its small size – barely 4 inches wide by 5 inches tall – suggests that it was intended for his personal devotion. One of its full-page drawings shows how computus interacts with Christian, and specifically Benedictine, contemplation. In this picture, Christ hangs on the cross crucified and flanked by the two virgins, Mary and John, the evangelist, both of whom are looking up at Christ. This scene of the three virgins is an image that recurs in many Benedictine texts, including several homilies of Ælfric.[11] In the space on the right and left above Christ sit two figures, one of whom is crowned and holds the sun, while the other holds the moon. The figures are in the register normally inhabited by heavenly figures such as angels, but instead they are in fact personified heavenly bodies. Since these two figures inhabit a position directly above Mary and John, respectively, they have a decided prominence in the picture, and the

9 N.R. Ker, *Catalogue of Manuscripts Containing Anglo-Saxon* (Oxford, 1957), no. 202; Helmut Gneuss, *Handlist of Anglo-Saxon Manuscripts: A List of Manuscripts and Manuscript Fragments Written or Owned in England up to 1100*, Medieval and Renaissance Text Studies 241 (Tempe, AZ, 2001), no. 380. An edition is available: Beate Günzel, ed., *Aelfwine's Prayerbook: London, British Library, Cotton Titus D. XXVI + XXVII*, Henry Bradshaw Society 108 (London, 1993).

10 Ker, *Catalogue*, 265. He was elevated to the position of abbot in 1031.

11 A description of this illumination and related pictures can be found in Barbara C. Raw, *Anglo-Saxon Crucifixion Iconography and the Art of the Monastic Revival*, Cambridge Studies in Anglo-Saxon England 1 (Cambridge, 1990), 129–31, with plates at VIII, IX, X.

computistical observance of the moon and sun is equated with the veneration of Mary, who held a central position in reformed houses in the late tenth and early eleventh centuries.[12] In its combination of devotional and liturgical material, such as the Offices of the Holy Cross, the Holy Trinity, and the Virgin; a collectar; and a litany, along with a range of computistical material, including a table giving the full calculation of Easter from 978 to 1097; this manuscript shows the close association between computistical study and the personal devotion of one Benedictine monk.[13]

In 1031 Ælfwine became the abbot of Newminster, a prominent Benedictine establishment, and the devotional aspect of computus perhaps relates back to the regulated orderly aspect of both computus and Benedictine monasticism, as we see in Cotton Tiberius A.iii. This manuscript joins Ælfric's *De temporibus anni* with such important Benedictine texts as the *Regularis concordia* and the Rule of St Benedict.[14] It seems that the observation of the orderly progression of the moon and the sun complements the orderly observance of life expected of Benedictine monks.[15] Computus may have been such an important activity for Benedictines because

12 For the connection of Mary to the Benedictine Reform, see Mary Clayton, *The Cult of the Virgin Mary in Anglo-Saxon England*, Cambridge Studies in Anglo-Saxon England 2 (Cambridge, 1990); Clayton, "Centralism and Uniformity versus Localism and Diversity: The Virgin and Native Saints in the Monastic Reform," *Peritia* 8 (1994): 95–106.

13 Roy Liuzza makes a similar argument about the prognostic material in this manuscript, a subject that he sees as growing out of the standardizations of the Benedictine Reform. "Anglo-Saxon Prognostics," 195–200.

14 Interestingly enough, this manuscript also includes a glossed copy of Ælfric's *Colloquy*, which is concerned with the order of society in slightly different ways. For more on these ideas of ordering society and the formation of novices, see Katherine O'Brien O'Keeffe, "'Esto quod es': Ælfric's *Colloquy* and the Imperatives of Monastic Identity," in *Stealing Obedience: Narratives of Agency and Identity in Later Anglo-Saxon England* (Toronto, 2012).

15 "Monastic discipline is first and foremost a temporal discipline of punctuality and accurate timekeeping. The spiritual life was shaped by the cycles of the calendar – fasts and feast, psalms and prayers, repentance and celebration were all performed according to calendrical calculations, and their observance was an outward sign of the universal unity of the church." Liuzza, "Anglo-Saxon Prognostics," 207. For a discussion of the importance of the Rule in ordering the life of the monks and its prescriptive detail, see Michael D.C. Drout, *How Tradition Works: A Meme-Based Cultural Poetics of the Anglo-Saxon Tenth Century*, Medieval and Renaissance Texts 306 (Tempe, AZ, 2006), 101–13, esp. 109–10. For a detailed account of a monk's daily life, see Mary Berry, "What the Saxon Monks Sang: Music in Winchester in the Late Tenth Century," in *Bishop Æthelwold: His Career and Influence*, ed. Barbara Yorke (Woodbridge, 1988), 150–1.

following the Benedictine rule required monks to focus very closely on both the seasons and the hours, since monastic observances must happen at specific times of day and change throughout the calendar year. Thus, Harley 5431, a deluxe copy of the Rule of St Benedict begins with a horologium, a chart that outlines the hours of the day. The other computistical texts and charts in this manuscript can be described as basic: a list of ferial regulars, epacts, and concurrents and a chart showing the age of the moon in twenty-nine- and thirty-day months. An Easter table is surprisingly absent from this list, despite the fact that the calculation of Easter is the telos of computus.[16] This manuscript also integrates computistical material into the decoration of the manuscript by adorning the text of the Rule and the other monastic works in the manuscript with elaborate initials containing motifs with interlaced birds and beasts. The computistical material is incorporated as part of this adornment, since these charts are richly decorated both in the ink for the letters, but also by thick coloured borders in red and purple, interlaced motifs, and animal decorations. In this colourful manuscript, the computistical material offers yet another adornment to what is otherwise a beautiful and decorated manuscript.

The computistical material in the manuscript Cotton Tiberius B.v may serve a similar decorative, rather than functional, purpose.[17] This manuscript is well known for its richly decorated miniatures illustrating the Wonders of the East and many other texts. The computistical material is equally richly decorated, but it is also defective. Patrick McGurk claimed that the computistical material in this manuscript was particularly incoherent:

> There is repetition of texts and a surprising division of others. Snippets from one of the texts ("De initio lunae quadragesimae") on the terms of the Easter moons recur four times on fols. 15, 18, and 18v (twice). Part of the text entitled "de celebratione paschae" is written twice on 18r and 18v. The supposed and well-known epistle of Theophilus of Alexandria to Theodosius on the decision of the council of Nicaea stops mid-way at the bottom of 17r and is separated from its sequel on 18r by some important tables on 17v, which

16 The formula for calculating Easter is notably absent from other computistical texts, such as Ælfric's *De temporibus*.

17 Ker, *Catalogue*, no. 193; Gneuss, *Handlist*, no. 373; a facsimile is available, P. McGurk, ed., *An Eleventh-Century Anglo-Saxon Miscellany*, Early English Manuscripts in Facsimile 21 (Copenhagen, 1983).

> suggests that the leaf with these tables may have been misplaced in a model or an archetype ... The general character of the entries on 18r and 18v suggests that these form an abbreviated, ill-arranged, repetitive, separate version of the computistical matter found in the Leofric [Missal]. Tiberius or its archetype stumbled on them, perhaps by chance, and merged them with the group ending on 17v, not apparently realizing that they were the same texts, only more incoherent and patchy even than the texts before 17v.[18]

Although the computistical material is visually appealing and ornamented, the text is corrupt and far less useful than it could be if it were copied with any care for the material. Furthermore, the Easter table (f. 16r) shows problems of careless and inadequate copying. According to McGurk, the table begins at 969. That date is written as "cccclxix" (469), since the roman numeral "D" (500) has been omitted. When the decennoval cycle is repeated in 988, the headings are renewed and the "D" is given for the first date only, which correctly reads, "Dcccclxxxviii." It is likely that in the exemplar, the "D" was given only for the first date at 969 and assumed after that, but the scribe's failure to copy it even for the first date presents serious problems of comprehension. More mistakes are introduced when the year 990 is reached, which reads "cccclxc." The roman numeral "l" for fifty is maintained as if it were part of the 400 from the previous year "cccclxxxix" (489), even though ninety is then correctly written as "xc." This intrusive "l" is maintained throughout the 990s, until 1000, which is blank rather than being an "M."

Furthermore, most of this error-filled Easter table was probably out of date by the time it was copied. The table begins at 969, the beginning of a decennoval cycle, a date of computistical importance, but of little relevance to the manuscript. Henel was the first to suggest that the manuscript must have been composed later than that. He argued that references in the manuscript to King Æthelred indicate that the text is from the latter part of his reign, specifically between 991 and 1016. Since the Easter tables run from 969 to 1006, the entire first decennoval cycle which ended in 987 had already passed before the earliest possible date for its completion. If the manuscript were completed towards the end of Henel's window, however, then the entire Easter table would have been exhausted by the time it was

18 Patrick McGurk, "The Computus," in *An Eleventh-Century Anglo-Saxon Miscellany*, 53–4 (specific page references to the Leofric Missal have been excised).

added to this manuscript.[19] The incomplete lists of the archbishops of Canterbury and the abbots of Glastonbury may function in the same way, resulting from a scribe's willingness to copy out-of-date and incoherent material from his exemplar without completing the information, rather than an early date for the manuscript.[20] In speaking of the incomplete state of the lists, Jacqueline Stodnick suggests that

> the significance of the material was more iconic than it was specific. In other words, the list collection in Tiberius B.v seems to be more important for what it displays than for the details it gives ... Given the apparent practical uselessness of some of the other materials in the manuscript, such as the computus texts, we have to wonder if other portions might share this largely iconic function. Rather than being preserved as a container for information, the manuscript (and the lists it contains) seems primarily to have been valued by its Anglo-Saxon users for its transformation of text into display – and the representation it is thus able to perform of knowledge, of history, and of place.[21]

The problems with the Easter table and the general incoherence of the computistical material in Tiberius B.v, an otherwise deluxe manuscript, encourages readers to explore the possibilities outlined by Stodnick that these computistical diagrams and text were added for their ornamental and "iconic" function, rather than their practical value.

The evidence of Tiberius B.v suggests that computistical texts were sometimes owned, but not used, as if the possessing of that material alone were enough. That principle is reaffirmed by the calendar and computistical material in a much less decorated MS: the tables contained in Cotton

19 Ker dated the manuscript even later, assigning a date of "s. xi^1," or "about the middle of the first half of the eleventh century"; *Catalogue*, 255–6. McGurk, the editor of the facsimile of Tiberius B.v, assigned an even later date to the manuscript, suggesting it was "perhaps nearer to 1050 than to 1025"; *Eleventh-Century Miscellany*, 33. According to Faith Wallis, copying out-of-date computistical material is not unusual. The Peterborough Computus was written c. 1120; its Easter tables contain dates for 988–1006, which would have been more than 100 years out of date at the time that it was copied. "Location and Dating," in *The Calendar and the Cloister*.

20 For the history of the lists in this manuscript, see David Dumville, "The Catalogue Texts," in *An Eleventh-Century Anglo-Saxon Miscellany*, ed. McGurk, 55–8.

21 "'Old Names of Kings or Shadows': Reading Documentary Lists," in *Conversion and Colonization in Anglo-Saxon England*, ed. Catherine E. Karkov and Nicholas Howe, Medieval and Renaissance Texts and Studies 318 (Tempe, AZ, 2006), 109–31, at 131.

Nero A.ii.[22] The Nero tables were likely once part of Cotton Galba A.xiv,[23] a prayer book once owned by a woman, who should never need to calculate Easter.[24] Although calendars are often richly decorated even in otherwise plain manuscripts, the kalendar in Nero A.ii can only be described as sloppy. Opening to the first page of January, the reader is confronted by a rough hand and plain black text, without the red, blue, or green ink that is normal in such calendars to distinguish columns of material. On the following page, for the month of February, some red annotations have been added, many but not all of which concern computistical information, such as the position of the bissextile day, rather than saints' days. These rubrics are in the same rough hand as the majority of the script. Following the calendar is a chart that lists epacts, concurrents, septuagessima,[25] terminus paschalis, and the day of Easter. Though such charts are usually very carefully ruled, this one seems to have been written freehand, and as a consequence the columns fail to line up. Furthermore, there seems not to have been enough room to include the day of Easter – arguably the most important part of an Easter table – so the roman numerals for the date are given, but not the month or the kalends, ides, or nones, as they are for the other dates.[26] This incomplete and poorly written Easter table suggests that ownership of this computistical knowledge was important, even when the material was neither useful nor decorative.

Computistical texts also appear accompanied by school texts that are connected to the Benedictine practice of learning hermeneutic Latin. Thus, computistical texts are found in Harley 3271,[27] a version of Ælfric's

22 Ker, *Catalogue*, no. 157; Gneuss, *Handlist*, no. 342.

23 An edition is available: Bernard James Muir, ed., *A Pre-Conquest Prayer-Book: (BL MSS Cotton Galba A.xiv and Nero A.ii (ff. 3–13))*, Henry Bradshaw Society 103 (Woodbridge, 1988).

24 According to Ker's *Catalogue*, "The oldest parts of it are probably of s. xi in., and may have been written for male use (ff. 7–37, 58–63^{v}, 65–70, 75), but the manuscript was extensively added to in s. xi^{1} for the use of a female member of a religious house, as appears from the feminine singular forms in texts on ff. 6^{v}, 53^{v}, 85^{v}, and 125^{v}, and the mention of 'hoc monasterium' (f. 89^{v})" (198). Bernard Muir argues that this book was originally bound as a blank book and entries were added in such a way as to suggest that it was "an 'exercise' book by those being taught in the monastery." *Prayerbook*, xvii.

25 I presume this is septuagesima, but the text reads, "xiiiil."

26 It is possible that the month names were cut off when this manuscript was trimmed to be rebound in its current form. However, there is space after the roman numerals to add kalends, ides, or nones, and in some cases to add the full names of the month, but these are nowhere included.

27 Ker, *Catalogue*, no. 239; Gneuss, *Handlist*, no. 435.

grammar combined with a Latin grammatical treatise and book 3 of Abbo's *Bella Parisiacae urbis*, a work read in the Anglo-Saxon period for its esoteric vocabulary and the elaborate glossing that surrounds the text.[28] In this manuscript, the Latin glossed text of Abbo is preceded by a bilingual (Latin and English) version of the text. In some manuscripts such as this one, computus seems to be an esoteric schoolroom exercise related to the study of glossed Latin texts with recherché vocabulary. In these manuscript contexts, mastery of computus's intricacies and complicated vocabulary can be as strongly connected to a monastic identity as mastery of the hermeneutic style.

While the provenance of each of these manuscripts is not known with certainty, they do demonstrate the range of possible, and largely non-scientific, roles that computistical material could play in a manuscript. While not all the manuscripts discussed in this section are specifically monastic, computus is often included alongside texts closely connected to the Benedictine Reform, such as the Rule of Benedict, and the study of computus seems to have occurred as an aspect of Benedictine personal devotion, as is demonstrated by small manuscripts, such as Cotton Titus D.xxvi, xxvii and Cotton Galba A.xiv, in addition to pedagogical works such as the *Enchiridion*. Since computistical works often appear in school texts alongside works connected to the cultivation of the hermeneutic style, knowledge of esoteric aspects of computus in Benedictine circles may serve the same function as the hermeneutic style in codifying Benedictine identity. Although computus was not restricted to the Benedictines in the same way that hermeneutic Latin was, the students of Byrhtferth's classroom seem to have been invested in showing that their computistical expertise surpassed that of their clerical counterparts, despite the fact that the evidence of computistical manuscripts, including the *Enchiridion*, shows that computus was not mastered by the vast majority of monastic scribes who were assigned to copy it. The desire to perform (or affect) a mastery of computus, even when the material is not fully understood, is not dissimilar to the role of the hermeneutic style in identity formation. As chapter 5 will explore, the vocabulary connected to hermeneutic Latin is often misused (which is one of Ælfric's objections), and the

28 For a discussion of this text's Old English gloss, see Patrizia Lendinara, "The Third Book of the *Bella Parisiacae urbis* by Abbo of Saint-Germain-des-Prés and Its Old English Gloss," *ASE* 15 (1986): 73–89. For more general information on school texts in the monastic curriculum, see David W. Porter, "The Latin Syllabus in Anglo-Saxon Monastic Schools," *Neophilologus* 78 (1994): 463–82.

evidence of glosses and manuscripts suggest that the monks' mastery of this esoteric style of Latin was never as complete as the reformers would have us believe.[29] The evidence of the *Enchiridion* and other contemporary manuscripts suggests that Byrhtferth's study of esoteric aspects of computus had less to do with preparing his students for the calculation of Easter and more to do with performing a certain level of cultural literacy that shows a strong monastic connection. In summation, the manuscript contexts suggest that Benedictines thought of computus as an object of study under their control, and knowledge of this subject and possession of manuscripts – even those so defective that they were not useful – were strongly connected to their self-identification. An argument for a strong monastic identity connected to computus, however, seems at odds with the vernacular language of the majority of the *Enchiridion*. If computus is taught in English, how can it be limited exclusively to monks?

The Politics of English

Throughout the *Enchiridion*, Byrhtferth provides a rich commentary on his project of translation from Latin to English and the value and use of English-language texts. These asides on vernacular translation have sometimes been read alongside Ælfric's very similar statements as an accurate depiction of early-eleventh-century attitudes towards language. As my argument heretofore has shown, Byrhtferth does not practise what he preaches; his overt comments about language in this text do not accord with his real actions while composing. This divergence between theory and practice encourages us to examine Byrhtferth's comments about language as a constructed position connected to his own identity as a Benedictine and devout follower of reformed monasticism. In addition, Byrhtferth's literary investment in English belies his stated opinions about English's role as a poor substitute for Latin. Furthermore, the monastic identity enacted by the performance of computistical knowledge conflicts with the recording of this knowledge in English, which is not typically the language of the monastic elite. The conflicted position inhabited by the vernacular

29 C.E. Hohler had a dim vim of the Latinity of reformed monks, claiming that their manuscripts might show the influence of "three gallons of beer a day." "Some Service Books of the Later Saxon Church," in *Tenth-Century Studies: Essays in Commemoration of the Millennium of the Council of Winchester and* Regularis Concordia, ed. David Parsons (London, 1975), 60–83, with quotation at 71.

reflects the many political tensions surrounding language, translation, and identity in the English Benedictine Reform.

Not surprisingly, many references throughout the *Enchiridion* suggest that Latin is the language of the educated, the *boceras* [learned in books], while English is a concession to those with less education: "Đas rædinga syndon wide cuðe on Lyden; forþan us gelustfullað þæt andgit nu eow gecyðan on Englisc þæt þa boceras cunnon on Lyden" (*BE*, 94) [These readings are widely known in Latin; for that reason it is pleasing to us to make known in English the knowledge that the scholars know in Latin]. This quotation goes beyond asserting that Latin is the appropriate language for the educated and also implies that knowledge in Latin is widely available, whereas knowledge in English is restricted and limited. Strictly speaking this is true, since those who were literate were usually also Latinate, and many more Latin manuscripts than vernacular existed, particularly in the field of computus. However, if the assertion that Latin writings are widely known is examined in the wider context of Anglo-Saxon society – beyond the limits of merely those who are literate and Latinate – to include those who are literate only in the vernacular or those who are not literate at all but could understand a text when read to them, Latin texts are not widely known, nor helpful. In fact, it is Latin scholarship that is limited to a few, while English could be available to a wider class of readers. Even in the monastic context of late Anglo-Saxon England, Latin is the language that restricts knowledge, not English, as the above statement implies. Byrhtferth's own writings confirm the accessibility and utility of the vernacular, since the majority of the *Enchiridion* is written in English, even portions specifically directed to a monastic audience.

Furthermore, Byrhtferth repeatedly asserts the inferiority of English as a language inadequate to the subtleties of the science he is trying to explain. He claims that he must mingle Latin terms with English, as in this sentence: "Me ys neod þæt ic menge þæt Lyden amang þissum Englisce" (*BE*, 104) [It is necessary for me to mix Latin among the English]. Although he claims that English cannot convey the technical vocabulary of Latin, his English computistical writing proves otherwise. While he does borrow and anglicize many computistical terms, such as "epacts,"[30] other Latin

---

30 For a discussion of how Byrhtferth anglicizes Latin words (most of which are technical computistical terms), see Peter S. Baker, "The Inflection of Latin Nouns in Old English Texts," in *Words and Works: Studies in Medieval English Language and Literature in Honour of Fred C. Robinson*, ed. Peter S. Baker and Nicholas Howe (Toronto, 1998), 187–206.

technical terms are rendered with commonly used Old English equivalents, like "equinoctium" [equinox] which is translated in Old English as "emniht" [literally: even-night] or "solstitia" [solstice] which appears in Old English as "sunnstede" [literally: sun-place or sun-stand] (*BE*, 8). The Old English words are calques on the Latin (i.e., *emn* = *aequus* and *niht* = *nox*; *sunn* = *sol* and *stede* = *-stitia*, from *sto*, meaning "to stand"), but Byrhtferth was not the first to use them in English. The *Dictionary of Old English Corpus* lists sixty-two occurrences of the word *emniht* in many sources, including the writings of Ælfric and Wulfstan and the E-text of the *Chronicle*.[31] The word *sunstede* is slightly less common, with nineteen occurrences, mainly in the writings of Ælfric and Byrhtferth.[32] Furthermore, Byrthferth's claim that English is a language not quite adequate to the translation of technical terms in Latin goes against the project of Winchester vocabulary, since the reformers created an English vocabulary for certain technical religious terms.[33]

Despite Byrhtferth's proclivity towards a very Latinate style of Old English, he does in fact translate many technical terms into English, contradicting his claim that "Þas þing synt earfoðe on Englisc to secganne, ac we wyllað þurh Cristes fultum hig onwreon swa wel swa we betst magon and þas meregrota þam beforan lecgan þe þisra þinga gyman wyllað" (*BE*, 66) [These things are difficult to say in English, but with the support of Christ we will reveal them as best as we can and (we will) lay the pearls before those who wish to take notice of these things]. In this statement, he suggests that great works of Latin learning are pearls, and although the exact wording of the text seems reminiscent of the biblical admonition against casting pearls before swine, the text is surprisingly gentle here, even suggesting his reader might be worthy of learning. While he protests

31 *Dictionary of Old English, Old English Corpus* [electronic resource], ed. Antonette diPaolo Healey (Ann Arbor, MI, 1998).

32 Ibid.; this includes one occurrence spelled "sunnstedas" in the *Enchiridion.*

33 For an explanation of Winchester words, see chap. 4, p. 136n5. The ninth-century translations commonly connected with Alfred did not hesitate to render complicated philosophical texts into English, such as Boethius's *Consolation of Philosophy* or the St Augustine's *Soliloquies.* See Janet Bately's "Uþwita/Philosophus Revisited: A Reflection on OE Usage," in *Essays on Anglo-Saxon and Related Themes in Memory of Lynne Grundy*, ed. Jane Roberts and Janet Nelson (London, 2000), 16–36; Nicole Discenza, *The King's English: Strategies of Translation in the Old English Boethius* (Albany, NY, 2005); and Discenza, "Writing the Mother Tongue in the Shadow of Babel," in *Conceptualizing Multilingualism in England 800–1250*, ed. Elizabeth M. Tyler, Studies in the Middle Ages (Turnholt, 2011), 33–55.

that the work is difficult, he still endeavours to translate the pearls of Latin learning into English for whoever is willing to contemplate them. This statement emphasizes the inadequacy of English as a technical language, but his own actions in translating and his adornment of his English-language text undermine the strength of this statement.

Despite the fact that Byrhtferth repeatedly protests that translating into English is tedious and that the language is incapable of conveying accurate translations of technical terms,[34] the number of times that he offers English equivalences of Latin and Greek words undercuts even this claim. Of the fifty-one times that Byrhtferth refers to the English language, twenty-six occurrences offer direct translations of Latin words, such as "þæt ys on Lyden solstitium and on Englisc midsumor" (*BE*, 74) [that is "solstice" in Latin and "midsummer" in English]. Many of these translations include a triplet with a lexis in Greek, Latin, and English, as in "Tomos on Grecisc on Lyden ys gereht diuisio and on Englisc todælednyss, and atomos on Grecisc <on Lyden ys gecweden> indiuisio, þæt ys untodælednyss" (*BE*, 110) ["Tomos" in Greek is rendered "division" in Latin and "division" in English, and "atomos" in Greek is said as "indivisio" in Latin, that is "in-divisibility"]. Statements like these suggest that the English language is capable of handling translation not only from Latin, but from Greek as well. Occasionally, these triplets include Hebrew instead of Greek, such as "þæt ciriclice leoð … þe Ebrei hatað Alleluia, and Lydenware hatað Laudate Dominum, and Englisce þeoda Godes lof gecigað" (*BE*, 154) [the spiritual song, which the Hebrews call "Alleluia" and the Romans call "Laudate Dominum" and the English name "Praise of God"], thus implying that the English language had expressions equivalent to each of the holy languages, Hebrew, Greek, and Latin, even for words specifically used to describe liturgical songs.[35]

---

34 "Vs þingð to langsum þæt we ealne þisne cwide on Englisc clericum geswutelion" (*BE*, 20) [It seems to us too tedious to translate this entire passage into English for clerics].

35 There is a precedent for this in King Alfred's preface to the *Pastoral Care*, "Ða gemunde ic hu sio æ was ærest on Ebreisc geðiode funden, & eft, þa þa hie Crecas geleornodon, þa wendon hi hie on hiora ægen geðiode ealle, &eac ealle oðre bec. And eft Lædenware swa same, siððan hi hie gelornodon, hi hie wendon ealla ðurh wise wealhstodas on hiora agen geðiode" [Then I remember how the law was first established in the Hebrew language, and afterwards the Greeks learned it, then translated it and all other books into their own language. And afterwards the Romans as well, after they learned it, they translated it all through their wise interpreters into their own language]. Henry Sweet, ed., *King Alfred's West Saxon Version of Alfred's Pastoral Care*, EETS, o.s., 45 and 50 (London, 1871), 4–6.

Byrhtferth's *Enchiridion* invests much space to vocalizing and thus reinforcing specific medieval hierarchies of language, especially the superiority of Latin, but when the text hits the page, different realities surface. The interchange between languages in the early parts of the *Enchiridion* shows this same conflict between theory and practice. While chapter 1 discussed how hierarchies of script reflect the relative status of languages, it is now time to examine the text more closely at the moment of linguistic instability, when the bilingual layout of the manual begins to unravel. Gradually, the English-language text leaves its role as a secondary translation and begins to supplant the Latin text by introducing new material along with embellishments and explanations not previously found. The first indication that English is becoming the dominant language is found when the transitions between languages are marked in English, not in Latin, as they have been in previous sections. This shift in the use of English to mark a change in language begins around page 47 in the manuscript, when the English phrase "Uton nu on englisc ymbe þys be dæle wurdlian" (*BE*, 32) [Let us now speak about this a little in English] marks the beginning of an English explanation. In previous sections such switches in language would be marked at the end of the Latin text in Latin, not in English. The manuscript layout is strange at this point as well because, although the Baker and Lapidge edition list this phrase on its own line as a separate paragraph, connected neither to that which precedes nor that which follows, the English phrase marking the change in language appears at the end of the Latin paragraph, clearly connecting it to the preceding Latin text and not to the subsequent English passage. The fact that language transitions are marked in the vernacular suggests that the Latin language is losing its position as the primary language of the text.

As this section continues, the Latin text becomes increasingly subordinated to the English, which begins to introduce changes not only in language, but in topic. Byrhtferth introduces the next computistical subject with the English words "Nu wė wyllað gecyðan hu man sceal mid þam concurrentium and þæra monða rihtingum findan hwylce dæge þa monðas gan on tun" (*BE*, 36) [Now we wish to make known how one should figure on what day the months appear to men using the concurrents and the month's regulars]. The word "concurrentium" embodies this unstable language dynamic because it is a Latin loan word that is being used in the dative plural, with a Latin ending that appears to be a genitive plural. In his catalogue of inflectional endings for Latin loan words, Peter Baker argues that incorrect genitive plural forms, such as this one, were used because they resembled the dative plural –um ending.[36] The somewhat imperfect adoption of this Latin word into the English inflectional system relates to other linguistic instabilities in the text, since earlier in the *Enchiridion*, a change in topic would have been signalled in the beginning of the Latin text and not at the end of the English one. Using the English language to introduce new topics begins to overturn the supposed language hierarchy of the *Enchiridion*, since it suggests that the Latin language is subservient to English and not vice versa. The next Latin section is even more clearly dependent on the English that precedes it. Baker and Lapidge punctuate the introductory English sentence with a colon after it, making the Latin text's dependency clear, "Gif þær beo læs þonne seofon, swylc dæg hyt byð; gif þær beoð seofon, þonne byð hyt Sæterndæg, swa þeos ræding ætywð" (*BE*, 36) [If there are less than seven, it is that day; if there are seven, then it is Saturday, as this reading shows]. The subsequent two changes in topic and the following diagram are also marked at the end of the preceding English-language text and not at the beginning of the ensuing Latin-language text.[37] Although material continues to be presented in Latin first and then translated into English, using an English-language text to signal textual changes indicates a kind of inverted hierarchy in which the Latin text becomes supplementary to the English, a kind of elaborate footnote, rather than the primary language, as it had been until this point.

The rising dominance of the English-language text can also be seen in the manuscript layout. At this point, Latin quotations and dialogues begin to be embedded within the English-language text without any markers to indicate the shift in languages. For instance, on page 50 of A, a single sentence reads, "We wyllað þæt hig understandon þisne cwide: 'Vasa fictilia tanto

36 "The Inflection of Latin Nouns," with several examples of "concurrentium" in the dative plural at p. 193 and summary of findings at p. 198.

37 The lunar regulars are introduced as "Vton awendan nu ure gesetnysse to þam rihtingum þe rimcræftige preostas cweðað lunares" (*BE*, 38) [Let us now turn our treatise to the regulars that clerics knowledgeable in computus call lunar]. Similarly, the epacts are introduced in English with "Wel geradlic hyt eac þingð us þæt we herto gecnytton þa epactas, þe wise preostas oft ymbe geradlice wurdliað" (*BE*, 40) [It also seems fitting to us that we add on to this the epacts, which wise priests often speak about intelligently]. The following diagram follows the English language text and is introduced as "Her we hig wyllað amearkian, þa epactas and eac þa regulares lunares, þæt hig openlicre and orpedlice standun beforan þæs preostes gesyhðe, þæt he mæge butan geswynce heora geryna ascrutnian" (*BE*, 44) [Here we wish to mark down the epacts and the lunar regulars, so that they may stand openly and boldly before the priest's sight, and he may without difficulty discern their mysteries].

solent esse utiliora quanto uiliora'" (*BE*, 36) [We wish that they understand this sentence: "Earthen vessels are more useful, the cheaper they are"]. In the manuscript, this statement is punctuated slightly differently, since medieval scribes did not use colons or quotation marks in the ways that modern convention allows. Rather, each half of the sentence is punctuated as if it were an independent, continuously flowing sentence with a final period. In this way, the Latin sentence intrudes into the English-language text without any markers to indicate that there is a shift in language. The script is the same in Latin as in English, and there is no coloured capital to set it apart, even though most language changes in the *Enchiridion* are marked by a new line and a coloured capital. Notably, this statement is not translated explicitly, but is explained with the following English words: "Þeah we wace syn and þas þing leohtlice unwreon, hig magon fremian bet þonne þa þe beoð on leoðwisan fægere geglenged" (*BE*, 36) [Although we are weak and treat these things slightly, [these writings] may accomplish more than those which are adorned beautifully with poetry]. Although leaving the Latin without a proper translation might imply a superior position for the Latin language, the subsuming of this text into an otherwise English-language text with an explanation that makes a full understanding of Latin unnecessary, shows the increasing dominance of English in this section.[38] The vernacular cannot be called supplementary, but rather the Latin begins to supplement it, and the more developed explanations in English slowly attenuate the need for a Latin-language text.[39] It is no wonder, then, that in only a few pages, the bilingual alternation of Latin and English will be replaced by a text that is almost entirely in English.

As the alternation of languages becomes unstable and breaks down, one can also trace a gradual transition from a bilingual text that prioritizes Latin to a text with a substantial creative investment in English. This same moment of linguistic instability begins with a Latin passage that Baker and Lapidge describe as "a paste-up of biblical quotations and allusions":[40]

---

38 Notably, however, this is a common biblical quotation and he may have expected his audience to know it without translation.

39 Cf. Rita Copeland's comments on Chaucer's *Legend of Good Women* and Gower's *Confessio Amantis*: "They also redefine the terms of vernacular translation itself: they use the techniques of exegetical translation to produce, not a supplement to the original, but a vernacular substitute for that original." *Rhetoric, Hermeneutics, and Translation in the Middle Ages: Academic Traditions and Vernacular Texts*, Cambridge Studies in Medieval Literature 11 (Cambridge, 1991), 179.

40 B&L, 266.

"Nunc speciosis pedibus uineam istius operis aggredi tempta<m>ur, quia iuxta uiam mendicando residemus. Rogitemus filium incliti Dauidis ut aperire dignetur nostros uisus quo absque errore hoc opus ualeamus exercere" (*BE*, 32) [Now we can attempt to enter the vineyard of this work with beautiful feet, because we sit down beside the road as one begging. Let us pray to the son of the shining David that he deigns to open our sight so that we will be able to exert ourselves in this work without error].

This learned combination of biblical images is translated relatively closely in the English, which reads: "Vton nu aginnan in to farenne to þisses wingeardes weorce mid wynsumum fotum, forðon we sittað ymb þam wege wædligende mid Timeus sunu. Vton biddan þæs æðelan Dauides sunu þæt he geopenige ure gesyhðe, þæt we butan gedwylde þæt weorc magon began þe we ongunnen habbað" (*BE*, 34)[41] [Let us now begin to enter into the work of this vineyard with beautiful feet, because we sit beside the way as one begging with the son of Timeus. Let us now pray to the son of noble David that he open our sight, so that we may attend to that work without error that we have undertaken].

The Old English translates the substance of the Latin, and while the Germanic language is not able to replicate the play on sounds in the Latin text, Byrhtferth instead indulged in rhetorical flourishes common to Old English, especially alliteration on "w." This adaptation shows a special attention to the literary development of the English-language text. Throughout the calculations in this passage, the vernacular diverges slightly from the Latin, first by directly addressing "la arwurða cleric" (*BE*, 34) [worthy cleric] and then by giving more specific directions for calculating the ferial regulars, offering calculations for April and May, in addition to more detailed instructions for March. As the section continues, the literary investment in English becomes stronger, while the Latin passages become more and more dependent on Byrhtferth's source.

Steadily throughout this section Byrhtferth invests increasingly less creativity in his Latin text, and larger running stints of the Latin text are either identical to or abbreviated from the computistical text as it appears in J, which is an adaptation of Helperic's *De computo* without Byrhtferth's characteristic stylistic embellishments. This method of offering a more or less exact Latin quotation and explicating it in rhetorically developed English

41 Although the text here in English and Latin clearly translates into "son," the reference is not to Solomon, but to the descendant of David, Jesus. The text Byrhtferth is adapting is part of Mark 10:47, which reads, "Fili David Iesu, miserere mei" [Jesus, son of David, have pity on me]. For a discussion of this passage, see B&L, 266.

problematizes the purpose of the *Enchiridion*. Rather than being a bilingual commentary on a computus, at this point the book becomes an English commentary on a pre-existing Latin text, since Byrhtferth did not draft the Latin, but is merely copying it from what is presumably his own abridgement of Helperic's text. Despite the scribal interference in this part of the text, the growing evidence points to a transition at this point in the manuscript to a text that, although it contains two languages, places English as the dominant one, rather than a Latin text with an English translation.

The fact that this shift is authorial and not scribal can be confirmed by Byrhtferth's creative and literary efforts, which seem to be focused more squarely on the English-language text as well. Section 1.2 presents a gradual progression from a work in which the primary creative impetus is focused on the Latin text and may or may not be translated into English, to a work that translates these rhetorical embellishments into English (thus indicating a stronger creative investment in English), and finally to a work that copies the Latin text almost directly from the source text with little embellishment, but invests a great deal of creative effort into adding both extra calculations and embellishments in English.

While Byrhtferth protests that English is an inferior language incapable of handling the technical vocabulary of Latin, his project of translation throughout the *Enchiridion* undercuts this claim. Through the act of translation, English is shown to be capable of expressing the truth of computus and translating each of the holy languages. Byrhtferth's conflicted view of the efficacy and value of English seems to be in line with the generally bifurcated view of the reformers, who recognized the utility of English at the same time that they inscribed a very difficult style of Latin with a strong monastic identity. Byrhtferth, however, is unique among the reformers in affecting a form of English replete with esoteric vocabulary akin to the reformers' hermeneutic Latin. Byrhtferth's English in particular is known for its unusual vocabulary, much of which is derived from glosses, especially those of Aldhelm.[42] The remainder of this chapter will examine Byrhtferth's "hermeneutic English" of book 3, that is, the English translation of Aldhelm's dismissal of the Muses. The fact that Byrhtferth attempts to replicate the hermeneutic style of Latin in the vernacular by imitating Aldhelm suggests the high value he places on English-language

---

42 "The most striking aspect of the vocabulary of [the *Enchiridion*] is its fondness for words that are more characteristic of glosses than of prose," B&L, cvi, with a further discussion of his unusual and gloss-derived vocabulary, pp. cvi–cxiv. For a discussion of Byrhtferth's use of glossed manuscripts in his work see Michael Lapidge, "Byrhtferth at Work," in *Words and Works*, 25–43.

composition, despite his repeated apologies for his English-language text. Furthermore, the fact that this Aldhelmian episode is embedded within a larger narrative about St Pachomius, a cenobitic saint closely connected to computus, inscribes the connection between hermeneutic English, monastic identity, and computistical study.

The Legend of St Pachomius and the Muses

Byrhtferth explores the position held by computus in the mythos of the monastic reform in his version of the Legend of St Pachomius, a monastic saint who received the correct calculation of Easter from God. According to the legend, this cenobitic saint is responsible for a relatively common set of computistical verses that begins "None Aprilis norunt quinos ..." (*BE*, 138).[43] Some version of this poem occurs in many computistical texts, since it aids a reader in the calculation of the Easter moon in the decennoval cycle, that is the nineteen-year cycle in which the Easter moons repeat.[44] Since this particular incident in the deeds of St Pachomius is recorded only in computistical texts and it is consequently not well known, it is worthwhile here to rehearse Byrhtferth's version of it:

> We witon geare þæt þær næs æt ne gediht ne Virgilius gesetnyss, ne þæs wurðfullan Platonis fandung oððe Socratis his lareowes smeagung, ac we prutlice gecyðað uplendiscum preostum þæt we be þissum circule gerædd habbað: "An abbod wæs on Egipta lande fullfremed on Godes gesihðe, Pac<o>mius genemed on naman gefege. He abæd æt þam mihtigan Drihtne mid eallum his munucheape þæt he him mildelice gecydde hwær hyt rihtlicost wære þæt man þa Easterlican tide mid Godes rihte, þæne Pascan, healdan sceolde. Him sona of heofena mihte com unasecgendlic myrhð, engla sum mid blisse, se þas word geypte and þæne abbod gegladode and þas uers him mid gyldenum stafum awritene on þam handum betæhte, þe þus wæron on his spræce gedihte:
>
> None Aprilis norunt quinos
> eall to þam ende." (*BE*, 138)
>
> [We know readily that there is no literary work nor composition of Virgil, nor logical treatise of Plato, nor investigation of his teacher Socrates concerning this cycle, but we proudly make known to the rustic clerics what we have

---

43 For the history of this legend see Charles W. Jones, "A Legend of St Pachomius," *Speculum* 18 (1943): 198–210.

44 According to Baker and Lapidge, "The verses are included in virtually every computus which we have seen" (B&L, 321).

read: "There was an abbot in Egypt who was perfect in God's sight, called Pachomius by name. He prayed to the mighty Lord with all of his company of monks that He mercifully make known to him where it was most correct to celebrate the Eastertide, or Paschal feast, according to God's ordinance. Immediately, by the power of heaven came unspeakable joy, an angel with grace, who made known these words and made the abbot glad and delivered these verses written with golden letters into his hands, which were thus composed in his language:

The nones of April know five ...
all the way to the end."]

Approximately half of the manuscripts that include the Easter verses also include the angelic visitation and divine inspiration of Pachomius. Since so many more manuscripts have the Easter verses than contain this particular legend, C.W. Jones has suggested that the poem is much earlier than the legend, and was only later attributed to Pachomius.[45] The legend was a favourite among regular clergy, such as Byrhtferth, because this legend shows that the ultimate authority on the celebration of Easter was given to a monk living in a cloistered monastic community. The secular clergy, by contrast, tended to prefer the version of the story that suggested the proper reckoning of Easter was decided by the Council of Nicea, an elected body that met long before the formation of monastic orders.[46] Byrhtferth of Ramsey emphasizes the distinctive contrast between regular and secular clergy in his version of the story, which he "prutlice gecyðað uplendiscum preostum" (*BE*, 138) [proudly makes known to rustic clerics], while at the same time emphasizing that Pachomius prayed with "eallum his munucheape" (*BE*, 138) [all his company of monks].

Images in eleventh-century manuscripts also emphasize the monastic connection of this episode's angelic authority for the celebration of Easter. The image in Cotton Caligula A.xv shows St Pachomius receiving a scroll with the Easter verses on it while surrounded by his monks.[47] Arundel 155 (the Eadwig Psalter) also shows Pachomius receiving a scroll from an angel in a register above arched columns containing these same Easter verses.[48] His monastic companions are clearly visible in outline behind him.

45 Jones, "St Pachomius," 201.

46 Ibid., 208–9.

47 Ker, *Catalogue*, no. 139; Helmut Gneuss, *Handlist*, no. 311.

48 Ker, *Catalogue*, no. 155; Gneuss, *Handlist*, no. 306. This image can be seen online at http://www.bl.uk/catalogues/illuminatedmanuscripts/ILLUMIN.ASP?Size=mid&IllID=3.

The Oxford manuscript St John's College 17, the computus most closely related to Byrhtferth's, contains no image of Pachomius, but emphasizes that he prayed "cum monachis suis"[49] (138) [with his monks]. Byrhtferth also emphasizes the firmly monastic connection of these verses by including this legend in book 3, which he directs to a monastic audience, claiming that the material is too complicated for the clerical audience who figures prominently in books 1 and 2.[50]

In these images, the Pachomius legend suggests that control of the date of Easter belongs in a monastic environment and even goes so far as to connect the monastic calculation of Easter with divine inspiration. This privileged position for both monasticism and computus would likely have been emphasized in Byrhtferth's own Benedictine classroom. Through these rhetorical moves, the Pachomius story takes a place of honour in a monastic identity formed around both computus and Latin-curriculum authors. The vernacular language, however, may seem to conflict with the argument for a strong monastic identification with computus. If computus were as important to monastic identity as I argue, then why would this section be written in English and not in a form of Latin more closely connected to the hermeneutic style? This section of the *Enchiridion*, though in English, does show features of the hermeneutic style, since the legend of Pachomius is immediately preceded by a passage that has been referred to as Byrhtferth's "hermeneutic English."[51] The passage is distinguished from other English writings of the reformers, since it resembles the esoteric Latin style of the Benedictine reformers, and is an English translation of Aldhelm's dismissal of the Muses from his *Carmen de virginitate*.

---

49 Ker, *Catalogue*, no. 360; an electronic edition is available on online at *The Calendar and the Cloister*.

50 See the discussion of audience in chapter 2, pp. 75–93; and Rebecca Stephenson, "Byrhtferth's Enchiridion: The Effectiveness of Hermeneutic Latin," in *Conceptualizing Multilingualism in England, 800–1250*, ed. Elizabeth M. Tyler, Studies in the Early Middle Ages (Turnhout, 2011), 121–44.

51 Malcolm Godden succinctly describes the difficulty of Byrhtferth's sometimes-inflated English prose style with the statement "The combination of exaggerated word-play, poetic and esoteric vocabulary, extravagant imagery and extensive intermingling of Latin words, produces the most extreme case of high style in Old English prose, matching the extravagance of the same author's Latin prose." "Literary Language," in *The Cambridge History of the English Language: Vol. 1, The Beginnings to 1066*, ed. Richard M. Hogg (Cambridge, 1992), 490–535, at 534. Peter Baker describes the style of some portions of the *Enchiridion* as "a highly ostentatious style that can best be compared to the hermeneutic style of Anglo-Latin writing." "The Old English Canon of Byrhtferth of Ramsey," *Speculum* 55 (1980): 22–37, at 28.

Despite the proximity of the Pachomius legend and the so-called hermeneutic English passage, these two sections have never been discussed together, because in the current edition the dismissal of the Muses occurs at the end of section 3.1, while the Pachomius legend opens 3.2. One of the main impediments to the interpretation of this passage is its placement in the current edition at the end of section 3.1. This position for the dismissal of the Muses is unusual because an invocation or a rejection of the Muses should appear at the beginning of a work, as it does in the Aldhelm's *Carmen*, not at the end of a section, relatively close to the middle of a larger book. This problem, however, may be an artificial one, since this section break is not extant in A and has been supplied by the editors. Elsewhere, I have argued that this particular section break must be misplaced by one or two paragraphs. [52] That piece, however, did not pursue what the implications might be of reading the dismissal of the Muses as the beginning of section 3.2 and as an introduction to the Pachomius legend.

Byrhtferth's dismissal of the Muses stands out in its context, not merely as a result of its odd placement at the end of a section, but also because the Muses do not seem to belong in a computistical text. Emily Thornbury, who traced the evolution of the Muses as a figure of poetic inspiration in Anglo-Saxon England, sees Byrhtferth's text as a dead end in their development. She states: "There was no pagan version of computus: Byrhtferth was hardly likely to be tempted to invoke pagan deities to his aid. He is asking the Holy Spirit for skill in speech, and decorating his prayer with the names of classical deities gleaned from Aldhelm. The Muses, in Byrhtferth's view, are merely ornamental statuary."[53] Thornbury is indubitably correct in claiming that the Muses are merely ornamental and relatively static in this episode. In fact, they do not seem to figure as real pagan deities at all, but as esoteric glosses in a kind of language game that shows the author's connection to the tradition of studiously glossing Aldhelm's manuscripts during the reform.[54]

---

52 "Reading Byrhtferth's Muses: Emending Section Breaks in Byrhtferth's 'Hermeneutic English,'" *Notes and Queries* 252.1 (March 2007): 19–22.

53 "Aldhelm's Rejection of the Muses and the Mechanics of Poetic Inspiration in Early Anglo-Saxon England," *ASE* 36 (2008): 71–92, at 91.

54 Mechthild Gretsch, *The Intellectual Foundations of the English Benedictine Reform*, Cambridge Studies in Anglo-Saxon England 25 (Cambridge, 1999), 332–83. The glosses are edited in *Aldhelmi Malmesbiriensis Prosa de Virginitate cum Glosa Latina atque Anglosaxonica*, ed. Scott Gwara, Corpus Christianorum Series Latina 124 and 124A (Turnhout, 2001).

The interpolation of the glosses in the main body of the text is easily seen in the full passage:

> Ic hate gewitan fram me þa m<e>remen þe synt si<ren>e geciged, and eac þa Castalidas nymphas (þæt synt dunylfa), þa þe wunedon on Elicona þære dune; and ic wylle þæt Latona (þære sunnan moder and Apollonis and Diane) fram me gewite, þe Delo akende, þæs ðe ealde swæmas gecyddon; and ic hopige þæt Cherubin se mæra ætwesan wylle and of þam upplican weofode mid his gyldenan tange þære gledan spearcan to minre tungan gebringan and þæs dumbes muðes <æ>ddran æthrinan, þæt ic forþam mæge argute arguto meditamine fari, þæt ys, þæt ic mæge gleawlice mid gleawre smeagunge þisne circul on Englisc awendan. (*BE*, 134)[55]

---

55 This passage is fairly closely adapted from Aldhelm's poetic version, which reads:

> Non rogo ruricolas versus et commata Musas
> Nec peto Castalidas metrorum cantica nimphas,
> Quas dicunt Elicona iugum servare supernum,
> Nec precor, ut Phoebus linguam sermone loquacem
> Dedat, quem Delo peperit Latona creatrix ...
> ... Quis poterit digne rerum misteria nosse
> Aut abstrusa Dei gnaro cognoscere sensu,
> Torridus altaris ni sumptus forcipe carbo
> Calculus aut ardens emundet spurca labella,
> Quo Seraphim quondam purgavit labra prophetae,
> Ut merito deinceps caelesti fomine flagrans
> Egregius doctor verbi clustella resolvat
> Et noxas populi scripturae torribus urat,
> Quatenus ad Christum convertat dogmate plures
> Ruricolas mutans ad caeli regna falanges?

(Ehwald, ed., *Aldhelmi opera*, 353, lines 23–30 and 356, ll. 74–83). [I do not ask for verses and phrases from the rustic Muses. Nor do I seek metrical songs from the nymphs of Castalia, whom they say perpetually preserve high Helicon. Nor do I pray that Phoebus, whom Latona (the mother) birthed on Delos, give a tongue loquacious with speech ... Who is able worthily to know the mysteries of things or to understand with a skilful intellect the hidden things of God, unless the hot coal, the burning stone, plucked from the altar with the tongs cleanse the unclean lips, as the Seraphim once cleansed the lips of the prophet, so that the distinguished teacher of the word may open the closed things and may burn the crimes of the people with the flames of scripture, until he converts the many rustic muses to Christ though his teaching, changing them into the ranks of the heavenly kingdom?]

[I command to depart from me the mermaids who are called Sirens and also the Castalian nymphs (who are mountain elves), who dwelled on Mount Helicon; and I wish to depart from me Latona (the mother of the sun, Apollo, and Diana), to whom Delos gave birth, as ancient triflers made known; and I hope that the excellent Cherubim will be present and with his golden tongs bring to my tongue the sparks of the embers from the highest altar and touch the vein of my dumb mouth, so that I may *argute arguto meditamine fari*, that is, that I may wisely with wise consideration translate this cycle into English.]

Although this passage is called "hermeneutic," no one has succinctly enumerated what causes it to merit that label beyond the blatant reworking of Aldhelm's poetry, the most important model for the hermeneutic style.[56] Finding a definition for a vernacular version of the hermeneutic style presents certain difficulties. In the introduction, I defined hermeneutic Latin as "a kind of Latin prose that affects an elevated register through importing poetic conventions into prose,"[57] and I extended the definition for the Latin style, however, to include "hyperbaton (or other instances of irregular syntax), rhyming prose, and other poetic references, especially allusions to Aldhelm."[58] Beginning with the last of these first, the matter of the text clearly invokes ideas of the hermeneutic style, since it translates an Aldhelmian passage that links the Muses to poetic inspiration in Isaiah and is heavily infused with poetic allusions. The syntax also shows the reformers' penchant for working with glossed manuscripts and invokes linguistic play that may have been common in their classrooms. Michael Lapidge was the first to point out that Byrhtferth's passage was based on a glossed text of Aldhelm, and though there is no manuscript with these exact glosses, the text does conform closely to the so-called Third Cleopatra Glossary (London, BL, Cotton Cleopatra A.iii, fols. 92–117), which was written in Canterbury in the mid-tenth century.[59] The slightly awkward syntax of

56 Admittedly, Aldhelm's prose was significantly harder and had more hermeneutic features than his poetry, but Aldhelm's model for poetry and the importance of the opus geminatum can be seen in Wulfstan of Winchester's metrical reworking of Lantfred's *Translatio et miracula S. Swithuni*. For more on the *opus geminatum* in England, see Gernot Wieland, "Geminus Stilus: Studies in Anglo-Latin Hagiography," in *Insular Latin Studies: Papers on Latin Texts and Manuscripts of the British Isles, 550–1066*, ed. Michael W. Herren (Toronto, 1981), 113–33; and Peter Godman, "The Anglo-Latin *opus geminatum*: From Aldhelm to Alcuin," *Medium Ævum* 50 (1981): 215–29.

57 See above, p. 19.

58 Ibid.

59 Lapidge, "Byrhtferth at Work," 36–7.

"m<e>remen þe synt si<ren>e geciged" [mermaids who are called Sirens], "Castalidas nymphas (þæt synt dunylfa)" [the Castalian nymphs (who are mountain elves)], "Elicona þære dune" [Mt. Helicon, and "Latona (þære sunnan moder and Apollonis and Diane)" [Latona (the mother of the sun, Apollo, and Diana)] result from glosses interpolated into Byrhtferth's adaptation of Aldhelm's text.[60] Interestingly enough, Byrhtferth has avoided using the word "Muses" explicitly. Instead, following Aldhelm, he referred to them with the more esoteric Latin borrowing of "Castalidas nymphas."[61] The Latin names in the Old English introduce a Latinate flavour to the paragraph, but Byrthferth goes even farther when he code-switches and introduces, "argute arguto meditamine fari" as a clause that completes the Old English phrase, with the infinitive form of the Latin verb "fari" prompted by the Old English modal, "mæge." The interpolation of the glosses and the insertion of Latin code-switching show the multilingual play in which Byrhtferth was engaged at this point in the text. Showing his knowledge of this tradition of glossing and his access to a glossed manuscript of Aldhelm was far more important than either closely following Aldhelm or developing the figures of the Muses as dynamic and viable instruments of poetic inspiration of the ancient world.[62]

Although the addition of the glosses could appear to be somewhat tedious, this passage is not without its own poetic embellishments, many of which connect it to the Pachomius passage that follows. For instance, Byrhtferth has introduced a poetic Latin line, and then imitates this line in English, "þæt ic forþam mæge argute arguto meditamine fari, þæt ys þæt

60 Ibid., 37.

61 Thornbury explains: "It was not the Muses' divine function, but their geographical associations, particularly with mountains that commanded the glossators' attention. In the classical world, the Muses were associated with springs like the Pirene at Corinth and the Castalia at Delphi"; "Aldhelm's Rejection of the Muses," 90. Note that "Castalidas nymphas" are the exact words with the same inflectional endings used in Aldhelm's Latin, even though the words here are considered by most scholars to be English. Baker argues that the accusative plural Latin ending in –as often remains in anglicized words because of the close correspondence to masculine a-stem nouns (even when the word should be feminine); "Inflection of Latin Nouns," 197.

62 As a result of the close correspondence between the glosses of this passage and those of the Third Cleopatra Glossary, Lapidge argues that Byrhtferth probably worked from a glossed manuscript of Aldhelm, since his knowledge of this curriculum author is thorough. He continues: "The best explanation is that the Aldhelm manuscript drawn on by the compiler of the 'Third Cleopatra Glossary' was subsequently used by Byrhtferth, but since that time has unfortunately perished." Lapidge, "Byrhtferth at Work," 37.

ic mæge gleawlice mid gleawre smeagunge þisne circul on Englisc awendan" (*BE*, 134) [so that I may *argute arguto meditamine fari*, that is, that I may wisely with wise consideration translate this cycle into English]. Baker and Lapidge reveal a little uncertainty about the origin of this Latin phrase, writing, "Evidently the cadence of a hexameter. We have been unable to identify its source; possibly it was composed by [Byrhtferth] himself" (BL, 320).[63] In Aldhelm's original the adjective *argutus* was used to describe Virgil as the "argutus poeta" [brilliant poet] who once said "Pandite nunc Elicona, deae cantusque monete"[64] [Open Helicon now, goddesses, and teach me your songs]. If this line was indeed Byrhtferth's own creation, or even if this is only his adaptation of another writer's poetic line, then he has transferred the reference of *argutus* from Virgil to himself. Notably, he does not ask for the gift of creating poetry, as Virgil did, but rather the gift of translation into English, which is reiterated from the following lines from Arator.[65] This reference to Virgil as an "argutus poeta" is referenced in the first line from the Pachomius episode, which claims that the divine inspiration of the Easter verses surpasses that of the Muses, "We witon geare þæt þær næs æt ne gediht ne Virgilius gesetnyss, ne þæs wurðfullan Platonis fandung oððe Soc̣ratis his lareowes smeagung, ac we prutlice gecyðað uplendiscum preostum þæt we be þissum circule gerædd habbað" (*BE*, 138) [We know readily that there is no literary work nor composition of Virgil, nor logical treatise of Plato, nor investigation of his teacher Socrates concerning this cycle, but we proudly make known to the rustic clerics what we have read]. Just as Byrhtferth dismissed the Muses before discussing the Easter cycle, he discounts the great ancient writers beginning with Virgil, replacing their pagan writings with his Christian interpretation of computus. In this moment, Byrhtferth redefines both what it is to be an author and the status that should be accorded to computistical inquiry.

Another possible connection between the Aldhelmian passage and the Pachomius legend could be read in the "gyldenum stafum" [golden letters] on which the Paschal verses were written. The letters, which are not called

---

63 B&L, 320.

64 Ehwald, ed., *Aldhelmi opera*, 353.

65 "Spiritus alme, ueni. Sine te non diceris umquam; / Munera da lingue, qui das <in> munere linguas" (*BE*, 136) [Come now, Holy Spirit. Without your presence, your name cannot even be said. Give the gift of tongues, you who give tongues as a gift]. The Latin lines come from Arator, *De actibus apostolorum*, 1.226–7.

golden in the source, closely parallel the "gyldenan tange" [golden tongs] with which the Cherubim remove the coal from the altar. Notably, the tongs were not golden in Aldhelm's original either, nor in the Isaiah version of this story. Byrhtferth's addition of the golden tongs and the golden letters opulently emphasizes the fact that Christian inspiration surpasses the prophetic power of the inert Muses and the pagan philosophers.

Relating the dismissal of the Muses to the Pachomius passage shows that Byrthferth rejects the poetic inspiration offered by the Muses in order to replace it with the divinely inspired Easter verses given to Pachomius by the angelic messenger. The lines from Arator invoking the Holy Spirit and his gift of translation serve as a bridge between the two incidents.[66] These two passages taken together connect the study of curriculum authors with the study of computus as two important pieces of monastic identity formation. For Byrhtferth, the Muses are not a real pagan threat, as Thornbury points out,[67] but just another piece of esoteric glossing that shows a relationship to a particular kind of training strongly connected to a specifically Benedictine identity. This discussion, however, has not grappled with perhaps the most important question that these passages raise: if hermeneutic Latin is central to the self-identification of Benedictine monks, then why are these two passages that are so closely connected to a monastic identity written in English?

As I argued in chapter 2, English in the *Enchiridion* is not merely for the benefit of the secular clergy. At the transition between books 2 and 3 (the only beginning of a book clearly marked with a rubric in A), Byrhtferth claims to switch audiences to focus solely on his monastic students and excludes the clerical students also present in his classroom.[68] Therefore, he claims that he will "iunge mynstermen to grettanne and mid twyfealdum este gefrefrian, þæt synt mid þam Easterlicum gerenum and mid eallum þam þingum þe behufuste synt þærto to witanne ... We byddað þa boceras and þa getydde weras þe þas þing fulfemedlice cunnon þæt heom hefelice ne þince þas þing þe we medomlice iungum cnihtum gesettað and sendað" (*BE*, 120) [greet young monks and comfort them with a twofold kindness, namely, with the Easter mysteries and all the things related to them that are necessary to know ... We ask the literate and the educated men who know

66 Lines and translation are cited above, n. 55.

67 See above, n. 53.

68 For quotation, see pp. 64 and 84.

these things completely that they do not regard these things as tedious, which we set down and send to young men]. As Byrhtferth turns to a more restricted monastic audience for book 3,[69] he again makes an apology for his English-language text, hoping that learned men would not feel that his English translation is too tedious, since this is intended merely for young men. In this modesty topos, Byrhtferth apologizes for English-language instruction in a manner similar to the statement that Ælfric offers at the beginning of his *Grammar*.[70] Although Byrhtferth will now turn to address monks in English, he assures his reader that it is for the young monks of his schoolroom, not the older monks, who should already know computus.

In the strictly monastic context of book 3, the hermeneutic English of the Aldhelmian passage is part and parcel of the same kind of monastic identity that I have suggested elsewhere is formulated by hermeneutic Latin. Byrhtferth's Aldhelmian English lines make sense only in the context of a previous knowledge of Aldhelm's *Carmen de virginitate*, preferably as it appeared in a glossed copy of the text, most likely held by a monastic house and studied by monks. The fact that this identity is being formed in English rather than in Latin is perhaps due to the intimacy of the environment of the monastic classroom in which Byrhtferth writes. It is possible that Byrhtferth translated this elite literary style because he never imagined an audience for the *Enchiridion* outside of a monastery, and the scope of his imagination may ultimately have been limited to his own classroom. Therefore, there is no conflict between Byrhtferth's practices and the linguistic policies of other reformers, since he is translating the most prestigious style of Benedictine monks for monks, not for the laity, nor even for the secular clergy. Even though this passage is in English, knowledge of Aldhelm would yet again separate monks from clerics, just as the Pachomius story emphasizes the divine inspiration that is available only to a prayerful monastic house.

---

69 For a more thorough discussion of the audience of book 3, see my "Effectiveness of Hermeneutic Latin," 138–41.

70 Although Ælfric expresses concern that "multos me reprehensuros" [many will censure me], he responds, "ego deputo hanc lectionem inscientibus puerulis, non senibus, aptandam fore" [I consider this reading to be appropriate to unknowing children, not to old men]. Jonathan Wilcox, ed., *Ælfric's Prefaces*, Durham Medieval Texts 9 (Durham, 1994), 114.

Conclusion

Byrhtferth's hermeneutic English reveals the extent of his literary investment in English-language composition. Although Byrhtferth may protest that English is a poor substitute for Latin, his actions suggest that English stands in very effectively for Latin and is worthy of the same level of language play that Byrhtferth explores in his hermeneutic Latin passages. The context of the passage and the connection to the monastic legend of Pachomius and to the *Carmen de virginitate* suggests that these language games were intended for the very monks who identified themselves so strongly with the hermeneutic style of Latin. In fact, much of Byrhtferth's English is sufficiently Latinized, either in vocabulary or subject matter, that it would not have been appreciated fully by a non-monastic audience.[71]

Although my studies into the *Enchiridion* originally began as an investigation into his deployment of the hermeneutic style as a mark of monastic identification, this research has shown the importance of English as an effective tool in the monastic classroom. Even beyond these practical considerations, these passages reveal the literary investment placed in English, even by Byrhtferth, a writer most known for his esoteric Latin texts. The prevalence of English in a strictly monastic context should cause modern scholars to re-examine many preconceived notions of Anglo-Saxon literature, especially the assumption that English-language works are intended for the laity or those who are otherwise uneducated in Latin. Although monks were expected to be able to read hermeneutic Latin, the very difficulty of this form required English-language supplementation. In other words, the esoteric nature of the monks' preferred Latin form actually encouraged the development of the vernacular, not just for the laity and secular clergy, but for the monks themselves, since their proficiency in this rarified style was probably never as thorough or widespread as Byrhtferth would have his readers believe.[72] Accordingly, Byrhtferth's discussion of the status of English should be read not as a realistic depiction of the Anglo-Saxon linguistic situation, but as a politically charged position that

71 See above, pp. 81–3.

72 For a similarly dim view of the monks' average Latinity, see Hohler, "Some Service Books."

reflects an attempt on the part of the monks to differentiate themselves from other clergy members whom they deemed to be inferior. Despite the denigration of English by Byrhtferth and other reformers, their English-language compositions show the importance of the vernacular as a literary product during the period. Regardless of the politics of the reformers' deployment of languages, the ideals of this linguistic policy did not work on the ground. Most monks probably could not read hermeneutic Latin proficiently, and this inconvenient fact may have led to Ælfric's abbreviations and translations. The next chapter will examine Ælfric's views on languages in his prefaces, many of which closely emulate Byrhtferth's.

PART TWO

4 The Politics of Ælfric's Prefaces

Ælfric of Eynsham inhabits an important position in the middle of the debate over the use and status of English in the late Anglo-Saxon period. He is a reformed monk, but as the next chapter will explore, he does not write in hermeneutic Latin, but in a simpler form of Latin and in English with words that he describes as "puris et apertis" [simple and clear] (*AP*, 111).[1] Although hermeneutic Latin is an important marker of affiliation with the Benedictine Reform, Ælfric's choice not to write in this distinctive style does not seem to indicate any distance from the reform movement. In his prefaces, Ælfric frequently described himself as a student of Æthelwold,[2] and he seems to have studied in Winchester sometime during that bishop's tenure, between 963 and 984. His devotion to Æthelwold in particular can be seen in his Latin *Life of St Æthelwold* and his English version of the *Life of St Swithun*, the patron saint of the Old Minster in Winchester.[3] Both of these lives contain references to Ælfric's participation in the monastic community of Winchester and his personal knowledge of

1 Jonathan Wilcox, ed., *Ælfric's Prefaces*, Durham Medieval Texts 9 (Durham, 1994), 111; hereafter this will be abbreviated in the text as *AP*. For a discussion of this phrase suggesting that English serves as a *sermo humilis*, see Robert Stanton, "Rhetoric and Translation in Ælfric's Prefaces," *Translation and Literature* 6 (1997): 135–48.

2 For instance, the preface to the first series of *Catholic Homilies* opens, "Ego Ælfricus, alumnus Æthelwoldi"; Wilcox, *Ælfric's Prefaces*, 107. There are other examples on pp. 115 and 124.

3 Michael Lapidge and Michael Winterbottom, eds, "Ælfric's Vita S. Æthelwoldi," in Wulfstan of Winchester, *The Life of St Æthelwold* (Oxford, 1991), 70–80, hereafter cited as Ælfric with a page number reference; and "Life of St Swithun" in Lapidge, *Cult of St Swithun*, 575–609. For further discussion of both Ælfric and Wulfstan of Winchester's versions of *The Life of St Æthelwold*, see chap. 5.

the reforming bishop, Æthelwold.[4] Traces of his Winchester education can also be seen in the language and style of his English texts, which contain so-called Winchester vocabulary.[5] In 987, Ælfric moved to the recently founded (or refounded) Cerne Abbas,[6] where he composed the two series of *Catholic Homilies* and also *Lives of Saints*,[7] the latter of which was

4 For instance, Ælfric explains his reasons for writing the so-called *Letter to the Monks of Eynsham* thus: "Fateor me ualde timide id praesumere, sed nec audeo omnia uobis intimare, quae in scola eius [scil. Æthelwoldi] degens multis annis de moribus seu consuetudinibus didici, ne forte fastidientes districtionem tante observantiae nec saltem uelitis auditum prebere narranti" [I confess that I undertake this project with great trepidation, but I do not dare to make known to you all the things that I have learned in Æthelwold's school about customs and usages while living there for many years, lest you shrink back from the strictness of so great an observance and not even wish to give me a hearing, when I speak]; Christopher A. Jones, ed., *Ælfric's Letter to the Monks of Eynsham*, Cambridge Studies in Anglo-Saxon England 24 (Cambridge, 1998), 110. In Ælfric's *Life of St Swithun*, he claims to have sung the *Te Deum* with monks of the minster, "Hi hit heoldon þa siððan symle on gewunan, swa swa we gesawon sylfe foroft, and þone sang we sungon unseldon mid him" [They kept it (the custom of singing the *Te Deum*) habitually always afterwards, as we ourselves have often witnessed, and we sang the song many times with them]; Lapidge, *Cult of St Swithun*, 600. Since his *Life of St Æthelwold* is so faithful to its source, his only direct reference to his time at Winchester occurs in the introduction, where he calls Æthelwold, "our father" [*noster pater*], Ælfric, 71. However, he also inserts the name of a thief (left unnamed in Wulfstan), which Lapidge and Winterbottom argue results from personal knowledge; Lapidge and Winterbottom, *Life of St Æthelwold*, 49 n. 6.

5 For Winchester vocabulary, see Helmut Gneuss, "The Origin of Standard Old English and Æthelwold's School at Winchester," *ASE* 1 (1972): 63–83; Walter Hofstetter, "Winchester and the Standardization of Old English Vocabulary," *ASE* 17 (1988): 139–61; Hofstetter, *Winchester und der spätaltenglische Sprachgebrauch: Untersuchungen zur geographischen und zeitlichen Verbreitung altenglischer Synonyme*, Münchener Universitäts-Schriften, Philosophische Fakultät, Texte und Untersuchungen zur englischen Philologie 14 (Munich, 1987); Mechthild Gretsch, *The Intellectual Foundations of the Benedictine Reform*, Cambridge Studies in Anglo-Saxon England 25 (Cambridge, 1999), esp. 89–131; and Gretsch, "Winchester Vocabulary and Standard Old English: The Vernacular in Late Anglo-Saxon England," *Bulletin of the John Rylands University Library of Manchester* 83.1 (Spring 2001): 41–87. For Ælfric's adaptations of Winchester vocabulary, see Malcolm Godden, "Ælfric's Changing Vocabulary," *English Studies* (1980): 206–23.

6 For a discussion of the arguments concerning the date of the founding of Cerne Abbas, see Jones, *Ælfric's Letter*, 7 n. 23.

7 The standard editions of these texts are Peter Clemoes, ed., *Ælfric's Catholic Homilies: The First Series*, EETS, s.s., 17 (London, 1997); Malcolm Godden, ed., *Ælfric's Catholic Homilies: The Second Series*, EETS, s.s., 5 (London, 1979); and Walter W. Skeat, ed., *Ælfric's Lives of Saints*, 2 vols., EETS, o.s., 76, 82, 94, 114 (London, 1881–1900; repr. as 2 vols, 1966).

dedicated to his patrons: Æthelweard, ealdorman of the western provinces, and his son, Æthelmær.[8] In 1005, Ælfric was appointed abbot of Eynsham, where his patron Æthelmær retired to live with the monks as "father and brother."[9]

Ælfric's avoidance of hermeneutic Latin seems especially strange in light of his patronage by these two important men. Not only was Æthelweard one of the most powerful men in the court of King Æthelred,[10] but he also composed the *Chronicon Æthelweardi*,[11] a hermeneutic Latin chronicle of English history (based on a lost version of the *Anglo-Saxon Chronicle*) for his kinswoman Matilda, abbess at Essen.[12] Æthelweard was succeeded as ealdorman of the western provinces by his son, Æthelmær, upon his death, which fell presumably in 998, the last year that he attested a charter.[13] Æthelmær was also an important man at court until his apparent fall from favour in 1005,[14] when he retired to Eynsham.[15] Despite these two men's political prominence, Æthelweard's own preference for hermeneutic Latin, and Ælfric's monastic connections, Ælfric avoided recherché vocabulary and cultivated a simple style in stark contrast to the flamboyant Latin of the period. Ælfric is known to modern audiences as primarily

---

8 "Ælfric gret eadmodlice Æðelwerd ealdorman, and ic secge þe, leof, þæt ic hæbbe nu gegaderod on þyssere bec þæra halgena þrowunga, þe me to onhagode on Englisc to awendene, for þan þe ðu, leof swiðost, and Æðelmær swylcera gewrita me bædon" [Ælfric greets alderman Æthelweard, and I tell you, dear man, that I have now gathered into this book the sufferings of the saints, which it seems appropriate to me to translate into English, since you dearest man and Æthelmer asked me for such writings]; Wilcox, *Ælfric's Prefaces*, 120.

9 For the evidence for Æthelmær's "retirement," see Simon Keynes, *The Diplomas of King Æthelred "The Unready," 978–1016: A Study in Their Use as Historical Evidence* (Cambridge, 1980), 209–13. For a discussion of the possible circumstances under which it occurred, see Jones, *Ælfric's Letter*, 5–15.

10 He was accorded the primacy among ealdormen from 993 to his death; see Keynes, *Diplomas of King Æthelred*, 192.

11 See above, p. 21n61.

12 Æthelweard's relationship to Matilda and his intentions in writing are outlined in the prologue to his chronicle; see Alistair Campbell, ed., *The Chronicle of Æthelweard* (London, 1962), 1–2. See also F.M. Stenton, *Anglo-Saxon England*, 3rd ed. (Oxford, 1971), 346–7.

13 Keynes, *Diplomas of King Æthelred*, 192 n. 139.

14 See above, n. 9.

15 However, Æthelmær reappeared in 1013 leading the western shires in submission to Swein Forkbeard. Charles Plummer, ed., *Two of the Saxon Chronicles Parallel*, vol. 1 (1892; repr., Oxford, 1952), 144.

a writer of English-language texts, since he wrote far more in English than in Latin, and these works were extensively copied.

The Anglo-Saxon abbot is also well known for his practice of writing prefaces that identify his position as author, his identity as a Benedictine monk, his teacher Æthelwold, the chain of authorities whom he follows, and his own techniques in translating. Not surprisingly, modern scholars have studied these prefaces seeking to elucidate the subject position of an author in late Anglo-Saxon England.[16] Embedded within Ælfric's discussion of each translation project is an elaborate discussion of the appropriate use of the vernacular and the proper audience for vernacular translations of religious works. Ælfric claims that he writes for the young, who have not yet learned Latin; for the laity, who cannot be expected to know Latin; and for his secular patrons (Æthelweard and his son Æthelmær), who wish to have translations of the texts studied by monks. There are two groups, however, that Ælfric almost never names explicitly in his prefaces as audiences for his English-language works: secular clerics and his fellow Benedictine monks.

In the case of the latter, scholars will readily assert that Ælfric did not translate for monks, especially not Benedictines, because they could read Latin.[17] In the case of the former, the secular clerics, Ælfric's failure to mention them as an audience in works beyond his pastoral letters is strange, since they were literate in the vernacular and were commonly depicted in monastic sources as having poor Latin. Furthermore, clerics were required to own books and had the leisure (and in some cases the requirement) to read them.[18] Since monks and clerics would have constituted the

16 For examples of such scholarship, see Richard Marsden, "Ælfric as Translator: The Old English Prose *Genesis*," *Anglia* 109 (1991): 319–58; Stanton, "Rhetoric and Translation"; and Jonathan Wilcox, "The Prefaces," in *AP*, 65–71.

17 Cf. Jonathan Wilcox's comments: "The explicit mention of nuns may provide a clue to Ælfric's reason for translating such a specifically monastic work into English" (*AP*, 52). The text is described as appropriate "to munecum and eac to mynecenum, þe regollice libbað for hyra Drihtnes lufe" (*AP*, 122) [for monks and nuns who live according to a rule for love of their Lord].

18 "Presbyter debet habere etiam spiritalia arma, id sunt diuinos libros, scilicet missalem, lectionarium, quod quidam uocant epistolarium, psalterium, nocturnalem, gradalem, manualem, passionalem, penitentialem, compotum, et librum cum lectionibus ad nocturnas" [A priest ought to have spiritual arms, that is divine books, namely a missal, a lectionary (which some call an epistolary), a psalter, the night office, a gradual, a book of saints' lives, a penitential manual, a computus, and a book of readings for the night office]. *Die Hirtenbriefe Ælfrics in altenglischer und lateinischer Fassung*, ed. B. Fehr, with suppl. by P. Clemoes, Bibliothek der angelsächsenischen Prosa 9 (Darmstadt, 1966), 2.137; similar lists exist at 1.52 and 2.157–8.

vast majority of literate members of Anglo-Saxon society,[19] Ælfric's omission of either of these groups as an audience in most of his works seems at the very least disingenuous, especially since, as Malcolm Godden argues, latter portions of the *Catholic Homilies* were directed at the secular clerics specifically, rather than a lay audience.[20] Ælfric's refusal to name an audience of monks and clerics for his English-language works, specifically his three homily collections, his *Grammar*, and his translation of Genesis, reflects not the reality of his readership, but Ælfric's elaborately constructed authorial position and vision of society, in which secular clerics are subjugated to a monastic priesthood.[21]

Conspicuous by Their Absence: Ælfric's Audiences

It is incredibly tempting to take Ælfric at his word when he describes his audience, since as Jonathan Wilcox points out that "attention to his audience, often explicitly expressed, is a hall-mark of Ælfric's writing."[22] However, despite this directness, Wilcox acknowledges multiple possible audiences, including eleven possible reading situations for the *Lives of Saints* beyond the explicitly stated environment of pious reading by Æthelweard and Æthelmær.[23] Given the many possible audiences for any medieval text committed to manuscript, it is interesting that Ælfric tends to be very specific when he names his imagined audience for each work. The *Catholic Homilies* are intended to be read in church to the faithful; the *Grammar* is written for the young; Genesis is translated at the behest of his patrons, Æthelweard and Æthelmær; *Lives of Saints* is said to be beneficial for the faithful, but is directly addressed to his secular patrons; and the *Admonitio*

19 For a brief overview of literacy in Anglo-Saxon England with a particular argument for an audience of clerics literate in English, see Jonathan Wilcox, "The Audience of Ælfric's Lives of Saints and the Face of Cotton Caligula A. xiv, fols. 93–130," in *Beatus Vir: Studies in Early English and Norse Manuscripts in Memory of Phillip Pulsiano*, ed. A.N. Doane and Kristen Wolf, Medieval and Renaissance Texts and Studies 319 (Tempe, AZ, 2006), 228–63, at 244–6.

20 "The Development of Ælfric's Second Series of *Catholic Homilies*," *English Studies* 54 (1973): 209–16.

21 On the tensions between the secular and monastic priesthood in Anglo-Saxon England and in Ælfric, see Christopher A. Jones, "Ælfric and the Limits of 'Benedictine Reform,'" in *A Companion to Ælfric*, ed. Hugh Magennis and Mary Swan, Brill's Companions to the Christian Tradition 18 (Leiden, 2009), 67–108.

22 Wilcox, *Ælfric's Prefaces*, 20.

23 "The Audience of Ælfric's Lives," 258–9.

ad filium spiritualem is appropriate for Benedictine monks and nuns. It is interesting that Ælfric never mentions the secular clerics as a potential audience for any of his homilies, translations, or pedagogical works.[24]

He does, however, express concern about their levels of education, especially in the preface to Genesis, in which he writes of a certain mass-priest, who was once his teacher and could understand Latin "be dæle" (*AP*, 116).[25] This mass-priest said that the patriarch Jacob "hæfde feower wif, twa geswustra and heora twa þinena" (*AP*, 116) [had four wives, two sisters and their maidservants]. Ælfric regretfully explains: "Ful soð he sæde, ac he nyste, ne ic þa git, hu micel todal ys betweohx þære ealdan æ and þære niwan" (*AP*, 116) [He spoke truly, but he did not know, nor did I know yet, how great a separation there is between the old law and the new]. This statement is often quoted as expressing his concern about the dangers of translating the Hebrew scriptures, and sometimes has been read, as it was by Gordon Whatley, as revealing anxieties about the conflict between Germanic marriage patterns and Christianity.[26] The concerns about marriage, however, come to a very specific point: clerical marriage.

---

24 The secular clerics are the audience for a series of pastoral letters published in Fehr, ed., *Hirtenbriefe Ælfrics*.

25 As Joyce Hill explains, "This may mean that he had an imperfect knowledge of Latin, understanding it only in part ('be dæle'), or that he knew the technicalities of Latin, understanding it according to its parts of speech ('be dæle'), but not knowing the principles of exegetical interpretation which would have allowed him to move beyond the literal, particularly when reading those parts of the Old Testament which were at odds with the teaching of the New. The second of these two interpretations is the more likely, because Ælfric used *dæl* in grammatical contexts to mean "part of speech," and because the immediate context of the statement about his first teacher is in his *Preface to Genesis* at the point where he discusses the difficulty of coming to terms with the information that Jacob had four wives." "The Benedictine Reform and Beyond," in *A Companion to Anglo-Saxon Literature*, ed. Phillip Pulsiano and Elaine Treharne, Blackwell Companions to Literature and Culture 11 (Oxford, 2001), 151–69, at 157.

26 "[Ælfric] worries about the likelihood that foolish (dysige) people will take the stories of the patriarchs literally instead of allegorically and use them as justification for various practices abhorrent to the Christian Church but not uncommon in early medieval societies, such as polygamy, concubinage, and incest or kin-marriages." E. Gordon Whatley, "*Pearls before Swine*: Ælfric, Vernacular Hagiography, and the Lay Reader," in *Via Crucis: Essays on Medieval Sources and Ideas in Memory of J.E. Cross*, ed. Thomas N. Hall with Thomas D. Hill and Charles D. Wright, Medieval European Studies 1 (Morgantown, WV, 2002), 158–84, at 162.

That Ælfric is more concerned with the marriage of the clergy, and not the potential incestuous marriage of the laity, is seen a little further down the passage, which reads,

> Ða ungelæredan preostas, gif hi hwæt litles understandað of þam Lydenbocum, þonne þincð him sona þæt hi magon mære lareowas beon... Hi cweþaþ eac oft be Petre, hwi hi ne moton habban [w]if, swa swa Petrus se apostol hæfde, and hi nellað gehiran [n]e witan þæt se eadiga Petrus leofode æfter Moises æ oþ [þ]æt Crist, þe on þam timan to mannum com and began [t]o bodienne his halige godspel and geceas Petrum ærest [h]im to geferan; þa forlet Petrus þærrihte his wif, and ealle þa twelf apostolas, þa þe wif hæfdon, forleton ægþer ge wif ge æhta, and folgodon Cristes lare to þære niwan æ and clænnisse." (*AP*, 117)
>
> [The unlearned clerics, if they understand some little part of a Latin book, then it seems to them immediately that they can be great teachers ... They say often concerning Peter, why may they not have a wife, just as Peter the apostle had, and they do not wish to hear nor know that the blessed Peter lived after Moses' law until Christ, who came to men at that time and began to preach his holy gospel and chose Peter first as his companion; then Peter left his wife at once, and all the twelve apostles who had wives left both their wives and their property and followed Christ's teaching to the new law and chastity.]

Although this passage is coded as a simple issue of interpretation, this discussion relates to larger issues of monastic identity, in that marriages of the secular clergy were a commonly repeated complaint of Benedictine monks. When the Winchester cathedral was reformed in 963, the secular clerics were forced to choose between their wives or their prebends.[27] Those who would not repudiate their wives were evicted from the minster. Although those who achieve the rank of mass-priest, that is, the sixth level of the priesthood, and are able to perform the sacraments are forbidden to marry, clerics in minor orders, who do not consecrate the Eucharist, may marry,

27 The expulsion is described in Michael Lapidge and Michael Winterbottom, eds, Wulfstan of Winchester, *The Life of St Æthelwold*, Oxford Medieval Texts (Oxford, 1991), 31–3. For the date for the expulsion of the canons, see the discussion in the same volume, pp. xlvi–xlvii. For a discussion of the consequences of the reform for property belonging to the monasteries, see Eric John, "The King and the Monks in the Tenth-Century Reformation," in *Orbis Britanniae and Other Studies* (Leicester, 1966), 154–80. For a more recent overview of the impact of the reform on communities and patronage, see John Blair, *The Church in Anglo-Saxon Society* (Oxford, 2005), 341–67.

if they choose. The Benedictines worked to abolish the practice of clerical marriage by implementing the Rule of Chrodegang, which would require clerics to live in celibate communities just as monks do.[28] While scholars are not wrong to cite this passage as warning of the dangers of improper interpretation, they should not overlook the fact that the interpretation of the secular clerics, and especially married clergy, has been warned against in particular. Thus, in this preface, Ælfric usurps the authority of the local clergy in order to create a translation that is authorized by his standing as a Latinate, celibate, Benedictine monk.[29]

It is interesting that when Ælfric lists the kinds of marriage that the uneducated reader might find confusing in the Old Testament, he lists various kinds of incest, claiming that in the early days "man ne mihte þa æt fruman wifian buton on his siblingum" (*AP*, 116) [one could not marry in the early days except for his own siblings]. In addition to men marrying their sisters, and fathers begetting children with their daughters, he also adds polygamy, all of which were taboo in Anglo-Saxon England. He does not mention other practices of the Old Law, the status of which was more precarious, like divorce. The great king Edgar himself seems to have been something of a serial monogamist,[30] since he had children with three different women, and the question of which of these marriages was legitimate played a major role in the succession dispute that followed Edgar's death.[31] Nor does Ælfric mention the fact that the sons of Levi and other Old Testament priests were permitted to marry. Ælfric, of course, spoke strongly against clerical marriage and is well known for the strictness of his

28 For an edition of the Rule see Brigitte Langefeld, ed., *The Old English Version of the Enlarged Rule of Chrodegang: Edited together with the Latin Text and an English Translation*, Münchner Universitätsschriften, Texte und Untersuchungen zur Englischen Philologie 26 (Frankfurt, 2004).

29 Robert Upchurch makes a similar argument in "For Pastoral Care and Political Gain: Ælfric of Eynsham's Preaching on Marital Celibacy," *Traditio* 59 (2004): 39–78.

30 According to Pauline Stafford, such serial monogamy was not that unusual in Wessex; see "The King's Wife in Wessex 800–1066," *Past and Present* 91 (1981): 3–27, at 13–14, with discussion of Edgar's wives at 14 n. 30. See also Barbara Yorke, "The Women in Edgar's Life," in *Edgar, King of the English 959–975: New Interpretations*, ed. Donald Scragg, Publications for the Manchester Centre for Anglo-Saxon Studies 8 (Woodbridge, 2008), 143–57.

31 For a discussion of how Archbishop Dunstan and Bishop Æthelwold found themselves on opposite sides of this dispute, see Barbara Yorke, "Æthelwold and the Politics of the Tenth Century," in *Bishop Æthelwold: His Career and Influence*, ed. Barbara Yorke (Woodbridge, 1988), 65–88, at 82–7.

expectations for even lay celibacy; he expected couples to abstain from sex after the woman was too old to produce children.[32] Robert Upchurch has connected the stringency of Ælfric's teaching on lay celibacy with a desire to undermine the authority of the secular clerics as teachers to the laity.[33]

Throughout his prefaces, however, Ælfric maintains that clergy – both secular and monastic – are set as teachers to uneducated people. In order to teach, these ecclesiasts need access to Ælfric's body of doctrine more than any other. It is therefore interesting that he does not name the secular clergy as an audience for his English-language works, when they certainly had more access to his homilies than the laity who attended services in their churches. In the first series of *Catholic Homilies*, one of Ælfric's earliest works, he claims to translate "ob edificationem simplicium, qui hanc norunt tantummodo locutionem" (*AP*, 107) [for the edification of the simple, who know only this language]. In other words, he will translate for those who know only English. The concern for those who cannot read Latin is similarly expressed in the corresponding English preface: "me ofhreow þæt hi ne cuðon ne næfdon ða godspellican lare on heora gewritum, buton ðam mannum anum ðe þæt Ledeon cuðon" (*AP*, 108) [It grieved me that they did not have the gospel teachings in their writings, except for those men who knew Latin]. The fact that his concern is more clearly focused on the laity who will listen to the sermons, rather than the secular clergy who will recite them, can be seen when he articulated his plan for this homily collection: "Quadraginta sententias in isto libro posuimus, credentes hoc sufficere posse per annum fidelibus, si integre eis a ministris Dei recitentur in ecclesia" (*AP*, 107) [We have placed forty homilies in this book, believing that this is able to be sufficient for one year for the faithful, if it is recited in entirety by the ministers of God in the church]. This statement suggests that he conceptualizes his audience as the flock of the faithful, rather than a seemingly inert cleric, who will read verbatim Ælfric's homilies to his lay audience. In this creation of audience, Ælfric emphasizes his final audience, those who listen to these sermons, above the clergy who must own and read this book for Ælfric's plan to come to fruition.

32 For a discussion of Ælfric's teachings on lay celibacy, see Upchurch, "For Pastoral Care," 39–78; for specific reference to Ælfric's departure from other church fathers by requiring celibacy after childbearing years, see pp. 49–54.

33 For the tradition of depicting the secular clerics as licentious in reformed texts, see chap. 2, pp. 68–70.

Ælfric's common warnings to scribes against making any changes can also be read as applying to the recitation of the homilies by secular clerics. In the first series, Ælfric warns, "Nu bydde ic and halsige on Godes naman, gif hwa þas boc awritan wylle, þæt he hi geornlice gerihte be ðære bysene, þy læs ðe we ðurh gymelease writeras geleahtrode beon. Mycle yfel deð se ðe leas writ, buton he gerihte, swylce he gebringe þa soðan lare to leasum gedwylde" (*AP*, 110) [Now I ask and entreat in God's name, if any wish to copy this book, that he eagerly correct it by the exemplar, lest we be blamed because of the actions of careless scribes. He who writes lies does great evil, and unless he corrects it, he brings true teaching to lying heresy]. It is almost certain that the scribe whom Ælfric warns here is a monk, since manuscripts were copied in monastic scriptoria, not by parish priests. The concern about maintaining the exact wording, however, could apply to a secular cleric who recites these words in front of a congregation. In fact, a sloppy reader/reciter could make the same kind of heretical intervention as a scribe by modifying the text during oral delivery. It is interesting that Ælfric does not refer to the possibility of oral mistakes, but instead focuses on the errors that can enter the written word, as if he did not even countenance the possibility that the cleric might not read the homilies exactly as they are written. By denying the agency of the cleric who reads the homilies and focusing instead on an ultimate lay audience, he supplants the local clergy by ventriloquizing their voice and forbidding them to take an active role in creating or restructuring the homilies for their individual churches and congregations.[34]

Tensions between secular clerics and monks mark many documents of the monastic reform, which attempted to draw a rigorous distinction between monks and secular clergy. Pastoral care is the responsibility of secular clerics, while monks should be cloistered and free to perform the *opus Dei*, that is, the rigid schedule of monastic prayers. Before the reform such distinctions were not generally observed, and even after the reform, as Mary Clayton has shown, the audience for mass in a monastic establishment could have included laity who would have had some portion of their pastoral care administered by monks.[35] Furthermore, Ælfric's

34 Donald Scragg asserts that Ælfric's homilies are copied more closely than the anonymous tradition, possibly because his collections were made in large centres by well-trained scribes. "Ælfric's Scribes," *Leeds Studies in English* 37 (2006): 179–89, at 185.

35 "Homiliaries and Preaching in Anglo-Saxon England," *Peritia* 4 (1985): 207–42.

own particular attention to pastoral care for the laity can be seen in his homily collections, which were sent to Canterbury and then circulated widely.[36] Wilcox's study of the dissemination of the *Catholic Homilies* in Dorset suggests that these homily collections constitute an ambitious project. He concludes:

> If Ælfric's homilies were disseminated as widely as I am suggesting, this would give flesh to the multiple fictive audiences that Ælfric himself envisages. In virtually every church, minster, and monastery throughout England, people of both sexes and all classes, in some places including among them communities of priests or monks and nuns, were assembling at the same hour on Sundays and festivals to hear the same moral, exegetical, and practical message preached at the same time. For all Ælfric's conservative orthodoxy, this achievement represents something quite revolutionary – the beginning of a form of mass communication that must have played a significant part in defining a sense of English identity at the turn of the millennium.[37]

In the midst of this revolutionary "mass communication" Ælfric has exerted monastic control over pastoral speech, and although the creation of these collections could be described as a concern for the local clergy, the wide circulation of homilies combined with a preface that explicitly forbids all interventions suggests that Ælfric's desires extend beyond simple "concern" into open colonization of the pastoral space that should be inhabited by clerics.

Ælfric's refusal to name a clerical audience seems to have less to do with the realities of Anglo-Saxon literacy and is related more closely to the space appropriate to the vernacular and his own identity as a Latinate Benedictine monk. Education – specifically a monastic education – was an important marker of monastic identification. Ælfric's own education and wide reading is a testimony to the availability of books in monastic houses and also the circulation of books among monastic houses, since neither Cerne nor Eynsham, where Ælfric wrote his extant corpus, were known to

36 Clemoes, ed., *Ælfric's Catholic Homilies: The First Series*, 134–68.

37 Jonathan Wilcox, "Ælfric in Dorset and the Landscape of Pastoral Care," in *Pastoral Care in Late Anglo-Saxon England*, ed. Francesca Tinti, Anglo-Saxon Studies 6 (Woodbridge, 2005), 62. For more on the division of labour between monks and clerics, see chap. 2.

have extensive libraries.[38] In the preface to his *Grammar*, Ælfric connects the educational renaissance of the late tenth century to the work of the monastic reformers Dunstan and Æthelwold. He claims: "nan Englisc preost ne cuðe dihtan oððe asmeagean anne pistol on Leden, oð þæt Dunstan arcebisceop and Aðelwold bisceop eft þa lare on munuclifum arærdon" (AP, 116)[39] [No English cleric knew how to write or read a letter in Latin, until Archbishop Dunstan and Bishop Æthelwold established the teaching of monastic life on this island]. The word "preost" here is important, because in Ælfric's writing (as in Byrhtferth's) this word refers specifically to members of the non-monastic, that is, secular, clergy.[40] Oddly enough, Ælfric never claims to translate for them, but rather for their charges, that is, the laity, who are likely to hear dubious teaching from these allegedly uneducated clerics. Since this construction of the "stupid secular cleric" mirrors that already explored in the works of Byrhtferth of Ramsey, I suggest that it is closely tied to the political tensions between monks and clerics in the late tenth century, specifically in the monks' desire to create for themselves an identity as owners of Latin religious knowledge.

---

38 Mechthild Gretsch goes so far as to say, "Ælfric's work on forging and refining English was no escapist occupation; nor was it a nostalgic commitment to ideas fostered by his teacher Æthelwold. It is rather a precious testimony to high-level scholarly activity being carried on in a time of national crisis and distress." "Ælfric, Language and Winchester," in *A Companion to Ælfric*, ed. Magennis and Swan, 137. Michael Lapidge uses Ælfric's wide range of scholarship in the *Catholic Homilies* as one evidence of the extensive library that must have existed at Winchester; *The Anglo-Saxon Library* (Oxford, 2006). However, determining the exact range of Ælfric's reading and library is difficult, since he tends to cite ultimate sources, not the compendia, florilegia, or homiliary that was open before him. Joyce Hill explains these complex problems with source study in "Authority and Intertextuality in the Works of Ælfric," *Proceedings of the British Academy* 131 (2005): 157–81. See also Cyril L. Smetana, "Ælfric and the Early Medieval Homiliary," *Traditio* 15 (1959): 164–204.

39 Notably this echoes Alfred's similar statement "ðætte swiðe feawe wæron behionan Humbre þe hiora ðenunga cuðen understandan on Englisc, oððe furðum an ærendgewrit of Lædene on Englisc areccan; & ic wene ðætte nauht monige begeondan Humbre næren" [that there were very few on this side of the Humber who could understand the service in English or could translate a letter from Latin into English, and I think there were not many on the other side of the Humber]; Henry Sweet, ed. *King Alfred's West Saxon Version of Alfred's Pastoral Care*, EETS, o.s., 45 (London, 1871), 2. It should be pointed out that Alfred did not specifically single out the clergy, either secular or monastic, but instead emphasized that learning should be pursued by all with the wealth and leisure to devote themselves to education. For more on the audience for Alfred's education reform, see Nicole Guenther Discenza, "Wealth and Wisdom: Symbolic Capital and the Ruler in the Translational Program of Alfred the Great," *Exemplaria* 13 (2001): 433–67.

40 See chap. 1, pp. 75–8.

What about the Monks?

Despite the frequency with which he mentions his own Benedictine affiliations as part of his authority for writing, Ælfric seldom names monks as his audience when writing in English. Only in the preface to his *Grammar* and the *Admonitio ad filium spiritualem* is a monastic audience even implied. In the case of the latter, Ælfric claims that this work is appropriate "to munecum and eac to mynecenum, þe regollice libbað for hyra Drihtnes lufe" (*AP*, 122) [for monks and nuns who live according to a rule for love of their Lord]. The strong Latinity of Benedictine monks is so entrenched in the scholarly mindset that at least one researcher has opined that this work is intended solely for nuns, since it is in English. Jonathan Wilcox suggests: "The explicit mention of nuns may provide a clue to Ælfric's reason for translating such a specifically monastic work into English" (*AP*, 52).[41] In my earlier chapters on Byrhtferth, I have argued that English translation was necessary, even for highly trained Benedictine monks, and perhaps an audience of monks and nuns (just as Ælfric describes) should not be dismissed too readily. The remainder of this section will pursue the possibility that monks were indeed the audience not just for this English-language translation, but for many other of Ælfric's translations in which they are not mentioned as an audience.

41 Wilcox further develops this argument in "The Audience of Ælfric's Lives," 253–4. Though evidence for Latin literacy among women in the late period is sketchy, in the earlier periods of Anglo-Saxon England, there is strong evidence for female Latin literacy; see Hugh Magennis, "Audience(s), Reception, Literacy," in *A Companion to Anglo-Saxon Literature*, ed. Phillip Pulsiano and Elaine Treharne, Blackwell Companions to Literature and Culture 11 (Oxford, 2001), 86–7; and Carol Neuman de Vegvar, "Saints and Companions to Saints: Anglo-Saxon Royal Women Monastics in Context," in *Holy Men and Holy Women: Old English Prose Saints' Lives and Their Contexts*, ed. Paul E. Szarmach, SUNY Series in Medieval Studies (Albany, 1996), 51–94, at 62–5. Although Æthelwold's translation of the Rule of St Benedict was adapted for use in female communities through the addition of feminine pronouns and additional material relevant to women, Rohini Jayatilaka cautions against assuming that the original translation was undertaken for female houses only; see "The Old English Benedictine Rule: Writing for Women and Men," *ASE* 32 (2003): 147–87. For the original view that Æthelwold's English translation was written specifically for women, see Mechthild Gretsch, "The Benedictine Rule in Old English: A Document of Bishop Æthelwold's Reform Politics," in *Words, Texts, and Manuscripts: Studies in Anglo-Saxon Culture Presented to Helmut Gneuss on the Occasion of His Sixty-fifth Birthday*, ed. Michael Korhammer, Karl Reichl, and Hans Sauer (Cambridge, 1992), 131–58. Aldhelm's correspondence with nuns in his own turgid style should certainly caution modern scholars against the idea that women could not read the highest styles of Latin when such styles were in vogue.

While the audience for the *Grammar* is not explicitly named as monastic, the reference to the young may imply a monastic schoolroom in which oblates were instructed in Latin. These young men were neither fully initiated into the ranks of manhood, nor had they fully achieved status as adult monks.[42] In this preface, Ælfric expresses concern that some will not approve of his translation, saying that "multos me reprehensuros" [many will censure me], but he responds that his translation is "inscientibus puerulis, non senibus, aptandam fore" (*AP*, 114) [appropriate for unknowing children, not the old]. The corresponding connections between English and youth, on the one hand, and Latin and age, on the other, seems to be part of the reason that Ælfric fears being rebuked: by making himself an author of English-language texts, he positions himself in a world dominated by children and appropriate to them. He risks infantilizing himself, at a time when most monks would prefer to be considered authors of more mature Latin-language texts.

In addition to the *Grammar* and the *Admonitio ad filium*, Ælfric's third homily collection, the *Lives of Saints* seems to have been intended at least in part for a monastic audience because its lengthy homilies must have been used for private reading,[43] and the saints it treats are those more appropriate to a monastic context.[44] Ælfric, however, does not name this audience nor address in his preface the circumstances in which these homilies are to be read or recited. Instead, he defends his project of translation by claiming that his lay patrons have compelled him to do so.[45] Specifically, Ælfric writes "eowerne geleafan to getrymmenne mid þære gerecednysse,

42 For a discussion of children's entry into a monastic community and of when they became full members of the community (with specific reference to early Anglo-Saxon England), see Sarah Foot, *Monastic Life in Anglo-Saxon England, c. 600–900* (Cambridge, 2006), 140–6.

43 Malcolm Godden, "Experiments in Genre: The Saints' Lives in Ælfric's *Catholic Homilies*," in *Holy Men and Holy Women*, ed. Paul E. Szarmach (Albany, NY, 1996), 261–87. For a discussion of several possible audiences for this work, see Wilcox, "The Audience of Ælfric's Lives," 246–55.

44 Joyce Hill, "Saint George before the Conquest," *Report of the Society of the Friends of St George's and the Descendants of the Knights of the Garter* 6 (1987): 284–95.

45 "Non mihi inputetur quod divinam scripturam nostrae lingue infero, quia arguet me praecatus multorum fidelium, et maxime Æþelwerdi ducis et Æðelmeri nostri, qui ardentissime nostras interpretationes amplectuntur lectitando" (*AP*, 120) [Do not blame me that I have translated the divine scripture into our language, since I have been persuaded by the prayers of many of the faithful, especially ealdorman Æthelweard and our Æthelmær, who have embraced our translations for reading enthusiastically].

þe ge on eowrum gereorde næfdon ær" (*AP*, 120) [to encourage your (Æthelweard and Æthelmær's) belief with the narrative, which you did not have earlier in your language]. Thus, he implies that his lay patrons cannot read these monastic texts because they are not available in English. Ironically, however, Æthelweard was perhaps one of the most educated laymen of the period. He wrote the *Chronicle of Æthelweard*, which is a Latin translation of the Anglo-Saxon chronicle, in the same very difficult style of Latin that was in vogue in monastic texts.[46] Although Æthelweard may not have had daily access to monastic libraries, he certainly could read Latin competently. Yet, Ælfric is comfortable suggesting that his secular patron requires translation, even while taking pains not to impugn the Latinity of his fellow monks, a fact which suggests that English is an acceptable language for instruction, so long as the immediate audience is not monastic.[47] As the earlier chapters on Byrhtferth suggest, the frequent naming of the clerical audience in the *Enchiridion* justifies the project of English composition, and for Ælfric the naming of Æthelweard functions in a similar manner. By naming an Anglo-Saxon ealdorman as the primary audience of this text, Ælfric is free to compose a translation that can also be read by monks. The main manuscript of the *Lives of Saints* (London, British Library, Cotton Julius E.vii), offers strong evidence of monastic readership, since it reached a monastic library shortly after its creation.[48]

In the case of the *Admonitio*, the *Grammar*, and the *Lives of Saints*, it is relatively safe to speculate about the existence of an audience of monks literate in English. When evidence from the study of the *Enchiridion* is added here as well, it is entirely plausible that monks who have been trained in Latin might choose to read an English-language text, whether or not they have limited or extensive proficiency in Latin. In fact, since books tend to be held in monastic libraries,[49] we should be especially sceptical of Ælfric's failure to name a monastic audience for the majority of his English-language works. Whether or not monks were the primary intended

46 The standard edition is Campbell, *Chronicle of Æthelweard*. For a good discussion of the careers of Æthelweard and his son Æthelmær, see Catherine Cubitt, "Ælfric's Lay Patrons," in *A Companion to Ælfric*, ed. Magennis and Swan, 165–92.

47 We see a similar trend in Byrhtferth's *Enchiridion* when he addresses an audience of secular clerics 73 times, but only addresses his monastic audience 12 times, although there were almost certainly as many monks as clerics in his classroom.

48 Whatley, "*Pearls before Swine*," 184.

49 For the evidence for libraries in Anglo-Saxon England, see Lapidge, *The Anglo-Saxon Library*.

audience of a piece, once a work was translated, Benedictines constituted a large percentage of the Anglo-Saxon population who were literate in either English or Latin. Furthermore, since monks had a requirement to read,[50] it is likely that some could have fulfilled this expectation through the perusal of English-language texts.

In conclusion, Ælfric's naming of audiences cannot be read as simply as he has named them. As literate members of the Anglo-Saxon population, Benedictine monks and secular clerics had to have been the largest audiences for any of Ælfric's works, despite his protestations to the contrary. Furthermore, just as Ælfric's descriptions of his audiences cannot be taken at face value, in a similar vein, his direct comments on the use and utility of English or Latin cannot be accepted without question. Ælfric's articulation of the role of English and Latin in the educational project of the Benedictine Reform has more to do with specific ideas about the structure of society and the position of languages within that society, rather than with actual language usage in late Anglo-Saxon England. It is through these comments on language that Ælfric constructs a specifically Benedictine identity both for himself and for his monastic readers.

Constructing a Benedictine Identity

Throughout his prefaces, Ælfric ties his credentials for writing to his identity as a Benedictine monk. Through this careful construction of his own authority, Ælfric creates a very specific portrait of the Benedictine educational reform and the intellectual achievements of its members. Not surprisingly, perhaps, Ælfric's construction of his own authority and the role of Benedictine monks in Anglo-Saxon England are subtly different depending on whether the preface is in Latin or in English. In English, he tends to reference his role specifically as a monk, as in the first and the second series of *Catholic Homilies* and the preface to *Genesis*. When writing in Latin he never uses the word "monachus," but instead tends to allude more peripherally to his monastic status by referencing his attendance at Æthelwold's school in Winchester, specifically in the first series of *Catholic Homilies*, his *Grammar*, the *Vita S. Æthelwoldi*, and the *Letter to the Monks of Eynsham*. The fact that these references appear only in Latin suggests that the place of Ælfric's schooling is more relevant to Ælfric's Latin audiences than to his English ones. Mary Swan explains that Ælfric

50 For a discussion of the monks' requirement to read, see chap. 2.

> is shaping an identity for himself relevant to the function of the text in question and at the same time is defining the identity of his addressee … In the prefaces to the *Catholic Homilies*, the *Lives of Saints* and *Genesis*, we see Ælfric configuring a powerfully Winchester reform–centred context for his authority and authorial activity, negotiating with great care his identity and status relative to that of the powerful men – Sigeric, Æthelweard, and Æthelmær – who receive and commission his work and are part of his ideological circle but who are dependent on his writings for authoritative spiritual instruction.[51]

In this close connection to Æthelwold's school, then, Ælfric redefines the role of teaching, as belonging not to clerics (as it would according to traditional delineations of clerical responsibilities) but to mass-priests and bishops, both categories that could be filled by monks.[52]

The fact that Ælfric defines himself as a teacher is a commonplace in scholarship.[53] His *Colloquy*, *Grammar*, and *Glossary* seem to be designed with a monastic classroom in mind. Throughout his works, he references the importance of his own role as teacher, a subject which Wilhelm Busse has catalogued in an extensive article detailing both Ælfric's and Wulfstan's self-representation.[54] Ælfric's relationship to his status as teacher, however, is not as transparent as it may seem. Some of his most famous comments about teaching occur in works ostensibly directed at a lay audience and not specifically intended for his monastic classroom. Furthermore, his comments about teaching often occur within close proximity to an overt criticism of the secular clerics' failure to teach correctly and to offer an acceptable example.

As a teacher of the laity, Ælfric's position is not wholly without ambivalence. His preface to the first series of *Catholic Homilies* shows Ælfric's earliest relationship to his own role as authority and teacher to a lay

51 Mary Swan, "Identity and Ideology in Ælfric's Prefaces," in *A Companion to Ælfric*, ed. Magennis and Swan, 268.

52 The reference to mass-priests and bishops comes from the particular wording of Ælfric's claim that the reformers were responsible for the tenth-century education renaissance.

53 For a recent survey of scholarship on Ælfric as a teacher, see Thomas N. Hall, "Ælfric as Pedagogue," in *A Companion to Ælfric*, ed. Magennis and Swan, 193–216.

54 Wilhelm G. Busse, "Sua gað ða lareowas beforan ðæm folce, & ðæt folc æfter: The Self-Understanding of the Reformers as Teachers in Late Tenth-Century England," in *Schriftlichkeit im frühen Mittelalter*, ed. Ursula Schaefer, ScriptOralia 53 (Tübingen, 1993), 58–106.

audience. Ælfric does not wholly embrace his role as teacher in this preface. In fact, Ælfric asserts that he is not a teacher, but a fighter of heresy: "ic ðas boc of Ledenum gereorde to Engliscre spræce awende, na þurh gebylde micelre lare, ac for ðan ðe ic geseah and gehyrde mycel gedwyld on manegum Engliscum bocum, ðe ungelærede menn ðurh heora bilewitnysse to micclum wisdome tealdon" (*AP*, 108) [I translated this book from the Latin language into the English speech, not for the purpose of compiling great learning, but because I saw and heard in many English books much heresy, which unlearned men counted as great wisdom as result of their simplicity].

He writes to present an authorized and orthodox teaching to a lay audience, who, perhaps, are not otherwise exposed to the theology present in reformed centres.[55] That Ælfric was successful in spreading these reformed doctrines beyond the monastery walls can be seen in the extensive and relatively rapid circulation of the first series. Busse suggests that Ælfric presents the reformers as teachers in a kind of apostolic succession normally reserved for priesthood. The emphasis on the apostle Peter in particular can be seen in the artwork of the reform, which often features Peter along with Mary in works such as the New Minster charter.[56] Both Peter and Mary also figure prominently in the dedication of the church at Thorney in which "the western part dedicated for use by the clergy and people was consecrated to St. Peter, while the eastern presbytery and northern porticus were consecrated to St. Mary and Benedict respectively."[57]

Ælfric as a mass-priest has authority derived from St Peter, and therefore must fill in as a teacher because those ordinarily appointed to teaching responsibilities, the secular clergy, are not doing a satisfactory job of teaching nor are they offering a profitable example. Some of the ways in which the secular clergy were falling short of the standards laid down by a strict Benedictine such as Ælfric have been handled by Upchurch.[58] In

55 Clemoes thought that Ælfric's work constituted a fully thought out educational program of Christian study. See below, p. 183.

56 Catherine Cubitt, "Images of St Peter: The Clergy and the Religious Life in Anglo-Saxon England," in *The Christian Tradition in Anglo-Saxon England: Approaches to Current Scholarship and Teaching*, ed. Paul Cavill, Christianity and Culture: Issues in Teaching and Research (Cambridge, 2004), 41–54.

57 Ibid., 46.

58 "For Pastoral Care."

Ælfric's emphasis on chastity – especially lay celibacy during liturgical seasons and during periods of infertility – he undermines the authority of secular clerics, who might potentially be married and have fathered children known in the region.[59] The rejoinder to the scribe in the first series of *Catholic Homilies* not to change a word can also be applied to the cleric responsible for giving the sermon in church; he is not to change anything and thus introduce error. In this first venture into homily creation represented by the first series, then, Ælfric enters into his role as teacher with a healthy level of ambivalence. He does not write to build great wisdom but to respond to heresy. In this position as a fighter of heresy, he can use his standing as a Winchester-trained monk to supersede the rights of the secular clerics to teach.

At the same time that Ælfric shows a certain ambivalence to his role as teacher, he claims that his authority in writing comes from how he has followed teachers who have come before him. He asserts that he followed "æfter geðungenra lareowa trahtnungum ... þæra lareowa naman ic awrat on ðære ærran bec on ðære Ledenan forespræce" (*AP*, 111–12) [after the exposition of excellent teachers ... the names of the teachers I wrote in my earlier book in the Latin preface]. According to Busse, "The reformers tried to establish a hierarchy exclusively founded on (patristic) erudition, with an individual's qualification according to clerical rank coming in second place only, after his learning."[60] Interestingly enough, he does not name his teachers at this point, but refers his readers to his earlier Latin preface for the first series. This cross-reference to a pre-existing preface in Latin is strange, since Ælfric's discussion of education and the importance of teachers occurs ordinarily in his English-language prefaces, not his Latin ones. Ælfric frequently takes pains to position himself as a teacher to those reading English-language works, but with the exception of the *Letter to the Monks of Eynsham*, written to adapt the *Regularis concordia* for practice at his own monastery, Ælfric does not customarily presume to adopt an authority for instructing those with fluency in Latin, as is exemplified in the preface to his *Grammar*, where Ælfric goes to great lengths to assert that he is a teacher of children, not adult monks.

However, this position is also a bit disingenuous, since Ælfric's authority is predicated upon his Latinity. It is not without consequence that each

59 Ibid., 44–8.

60 Busse, "Sua gað ða lareowas," 76.

of his three homily collections begins with a Latin preface, followed by an English preface. His role as teacher, however, is never discussed in Latin, but in English, as if he does not need to justify his role as teacher to other monks, but only to his vernacular audience. The fact that his discussion of teaching is in English suggests that he is not arguing for permission to teach from monastic superiors, but rather is constructing his own role as author/teacher, while at the same time configuring an audience of ideal learners. He is teaching the students how to be taught and at the same time by whom they should be taught.[61] Since he conducts this important identity-formation in English, he is simultaneously constructing an identity for English-language instruction and English-language compositions.

One of the identities created for English is that of a transitional language used in a period of infancy before the more adult study of Latin texts, and this identity is reiterated throughout both the English and the Latin prefaces to the *Grammar*. Ælfric claims to translate the *Excerptiones de Prisciano* into English for "vobis puerulis tenellis ... usque quo ad perfectiora perveniatis studia" (*AP*, 114) [you tender youths ... until you achieve a more perfect study]. The "perfectiora" ("more perfect" or "more complete") study to which Ælfric refers probably implies the study of the Latin scriptures.[62] In the English preface to the *Grammar*, Ælfric elaborates on the distinction between the duties appropriate to youth and maturity: the young are to learn, while the old are to teach. Ælfric writes: "Iungum mannum gedafenað þæt hi leornion sumne wisdom, and ðam ealdum gedafenað þæt hi tæcon sum gerad heora iunglingum, for ðan ðe ðurh lare byð se geleafa gehealden" (*AP*, 115) [It is fitting for young men to learn some wisdom and for old men to teach some counsel to their youths, because the faith is maintained through teaching]. Ælfric's teaching is part of his own role in maintaining the faith, which he deems to be

61 My thinking on this point has been influenced by Katherine O'Brien O'Keeffe's work on Ælfric's Colloquy; "'Esto quod es': Ælfric's *Colloquy* and the Imperatives of Monastic Identity," in *Stealing Obedience: Narratives of Agency and Identity in Later Anglo-Saxon England* (Toronto, 2012).

62 Note the similar comments in his preface to *De grammatica* from Alcuin, who described grammar as a step in the educational process for youths "donec perfectior aetas et animus sensu robustior ad culmina sanctarum Scripturarum perveniat" [until a more perfect age and a spirit with a more robust sense arrives at the peak of Holy Scriptures]. *Library of Latin Texts – Series A: Database for the Western Latin Tradition* (Brepols, 2009), col. 854 (accessed 14 February 2012).

in jeopardy. He asks, "hu mæg se geleafa beon forðgenge, gif seo lar and ða lareowas ateoriað?" (*AP*, 115) [How may the faith be advanced if the learning and the teachers diminish?]. Ælfric resolves the conflict between his own Benedictine identity, which requires Latinity, and his English-language translations by constructing himself as a teacher. Therefore, he translates because he is required to teach those who must do their part to maintain the faith.[63] But within these comments on the necessity of teaching still rests an insinuation that the correct example is not being offered by the secular clergy, who are supposedly designated as the teachers to the laity. Ælfric must take up this role because the appointed pastors have failed in their responsibilities to master the Latinity and educational achievements expected of a reformed monk.

Ælfric compensates for his reluctance to accept the role of teacher by agreeing to translate only the "naked narrative,"[64] with the truth locked away. The next chapter will explore how Ælfric's adaptation of Wulfstan of Winchester's *Vita S. Æthelwoldi* used a vocabulary that attempted to replicate a univalent narrative structure by limiting interpretation, but this emphasis on a safe interpretation that limits misunderstanding perhaps overlooks an important aspect of the prefaces to Genesis and the *Grammar*, namely, that Ælfric teaches a form of interpretation here. He claims that grammar is the key that unlocks the text. Thus, his whole project of writing and adapting the *Grammar* teaches a specific kind of biblical exegesis. Equally in the preface to Genesis, the longest preface that Ælfric wrote, he digresses on some appropriate methods of interpretation. While these attempts at instruction are relatively abbreviated so as to be adaptable to a preface, they do indicate that as much as Ælfric apologized for his English-language instruction and warned of its dangers, at the same time, he attempted to teach an English-only audience how to interpret scripture in

63 Notably, Melinda Menzer reads the Grammar as a key to Ælfric's body of English-language works as the first phase in the teaching of interpretation. "Ælfric's English *Grammar*," *JEGP* 103 (2004): 106–24.

64 Ælfric's reference to the naked narrative appears in the following context: "We secgað eac foran to þæt seo boc is swiþe deop gastlice to understandenne, and we ne writaþ na mare buton þa nacedan gerecednisse. Þonne þincþ þam ungelæredum þæt eall þæt andgit beo belocen on þære anfealdan gerecednisse, ac hit ys swiþe feor þam" (*AP*, 117) [We say also before undertaking this translation that the book has a very deep spiritual meaning, but we write no more than the naked narrative. Then it seems to the uneducated that all the meaning is contained in the univalent narrative, but it is very far from that].

an orthodox way. The implicit assertion that English can function in such an important task undercuts the claims that he makes about the inadequacy of the English language and his own claims about his ambivalence towards teaching. Notably, it is in his prefaces to the *Grammar* and to Genesis that Ælfric attacks the teaching of the secular clergy most strongly. Ælfric's ambivalent acceptance of his role as a teacher seems always to go hand in hand with his usurpation of the secular clergy in their more usual pastoral role.

Conclusion

Ælfric's positioning of himself as a teacher is not a neutral act. Rather, he is creating a Benedictine identity that usurps the authority of the secular clergy, while subjecting these same clerics to the *auctoritas* of reformed monks. Furthermore, the inconsistencies between Ælfric's statements about the vernacular and his actual practices as a translator arise from his construction and positioning of his two main audiences: the secular clergy and reformed monks. Like many Benedictines, Ælfric establishes his monastic identity and authority by defining himself in opposition to secular clerics, whom he depicts as liable to introduce heresy because of their poor education. Conversely, because he claims that the monks' authority rests in their superior Latinity, he must also assert that English translations are not intended for a Benedictine audience, just as Byrhtferth did. The truth of the matter seems to be quite the opposite. Even if it is accepted that Ælfric writes English homilies for the laity, this imagined lay audience almost certainly received his message only when mediated through an ecclesiast, either secular or monastic. In addition, the prefaces, unlike the homilies, conform to the expectations of a written genre generally intended for private contemplation, and monks have the leisure, access, and even the requirement to perform such study. When the audience for Ælfric's remarks on the value of the vernacular is read as literate and probably ecclesiastic, his description of the vernacular can be seen for what it is: a very specifically articulated language politics that provides a rationale for the pre-eminence of Latinate Benedictines, who are shown to be leaders of the people and superior to the secular clergy.

Speaking of the superiority and importance of Latinity among Benedictines presents a decided problem for a figure such as Ælfric, who is almost exclusively a vernacular author. Despite the fact that Latinity was so important in his construction of the language dynamics of the reform, Ælfric never composed in the hermeneutic style commonly called the badge of a reformed monk. The next chapter considers why Ælfric's Latin-language production does not match Benedictine expectations in this regard, even when dealing with subjects dear to the hearts of reformers, such as the life of the reforming bishop Æthelwold. In a close study of Ælfric's adaptation of this life, the political articulations of his prefaces can be set against the more practical considerations that Ælfric undertook while translating. Placing ideology next to utility in the work of such a prominent author as Ælfric goes a long way towards illuminating the linguistic hierarchies in the historical and social context of the late Anglo-Saxon period.

5 Unravelling the Hermeneutic Style: Ælfric's Latin Epitomes and English Translations

Reading Ælfric's English audience as composed of literate ecclesiasts, both monks and secular clergy, demands a reconsideration of the audience and purpose of his Latin works as well, particularly since they avoid the hermeneutic style so common among his peers, such as Byrhtferth.[1] Nearly every other Benedictine author during this period attempted hermeneutic prose or verse.[2] Ælfric, however, wrote "non garrula verbositate aut ignotis sermonibus, sed puris et apertis verbis" [not with wordy verbosity or unknown speech, but with clear and open words].[3] Although these words refer to Ælfric's project of vernacular translation, not his Latin-language compositions, many scholars have noted the similarity between Ælfric's plain style in Old English and his unadorned Latin prose.[4] The connection between the styles in both languages should not be made so quickly, since

1 Christopher A. Jones has argued that Ælfric's stylistic choices were based on the fact that he began his Latin training late in life; "*Meatim Sed et Rustica*: Ælfric of Eynsham as a Medieval Latin Author," *Journal of Medieval Latin* 8 (1998): 1–57. I disagree with that assertion and presented my rebuttal in "Ælfric of Eynsham and Hermeneutic Latin: *Meatim Sed et Rustica* Reconsidered," *Journal of Medieval Latin* 16 (2006): 111–41. That article is an earlier version of this chapter. There I countered Jones's thesis that Ælfric's insufficient youthful education led to his inability to compose in hermeneutic Latin. I argue that Ælfric's stylistic choices did not result from a poor education, but from a very specific idea about how a narrative should function.

2 See discussion in chap. 1, pp. 20–1.

3 Jonathan Wilcox, ed., *Ælfric's Prefaces*, Durham Medieval Texts 9 (Durham, 1994), 111. All translations are my own unless otherwise noted.

4 "As in Old English, so also in Latin, [Ælfric] strove always for brevity, clarity, and simplicity, but without neglect of a spare but elegant rhetoric." Milton McC. Gatch, *Preaching and Theology in Anglo-Saxon England: Ælfric and Wulfstan* (Toronto, 1977), 131.

other reformers affected a plain English style, despite their preference for turgid Latin.[5] As Byrhtferth's writings exemplified, a readable style of Old English coupled with an esoteric Latin vocabulary is a hallmark of the texts connected to the reform.

Yet Ælfric's writing shows no trace of the flamboyancy characteristic of the period, and many scholars have commented on its tendency to follow in the tradition of Bede and Alcuin, rather than that of Aldhelm.[6] Ælfric's style is often described as simpler than that of his counterparts, such as Byrhtferth, who preferred esoteric vocabulary and endless amplification. This dichotomy between Ælfric and Byrhtferth (or between Bede and Aldhelm) has caused Ælfric's syntactical complexity not to be appreciated. Rhythmical *cursus*, alliteration, and complicated syntax can be found in Ælfric's writing, despite the fact that these traits are more typically associated with the hermeneutic style inspired by Aldhelm. I have argued elsewhere that Ælfric's writing has more complex syntactical structures than his sources, especially when those texts are in the hermeneutic style, precisely because of their concision, which compresses complex grammatical structures.[7] In other words, the traits that make Ælfric's work appear to be simpler, or merely easier to read, make it grammatically more challenging. What sets Ælfric's writings apart, however, is that they meticulously avoid Grecisms and esoteric words characteristic of Aldhelm and other hermeneutic writers, and Ælfric seems to have particularly enjoyed removing the redundancies characteristic of the hermeneutic style.

Ælfric's difference in style seems to be closely keyed to a difference in purpose. Many texts in the hermeneutic style memorialize important moments or people of the reform, such as Lantfred's *Translatio et miracula sancti Swithuni*, which simultaneously records a hagiography of Swithun, bishop of Winchester, and commemorates the Benedictine reformation of the Old Minster by Æthelwold.[8] Although Ælfric frequently adapts and rewrites these very same monastic texts, his versions seem to be more

5 Æthelwold, for example, composed the preface to the *Regularis concordia* in hermeneutic Latin, but the translation of the Rule of Benedict in simple English. For the disparity between these two styles, see Michael Lapidge, "Æthelwold as Scholar and Teacher," in his *Anglo-Latin Literature, 900–1066* (London, 1993), 183–211, at 98–103. See also Christopher A. Jones, ed., *Ælfric's Letter to the Monks of Eynsham*, Cambridge Studies in Anglo-Saxon England 24 (Cambridge, 1998), 52 n. 135.

6 For an example of this characterization, see Alistair Campbell, *The Chronicle of Æthelweard* (London, 1962), xlv.

7 "Ælfric of Eynsham," 117–24.

8 See discussion in Introduction, pp. 1–14.

workaday, since the creation of the Latin text was a middle stage in his process of preparing an English-language abbreviation and translation for his homily collections. For instance, before translating his English-language *Life of St Swithun* from Lantfred's *Translatio* (as discussed in the Introduction), Ælfric seems to have first created a Latin epitome in which he greatly reduced the length of the work and removed hermeneutic vocabulary.[9] This Latin epitome exists in a single manuscript, Paris BNF Lat. 362, which Michael Lapidge has argued is a commonplace book in which Ælfric collected and abbreviated Latin versions of the Anglo-Saxon saints' lives that he later translated in his *Catholic Homilies* and *Lives of Saints*.[10] As a medial stage in the translation process, these texts offer a missing link in the relationship between Latin lives in the hermeneutic style and their English-language translations because they allow us to see what Ælfric had to remove from a text in order to make it appropriate to the English language. It is especially interesting that he did this linguistic surgery in Latin first and then translated the epitome into English.

This chapter turns to a single text in that manuscript, *Vita S. Æthelwoldi*, the only one for which Ælfric authored one of his famous prefaces and which is therefore indisputably his. Unfortunately, no English version of this epitome survives, and it is difficult to be certain that this particular text was intended for English-language translation. Yet the life of every other saint dealt with in this manuscript has been translated into English. As Lapidge emphasizes,

> Leaving aside St. Æthelwold … Ælfric treated the remaining six saints – Cuthbert, Edmund, Oswald, Birinus, Swithun, and Æthelthryth – either in his *Catholic Homilies* (Cuthbert) or in his *Lives of Saints* (Edmund, Oswald, Swithun, Æthelthryth; an account of Birinus is incorporated into his "Life of St Oswald"). It was these six Anglo-Saxon saints, and only these saints, which Ælfric treated in his vernacular hagiography.[11]

These comments point to the homogeneity of the manuscript as a collection of texts that Ælfric otherwise used in their entirety for his vernacular homilies. It should be acknowledged, however, that Lapidge was arguing

9 A full discussion of the changes can be found in Michael Lapidge, ed., *The Cult of St Swithun*, Winchester Studies 4.2 (Oxford, 2003), 558–61.

10 Lapidge, *Cult of St Swithun*, 555–7.

11 *Cult of St. Swithun*, 556.

for Ælfrician authorship for the entire manuscript, not that the *Vita S. Æthelwoldi* was intended for English-language translation, as I am suggesting. While it cannot be proved that this particular text was ever translated (or prepared for translation), Ælfric's method of epitomizing is so regular as to be almost mechanical (as will be explained in detail below), and this text may still offer a clue to Ælfric's goals in his reworking of hermeneutic texts and his subsequent creation of English-language homilies.[12]

The time is ripe for a deeper evaluation of Ælfric's process and procedure in translating, since his changes while translating have been a particularly popular topic. *The Year's Work in English Studies* lists two articles on this subject in 2010 alone, and another two in 2011.[13] Although all these articles provide insight into changes and adaptations that Ælfric made to his source, their conclusions are fundamentally limited because these scholars do not ordinarily work on Anglo-Latin texts and only one seemed to be aware of the pieces in which Michael Lapidge or Christopher A. Jones discuss Ælfric's mechanical methods of translation.[14] These recent studies speak to the need for scholarship that pushes forward the study of hermeneutic Latin in terms intelligible to scholars who work primarily on English-language texts. This chapter then will examine the changes that Ælfric made to his version of the *Vita S. Æthelwoldi* when he abbreviated it from Wulfstan of Winchester's more flamboyant hermeneutic version. In its liminal position as a Latin text that stands alone (as demonstrated by

12 While the hagiography of Swithun might be a better starting point for this research, since it is available in the hermeneutic style, a Latin epitome, and an English version, an edition was not available at the time I began my research, nor is the case for Ælfrician authorship as definitive as for the *Vita S. Æthelwoldi.*

13 Philip Shaw and Rebecca Stephenson, "Early Medieval," *YWES* 91 (2012): 1–29, at 25–6; Shaw and Stephenson, "Early Medieval," *YWES* 92 (2013): 1–35, at 31–2; Kiriko Sato, "Ælfric's Lexical Alterations in His Adaptations from the Old English Boethius," *Neophilologus* 95 (2011): 305–11; Stewart Brookes, "Reading between the Lines: The Liturgy and Ælfric's Lives of Saints and Homilies," *Leeds Studies in English* 42 (2011): 17–28; Hiroshi Ogawa, "Sententia in Narrative Form: Ælfric's Narrative Method in the Hagiographical Homily on St Martin," *Leeds Studies in English* 42 (2011): 75–92; Robert K. Upchurch, "A Big Dog Barks: Ælfric of Eynsham's Indictment of the English Pastorate and Witan," *Speculum* 85 (2010): 505–33; Don Chapman, "Uterque Lingua / Ægðer Gereord: Ælfric's Grammatical Vocabulary and the Winchester Tradition," *JEGP* 109 (2010): 421–45.

14 See Lapidge and Winterbottom, *Life of St Æthelwold*, cl–cliii. For Ælfric's use of this method in his redrafting of the *Regularis concordia*, see Jones, *Ælfric's Letter*, 18–60 and "*Meatim Sed et Rustica*," 21–41. Upchurch seemed to be the only scholar aware of Ælfric's translation techniques.

its carefully crafted preface) but may have also been intended for eventual English-language translation (as its manuscript placement suggests), Ælfric's *Vita S. Æthelwoldi* offers insight into the dynamic relationship between the complexity of the hermeneutic Latin style and the simpler English style favoured by reformers.

Ælfric's Method of Abbreviation and Translation

Among the two lives of St Æthelwold written by first-hand witnesses (i.e., Wulfstan and Ælfric), Ælfric's *Life* is read more frequently by modern scholars because of its clarity and brevity,[15] and the long-held belief that it was composed first, and that Wulfstan later embellished it with hermeneutic Latin.[16] Some have even suggested that Wulfstan's edition is a twelfth-century forgery based on Ælfric's *Life*, since none of the manuscripts of Wulfstan's texts were written before the twelfth century.[17] However, Lapidge and Winterbottom have shown that Wulfstan's *Life* was more widely read and was more influential throughout the Middle Ages than Ælfric's abbreviation.[18] While Ælfric's *Life* exists in only one manuscript, Wulfstan's *Life* is extant in five, and evidence from indirect witnesses suggests that it was the "most widely read of all pre-Conquest Anglo-Latin saints' *vitae*."[19] Furthermore, Lapidge and Winterbottom have shown that Ælfric abbreviated Wulfstan's *Life*, not the other way around.

The most striking aspect of Ælfric's method of abbreviation (both in this text and elsewhere) is that he tended to preserve the original words of his source while omitting unnecessary verbiage. Instead of recasting the *Life* in his own words, Ælfric adapted the words of his source, changing them to fit new grammatical positions in a process akin to working a jigsaw puzzle: rearranging parts of the sentence so that the original words of the source can be retained, despite the fact that significant portions of each sentence are left out. This operation can best be shown visually. Below is

15 E.g., David Knowles, who repeatedly cites Ælfric's *Life*, but not Wulfstan's; see *The Monastic Order in England: A History of Its Development from the Times of St Dunstan to the Fourth Lateran Council, 940–1216*, 2nd ed. (Cambridge, 1963), 39–41.

16 D.J.V. Fisher, "The Early Biographers of St Ethelwold," *English Historical Review* 67 (1952): 381–91.

17 J.A. Robinson, *The Times of Saint Dunstan* (Oxford, 1923), 107–8. For a list of manuscripts, see Lapidge and Winterbottom, *Life of St Æthelwold*, clxviii–clxxix.

18 Lapidge and Winterbottom, *Life of St Æthelwold*, clxvii.

19 Ibid.

an excerpt that captures the flamboyancy of Wulfstan of Winchester's *Life of St Æthelwold* with the corresponding text in Ælfric's version:

Erant igitur *parentes sancti* pontificis *Æthelwuoldi* ex ingenua Christianorum propagine oriundi, *Wentanae ciuitatis* urbani, *temporibus* senioris *Eaduuardi regis Anglorum florentes,* in mandatis et iustificationibus Domini sine querela fideliter incedentes. Qui dum cotidianis bonorum operum pollerent incrementis, *eximio Dei* munere *decorati* sunt *quo talem mererentur* gignere sobolem, cuius eruditione et exemplis *non solum populi praesentis aeui sed etiam futuri* peruenirent ad noticiam ueri luminis, ut exuti *caligine* tenebrosi *erroris* gloria fruerentur aeternae claritatis.[20]

[Therefore, the parents of the holy bishop Æthelwold arose from the noble stock of Christians, were dwellers in the city of Winchester, lived in the time of Edward the Elder king of the English, and advanced in the commands and justifications of the Lord faithfully without complaint. While they were powerful in the daily additions of good works, they were adorned with the extraordinary gift of God in that they deserved to give birth to such offspring, by whose learning and example not only the people of the present age, but also the future might arrive to the acquaintance of the true light, so that they might enjoy the glory of eternal splendour, after the darkness of shadowy error had been extinguished.]

Erant autem parentes sancti Æthelwuoldi habitatores ciuitatis Wentae, tempore Eaduuerdi regis Anglorum florentes, eximio Dei dono decorati quo talem meruissent prolem generare, cuius documentis non solum praesentis aeui populi sed etiam futuri caligine caruissent erroris.[21]

[However, the parents of holy Æthelwold were inhabitants of the city Winchester, living in the time of Edward, king of the English. They were distinguished by an extraordinary gift of God in that they deserved to give birth

20 Michael Lapidge and Michael Winterbottom, eds, Wulfstan of Winchester, *The Life of St Æthelwold* Oxford Medieval Texts (Oxford, 1991), 2–4; hereafter the text of this saint's life will be cited as "Wulfstan" with a page number, while the editorial material of the volume will be cited with reference to the editors' names.

21 Michael Lapidge and Michael Winterbottom, eds, "Ælfric's Vita S. Æthelwoldi," in Wulfstan of Winchester, *The Life of St Æthelwold* (Oxford, 1991), 70–80, at 71; hereafter cited as Ælfric with a page number reference.

> to such a son, by whose teachings not only the people of the present age, but also the future are deprived of the darkness of error.]

The words italicized in Wulfstan's text were retained in toto by Ælfric, in what Lapidge and Winterbottom call the "red-line" method of abbreviation, since Ælfric could have drawn a red line through the undesirable words and copied the remaining selection.[22] This method of epitomizing is so faithful to the exact words of the original text that Ælfric even retains the inflectional endings, causing him to execute a complex reworking of the grammar. At the same time that Ælfric reworks the grammar, he often excises the amplification and redundancy characteristic of the hermeneutic style. For instance, Wulfstan's passage begins with the verb *erant* [they are] followed by four nominative plural adjectives or participles, *oriundi* [arisen], *urbani* [city dwellers], *florentes* [flourishing], and *incedentes* [advancing], that modify the subject, *parentes* [parents]. Ælfric omitted two of these participles and their phrases in their entirety, and exchanges *urbani* for the synonym *habitatores*, but otherwise leaves the remaining two phrases intact. This careful cutting highlights the repetitiveness of the hermeneutic style, since Ælfric's text retains all the essential information without the extra verbiage.

Ælfric is so faithful to the exact words of the text, even their inflectional endings, that it is easy to miss the words that he changes, such as substituting *habitatores* for Wulfstan's *urbani*. Technically speaking, the words that Ælfric changes are not hermeneutic. Despite Wulfstan's preference for amplification, his vocabulary is considerably less exotic than Byrhtferth's, and the text contains only four Grecisms, all of which were in fairly common use in the later tenth century.[23] But despite the "modesty" and "sobriety" that characterize Wulfstan's vocabulary, many otherwise inoffensive words seem to be not to Ælfric's taste.[24] The replacement of many of these words does not seem to be motivated by their frequency in the Latin

22 Lapidge and Winterbottom, *Life of St Æthelwold*, cxlvii–cxlix; Lapidge, *Cult of St Swithun*, 558–61. In addition to Paris BNF Lat. 362, this mode of abbreviation was also used in *Ælfric's Letter to the Monks of Eynsham*. For a discussion of Ælfric's changes to this text, see Jones, "*Meatim Sed et Rustica*" and *Ælfric's Letter*, 18–60.

23 Lapidge and Winterbottom, *Life of St Æthelwold*, cix–cx.

24 Lapidge and Winterbottom describe Wulfstan's style thus: "In an age when most Latin prose was characterized by ostentatious, hermeneutic vocabulary, Wulfstan's prose stands out for its modesty and sobriety. Wulfstan was not as severe a stylist as Ælfric, who in his redaction of the *Vita S. Æthelwoldi* found much to excise; but in comparison (say) with the Aldhelmian pomposity of Byrhtferth, Wulfstan is a master of restraint." Ibid., cxi.

corpus, but rather by the precision of their meaning. Ælfric often changed Wulfstan's multivalent words to more concrete words with a single and precise meaning. For instance, in the passage above the words italicized in Ælfric's text have been altered from the original source. Listing the Ælfrician word first, they are

autem = igitur
habitatores = urbani
dono = munere
prolem = sobolem
generare = gignere
documentis = eruditione et exemplis.[25]

The substitution of *autem* [however] for *igitur* [therefore] shows a higher level of semantic precision, since the postpositive particle *autem* indicates a transition between sections, and here it specifically signals the transition from the prologue to the main text of the *Life*.[26] In a similar vein, the next four words show an interesting tendency that continues throughout the work:[27] Ælfric preferred words with a singular transparent meaning and frequently replaced words with multiple meanings in Wulfstan with more precise words. Wulfstan's word *urbani* can mean "an inhabitant of a city" or "polished, refined, cultivated," but Ælfric's word *habitatores* refers only to the inhabitant of a place without the additional connotation of sophistication. Wulfstan's word *munere* also has two possible meanings: (1) "a gift" and (2) "a service, office, or post." By changing to the word *dono*, Ælfric has focused on the definition that he wished to highlight, i.e., "a gift." The next two examples are similar. Wulfstan's *sobolem* means "a twig" or "an offshoot," but by transference it is used in poetry to mean "offspring or progeny."[28] By contrast, the word that Ælfric

25 I have omitted the word *caruissent* because it is part of a major grammatical revision, and is discussed in my "Ælfric of Eynsham," 123.

26 See the entries in the *Thesaurus Linguae Latinae* for "autem" and "igitur." However, Jones could not always find such obvious reasons for the alteration of conjunctions in Ælfric's *Letter to the Monks of Eynsham*; see "*Meatim Sed et Rustica*," 28–9.

27 The replacement of *gignere* for *generare* does not follow this pattern, since *gigno* is far more common than *genero*. However, in the Vulgate, *gigno* normally appears in its perfect form *genuit*, cf. the first chapter of Matthew and the third chapter of Luke. I suggest that the change in stem from *gigno* to *genui* might have caused Ælfric to choose a comparable verb with a more regular stem, i.e., *genero*.

28 The use of vocabulary more commonly connected to poetry is a hallmark of the hermeneutic style. See Introduction, pp. 18–19.

chose, *prolem*, literally means "that which grows forth" and is used almost exclusively to refer to offspring or progeny.[29] The final word on the list, *documentis*, shows a similar trend towards specificity, because it replaces *eruditione et exemplis*: general words that refer to learning/knowledge and examples/patterns, respectively. Ælfric's more specific word comes from *doceo* [to teach] and means a lesson or example used in instruction or as a warning. Whereas Wulfstan's words vaguely refer to Æthelwold's learning and good life, Ælfric has focused specifically on his role as a good teacher. These words taken together show a general tendency in many of the small alterations of vocabulary that Ælfric made throughout this work: when Ælfric encountered a word in his source that was vague or multivalent, he replaced it with a specific word that focused on the single meaning that Ælfric wished to highlight. His precision of wording is in striking contrast to the normal practice of amplification in hermeneutic Latin, which emphasized the use of polysyllabic synonyms even when the meaning of the words was not exactly appropriate for the context, as is common in Byrhtferth's writing. It seems that Ælfric could not tolerate this linguistic imprecision in spite of its frequency in many documents connected to the monastic reform. The alterations that Ælfric introduced into the text show an interest in both the syntactical and poetic nuances of words, and this is an interest shared by the more elaborate writers of the reform, such as Wulfstan. However, Ælfric seems concerned with precision in the use of Latin, not flamboyancy.

The passage above also contains two words that illustrate Ælfric's interest in self-explanatory etymologies, *prolem* and *documentis*. Both of these words seem to have been preferred in their specific contexts because of the precision of their roots. Throughout the *Life of Æthelwold*, we see polysyllabic words whose meanings differ from their uncompounded roots replaced with more self-explanatory compounds. For instance, Ælfric changes *prosilire* [to burst forth, lit. to jump forward] to *exire* [to go out],[30] *optinuit* [he possessed, lit. he held towards or on account of] to *adquisiuit*

29 See also below, pp. 166–7, for Ælfric's tendency to replace certain Latin compounds with other compounds that are self-explanatory. Notably, *soboles* is more correctly spelled *suboles* and is a compound of *sub* [under] + *olesco* [to grow], whereas *proles* comes from *pro* [forward] + *alo* [to nourish], of which *olesco* is the frequentative.

30 Wulfstan, 4; Ælfric, 71. This particular change is also part of Ælfric's tendency to downplay the miraculous elements of the text. See below, pp. 174–7.

[he acquired, lit. he moved towards acquiring],[31] *appellatur* [lit. he is addressed] to *nominatur* [he is named],[32] *adtendens* [here: watching, lit. stretching towards] to *ammirans* [wondering at],[33] and *praesumpsisti* [you presumed, lit. you have taken beforehand] to *ausus fuisti* [you dared].[34] In the list of words above, the meaning of the word that Ælfric has chosen can be gleaned from its constituent parts. Ælfric, the schoolmaster, may have been concerned about the confusion potentially caused by these non-literal compounds and consequently chose words that were self-explanatory in order to assist his readers.

Ælfric's desire for precision and proper semantics is especially pronounced in words related to religious functions.[35] For instance, Ælfric routinely replaced Wulfstan's *antistes* or *pontifex* (and forms of these words) with *episcopus* (and forms thereof).[36] Ælfric seemed to object to other religious words as well. He preferred the construction *fecit abbatem* [made an abbot] to *constituit abbatem* [established an abbot] or *ordinauit abbatem* [ordained an abbot].[37] It seems that abbots were

31 Wulfstan, 40; Ælfric, 76.

32 Wulfstan, 40; Ælfric, 76.

33 Wulfstan, 52; Ælfric, 78.

34 Wulfstan, 54; Ælfric, 78. There are many other examples that are perhaps less clear: e.g., Wulfstan, 6, *referebant*, Ælfric, 72, *narrauit*; Wulfstan, 12, *alloquitur*, Ælfric, 72, *dixit*; Wulfstan, 12, *interrogo*, Ælfric, 72, *inquit*; Wulfstan, 20, *consentiente*, Ælfric, 73, *permittente*; Wufstan, 20, *praenotati*, Ælfric, 73, *praefati*; Wulfstan, 30, *detestandos*, Ælfric, 75, *nefandos*; Wulfstan, 40, *coadunauit*, Ælfric, 76, *congregauit*; Wulfstan, 52, *perrexit*, Ælfric, 78, *iuit*; Wulfstan, 54, *sustinerit*, Ælfric, 79, *perpessus sit*. I am not suggesting that Ælfric always avoided the above words, but only that he has chosen a compound that is more appropriate for each context.

35 Jones also noted this in his research of Ælfric's *Letter to the Monks of Eynsham*; see "*Meatim Sed et Rustica*," 30–2.

36 Ælfric's preference in the case may be related to roots of the words, since Isidore of Seville wrote that "pontifex princeps sacerdotum est," and that "antistes sacerdos dictus ab eo quod ante stat. Primus est enim in ordine Eccleisiae," while "Episcopi autem Graece, Latine speculatores interpretantur; nam speculator est praepositus in Ecclesia; dictus eo quod speculatur, atque praespiciat populorum infra se positorum mores et vitam." W.M. Lindsay, ed., *Isidori Hispalensis episcopi etymologiarum sive originum libri XX* (Oxford, 1911), VII.xii.12, 13, and 16. It is Æthelwold's role as watcher and protector of the flock that Ælfric generally emphasizes. However, in earlier prefaces, Ælfric used *presul* instead of *episcopus*. See Wilcox, *Ælfric's Prefaces*, 107 and 115.

37 Wulfstan, 36, *constituit*, Ælfric, 76, *fecit*; Wulfstan, 38, *ordinauit*, Ælfric, 76, *fecit*; Wulfstan, 28, *ordinatum*, Ælfric, 74, *factum*.

appointed, not established or ordained, according to Ælfric's understanding of church structure.[38] Ælfric also preferred to call nuns *monialia*,[39] rather than *sanctimonialia*, despite the fact that the latter word is more common in the *Regularis concordia* and in Wulfstan's *Life*.[40] In addition, Ælfric altered *canonicus* to *clericus* in every case that it occurs.[41] This change is unusual in that it replaces the more precise word, canon, a cleric who served in the bishop's *familia*, with the more general word, cleric, which describes a religious person who is not a monk. Furthermore, the presence of *canonicus* once led J.A. Robinson to argue that Wulfstan's text was a product of the twelfth century, since he claimed that this word was not used in England during the tenth century.[42] However, as Michael Lapidge has shown, *canonicus* is also used in Lantfred's *Translatio et miracula Sancti Swithuni* (c. 975) and Wulfstan's *Narratio de Sancto Swithuno* (992 X 996), that is to say, in Winchester texts of the generation before Ælfric.[43] Although the reasons for the words Ælfric selected are unclear, since they do not conform to typical usage in Winchester or other reformed centres, it is obvious that Ælfric sought a uniformity in language relating to the church in his writings. Such standardization is in accordance with the general tendency of the Benedictine Reform to seek uniformity, as in the single practice for monks embodied in the text of the *Regularis concordia.* However, there is no evidence that other reformers attempted a similar project. This standardization of religious language seems to have been Ælfric's invention.

This emphasis on the precision of language, especially regarding religious words, is not without precedent in the monastic reform, in the

---

38 This contradicts usage in the Rule of St Benedict, which uses the word *ordinatio* for the appointment of the abbot and stipulates that he must be chosen by the members of the community; see Justin McCann, *The Rule of St Benedict* (Westminster, MD, 1952), 144. The *Regularis concordia* stipulates that the *electio* of the abbot should be carried out with the consultation of the king. Symon, Spath, et al., *Regularis concordia*, 74–5.

39 By nuns, I mean cloistered women that were the equivalents of monks; cf. Sarah Foot's discussion of the terms to describe female religious women in Anglo-Saxon England and their modern English translations, in *The Disappearance of Nuns from Anglo-Saxon England*, vol. 2 of *Veiled Women*, Studies in Early Medieval Britain (Aldershot, 2000), 104–10.

40 Wulfstan, 42, Ælfric, 77; Wulfstan, 44, Ælfric, 77. For a discussion of the terms describing female religious in Latin and English, see Foot, *Veiled Women*, 96–104.

41 The single exception is in the miracle story cited below, pp. 172–3.

42 See above, p. 162.

43 Lapidge and Winterbottom, *Life of St Æthelwold*, clv. Editions of both of these works are available in Michael Lapidge, *The Cult of St Swithun*, Winchester Studies 4.2 (Oxford, 2003), 252–333 (Lantfred) and 372–551 (Wulfstan).

so-called Winchester vocabulary of Old English.[44] This particular set of vernacular words was first noticed by Helmut Gneuss in texts associated with Winchester.[45] Walter Hofstetter later identified thirteen groups of words that appear in texts related to Winchester but not in other non-monastic texts.[46] These mostly religious words seem to have arisen from Latin glosses and translations,[47] and were an attempt to create technical religious vocabulary in English in order to facilitate the translation of spiritual texts into the vernacular.[48] For instance, the Winchester word *wuldorbeag* translates the Latin *corona*, but only when *corona* refers to the crown of life worn by martyrs (i.e., *corona vitae aeternae*), not when it refers to the crown worn by a king.[49] In this case, the reformers have coined an Old English word that was more specific than the Latin word it translated.[50] Mechthild Gretsch has argued that Dunstan and Æthelwold first began to experiment with this vocabulary while they were in Glastonbury creating glosses to Latin religious texts, such as the Royal Psalter (the so-called D gloss) and the Aldhelm glosses.[51] These Winchester vocabulary words were certainly taught at Winchester during Ælfric's time there under Æthelwold's tutelage. The influence of Winchester vocabulary on Ælfric can be seen in his relatively consistent use of these words in his prose.[52]

44 For Winchester vocabulary, see above p. 136n5.

45 Helmut Gneuss, "The Origin of Standard Old English and Æthelwold's School at Winchester," *ASE* 1 (1972): 63–83.

46 For the descriptions of these thirteen categories, see Walter Hofstetter, *Winchester und der spätaltenglische Sprachgebrauch: Untersuchungen zur geographischen und zeitlichen Verbreitung altenglischer Synonyme*, Münchener Universitäts-Schriften, Philosophische Fakultät, Texte und Untersuchungen zur englischen Philologie 14 (Munich, 1987), 4–20.

47 Mechthild Gretsch, "Winchester Vocabulary and Standard Old English: The Vernacular in Late Anglo-Saxon England," *Bulletin of the John Rylands University Library of Manchester* 83.1 (Spring 2001): 41–87.

48 For more on the idea of technical vocabulary, see Gretsch, "Winchester Vocabulary and Standard Old English" and *The Intellectual Foundations of the English Benedictine Reform*, Cambridge Studies in Anglo-Saxon England 25 (Cambridge, 1999), especially the discussion of *ecclesia* on p. 112.

49 Gretsch, "Winchester Vocabulary and Standard Old English" and *Intellectual Foundations*, 98–104.

50 Sarah Foot has also noted that the terminology for women religious is more specific in Old English than in Latin; see *Veiled Women*, 96–104.

51 Gretsch, *Intellectual Foundations*, 381–3.

52 Walter Hofstetter, "Winchester and the Standardization of Old English Vocabulary," *ASE* 17 (1988): 139–61, at 139.

I suggest that Ælfric's regular employment of Winchester vocabulary in his English writings can be connected with the pursuit of semantic precision in his Latin texts. Ælfric's tendency to prefer specific words for religious functions, when multiple words existed for the same function, such as *episcopus* instead of *antistes* and *pontifex*, or *monialis* instead of *sanctimonialis* or *monacha*, may have arisen from an attempt to approximate the semantic regularity of Winchester vocabulary in Latin. In fact, the latter example finds a direct analogue in the Old English word *mynecenu*,[53] a word used in the tenth century to distinguish the female equivalent of a Benedictine monk from a *nunne*, a secular vowess who was the female equivalent of a cleric.[54] Before the monastic reform, there was no linguistic means to distinguish between these two groups of women, nor did a clear distinction ever exist in Latin texts of the tenth century. In Latin both groups were referred to with the general term *sanctimonialia*,[55] which has led to a great deal of confusion among modern historians, since it is difficult to determine the location or nature of women's houses in later Anglo-Saxon England owing to the ambiguity of the terms that describe them.[56] Ælfric may have attempted to replicate the precision of the Old English *mynecenu* by using *monialis* in Latin.[57]

Ælfric's preference for self-explanatory compounds and univalent words may reflect an early stage in the codification of his own version of

53 Since this word is not included in Hofstetter's study, it is not properly speaking a "Winchester word." However, Sarah Foot has argued that the distinction between *mynecenu* [female monks] and *nunnan* [secular vowesses] did not exist before the monastic reform; see *Veiled Women*, 96–104, and "Language and Method: *The Dictionary of Old English* and the Historian," in *The Dictionary of Old English: Retrospects and Prospects*, ed. M.J. Toswell, Old English Newsletter Subsidia 26 (Kalamazoo, MI, 1998), 73–87, at 80–1.

54 Ibid.

55 Foot, *Veiled Women*, 101–4.

56 Ibid., 96–104 and passim.

57 In both cases where Ælfric used this word, it replaced *sanctimonialis*. In the first instance, it definitely referred to *mynecenu*, who "*regulariter viventibus*"; Wulfstan, 42. The second case is not as clear, since it is part of a series of titles in Wulfstan, "Pater erat et pastor monachorum, peruigil sacntimonalium protector et uirginum" (44) [He was father of monks and ever watchful guardian of sanctified virgins]. However, Ælfric has shortened the list and made *monialis* much more clearly parallel to monks, "Pater erat monachorum et monialium" (77) [He was father of monks and nuns]. *Monialis* is the normative word used to describe religious women in the Domesday Book; see Foot, *Veiled Women*, 103–4.

a Latin-language equivalent to Winchester vocabulary, a move that may have been motivated, in part, by his possible intention to translate this piece into English later.[58] Therefore, understanding Ælfric's obsession with precise Latin vocabulary aids our understanding of his word choices in his English-language translations. It is important to remember that Ælfric experimented with and refined Winchester vocabulary in order to make it more precise.[59] The pursuit of words with distinctive meanings in Latin and Old English may have been the "naked text" [*naced gerecednis*] that Ælfric discussed in his *Old English Preface to Genesis*.[60] Ælfric's attention to the precise denotation of Latin words also affects the narrative, and here too, the text tends to be "naked" and univalent, as the next section will contend

The *Life of St Æthelwold* and Narrative

Ælfric's faithfulness to the exact words of his source conceals many subtle changes that affect the narrative of the text, either in ordering or in content. Ælfric was not an artless abbreviator who mindlessly copied what was before him after excising the more difficult vocabulary. On the contrary, he adapted the meaning of his text by removing most of the literary allusions that encouraged readers to interpret the text on multiple levels. Ælfric also excised much of Wulfstan's extraneous commentary in order to focus the text on the specific aspects of Æthelwold's life that Ælfric wished to highlight. In this way, Ælfric attempted to create a narrative that functioned only on the literal level, without a spiritual understanding that could be misconstrued.

In order to emphasize the literal level of the text, Ælfric created a more logical narrative order in the text by resequencing conjunctions and

58 According to Gretsch, there were many stages in the creation of Winchester vocabulary: see *Intellectual Foundations*, 95. For a discussion of Ælfric's adaptation of it, see Malcolm Godden, "Ælfric's Changing Vocabulary," *English Studies* (1980): 206–23.

59 Note especially changes in the use of "martyr." Godden, "Ælfric's Changing Vocabulary," 208–9 and 220.

60 "We secgað eac foran to þæt seo boc is swiþe deop gastlice to understandenne, and we ne writaþ na mare buton þa nacedan gerecednisse. Þonne þincþ þam ungelæredum þæt eall þæt andgit beo belocen on þære anfealdan gerecednisse, ac hit ys swiþe feor þam." Wilcox, *Ælfric's Prefaces*, 117. I acknowledge, when Ælfric made this statement, he referred to composition in English. This preface will be discussed in detail below, pp. 184–6.

adverbs.[61] In the following passage, the narrative words that Ælfric changed or added are in italics:

> Contigit *aliquando* clericum eius, cui designatum erat *ampullam eius ferre*, minus olei accipere quam necessitas poscebat, et hoc ipsum in itinere perdidisse. *Veniens* autem *episcopus* ad locum destinatum, *cum uellet habere crisma, non habuit*. Turbatus *tunc* clericus *repedauit* iter *quo*[62] uenerat, et inuenit ampollam plenam olei iacentem, quae nec medietatem antea habuerat.[63]
>
> [Once it happened that his cleric who had been designated to carry the ampulla took less oil than necessity required, and even this oil he lost along the way. As the bishop arrived at the appointed place, when he wished to have chrism, he did not have it. The agitated cleric retraced the path by which he had come and he found the ampulla (which before had been only half-full) lying completely filled with oil.]

With the exception of *episcopus*,[64] all the words that Ælfric changed in this section improve the narrative flow of the story. While Ælfric wrote a very clear and succinct portrait of a miraculous event where a lazy cleric found the chrism that he had lost in his negligence, Wulfstan wrote a confusing sequence of events that is twice as long and filled with praise of Æthelwold:

> *Placuit inter haec omnipotenti Deo ut caelesti etiam monstraretur indicio quod ei beneplacitum esset habitare in sancto suo. Nam cum iter quoddam sacer antistes ageret ut in agro Dominico semen uerbi Dei spargeret,* contigit clericum eius, cui *sanctum crisma* fuerat designatum, minus olei quam necessitas poscebat accepisse, et hoc *parum quod acceperat* in ipso itinere perdidisse. *Cumque Christi famulus* ad destinatum *peruenisset* locum, *post missae celebrationem postque dulcia sanctae praedicationis alloquia, iussit ex more ad confirmandos pueros oleum sibi exhibere. Sed* clericus *qui ampullam se secum ferre aestimabat repente quod eam perdidisset agnouit.* Turbatus ergo celerrime repetiit iter unde uenerat, et *diligenter huc illucque circumspiciens* inuenit ampullam *crismatis in*

61 Ælfric's change of conjunctions did not always work to great effect. Jones discusses some of the less effective changes in Ælfric's *Letter to the Monks of Eynsham*, in "*Meatim Sed et Rustica*," 28–30.

62 Although the authorial reading in Wulfstan seems to be *unde* at this point, there is a manuscript variant for *quo*; see Lapidge and Winterbottom, *The Life of St Æthelwold*, 48.

63 Ælfric, 77.

64 For why Ælfric changed this word, see above, pp. 167–8.

> *uia* iacentem oleo plenam, cuius nec medietas *quidem paulo* ante *quicquam liquoris* habuerat. *Qua assumpta 'cum timore et gaudio magno' reuersus est, sancto antistiti satisfaciens et caelestis stillicidii miraculum ueraci relatione pandens. Quod Dei nutu gestum esse probatur, ut qui spiritus sancti gratia perfundebatur, eiusque unctione corda et facies multorum exhilarabat, ipse non solum interius sed etiam exterius oleo supernae laeticiae remuneraretur.*[65]
>
> [At that time, it was pleasing to the omnipotent God that he show with a celestial sign that it was very well-pleasing to him to dwell in his holy man. For when the holy bishop went on a certain journey so that he might scatter the seed of the word of God in the Lord's field, it happened that his cleric, to whom the holy chrism was appointed, took less oil than necessity required, and what little bit he took he lost along the way. And when the servant of Christ had come to the appointed place, after the celebration of the mass and after the sweet exhortation of his holy sermon, he ordered that the oil be shown to him so that he could confirm the boys, as was the usual custom. But the cleric, who thought that he carried the ampulla with him, suddenly realized that he had lost it. Troubled, he quickly went back down the path from whence he had come, and diligently looking around here and there, he found the bottle of chrism lying on the road full of oil, although earlier it had been a little less than half full of liquid. Picking up the container "with fear and great joy," he returned begging the pardon of the holy bishop by revealing the miracle of the heavenly moisture in a true narrative. This thing is proved to have been done by the will of God, so that he, who was imbued with the grace of the holy spirit and made happy the faces and hearts by its unction, might be repaid not only inwardly, but also outwardly by the oil of heavenly happiness.]

Ælfric distilled this longer version of events by adding temporal conjunctions that clarify the ordering of events (*aliquando*, *cum*, and *tunc*) while simplifying the facts of the case. Rather than Wulfstan's elaborate explanation of when the cleric discovered the chrism to be missing, "Cumque Christi famulus ad destinatum peruenisset locum, post missae celebrationem postque dulcia sanctae praedicationis alloquia, iussit ex more ad confirmandos pueros oleum sibi exhibere"[66] [And when the servant of Christ had come to the appointed place, after the celebration of the mass and after the sweet exhortation of his holy sermon, he ordered that the oil be

65 Wulfstan, 48.
66 Ibid.

shown to him so that he could confirm the boys, as was the usual custom], Ælfric stated simply, "cum uellet habere crisma, non habuit"[67] [when he wished to have the chrism, he did not have it]. Furthermore, Wulfstan's text said that the cleric in question was the one "cui sanctum crisma fuerat designatum"[68] [to whom the holy chrism was assigned]. However, what the cleric was to do with the chrism is unexplained (perhaps because a monastic audience would already know the job of the cleric with such an assignment). Ælfric, by contrast, at this point clarified the job of the cleric, "cui designatum erat ampullam eius ferre"[69] [to whom it was assigned to carry his ampulla]. By explaining that the cleric was responsible for filling and maintaining the ampulla at the beginning of the story, the moments of loss and recovery are more easily understood. Until the chrism is recovered in Wulfstan's text, it is unclear whether the oil or the container has been lost. By clarifying the material facts and adding temporal modifiers that sequence the action, Ælfric presented a miracle that was more readily understood.

Furthermore, Wulfstan emphasized more pointedly the personal piety of Æthelwold, while Ælfric related only the concrete facts of the story. In Ælfric's version, we see no reference to heavenly approval or celestial signs, whereas Wulfstan said this miracle occurred "Dei nutu" [with God's approval], as a "caelesti … indicio" [heavenly sign], that "placuit … omnipotenti Deo" [was pleasing to the omnipotent God]. Also, Wulfstan called Æthelwold "sancto suo" [his holy man], "sacer antistes" [holy bishop], and "Christi famulus" [Christ's servant], while Ælfric referred to Æthelwold as merely "*episcopus*" [bishop]. In addition, Ælfric removed in entirety the first and last sentences of this paragraph, which explicitly state the heavenly nature of this miracle. Whereas in Ælfric's text we see a well-ordered and clear rendition of a miraculous event without any commentary upon it, in Wulfstan's version, we have a lengthy meditation upon the personal virtue of Æthelwold that this miracle evidenced.

Ælfric's discomfort with miracles is well documented, both in his own writings and by modern scholars.[70] In his Homily for Ascension Day, Ælfric discussed the concern that magicians can enact miracles – or things

67 Ælfric, 77.

68 Wulfstan, 48.

69 Ælfric, 77.

70 Malcolm R. Godden, "Ælfric's Saints' Lives and the Problem of Miracles," in *Old English Prose: Basic Readings*, ed. Paul Szarmach, Basic Readings in Anglo-Saxon England 5 (New York, 2000), 287–309.

that appear to be miracles.[71] Therefore, Ælfric defined magic as that which is enacted by an individual, while a miracle is that which is done by God in order to show his approval for a person or a situation.[72] In Ælfric's stories, a saint can be an agent for a miracle, but as in the *Life of St Æthelwold*, the miracles frequently occur around the saint without any direct action on his part. It seems that Ælfric's personal knowledge of Æthelwold further dampened his enthusiasm about the bishop's miraculous deeds. Throughout the work, Ælfric seldom called Æthelwold "*sanctus vir*," although this appellation appears routinely in Wulfstan's work. Instead Ælfric generally referred to Æthelwold by his name or his ecclesiastical title, *episcopus* [bishop].[73] Similarly, Ælfric has limited the miraculous quality of the deeds that Æthelwold performs. As Malcolm Godden pointed out,

> Only two of the miracles which Ælfric describes in his life of St. Æthelwold occur after the saint's death, yet it is perhaps significant that the others are not, in the strict sense, performed or worked by the saint. Three of them are experienced by his mother before or soon after his birth; others involve the monastic community rather than the saint himself; only one is even a response to his prayer.[74]

The difference between the miracles that Ælfric described and the miracles as told by Wulfstan shows that Ælfric did not place the same narrative importance on the personal sanctity of Æthelwold. In the following example, we see how Ælfric played down a miracle to make Æthelwold's personal role less important:

> Accidit *namque* quadam solenni die, sedenti *matre* domi et in gremio infantem tenente, *tempestuosam auram adsurgere*, *in tantum ut ipsa*, *sicuti* decreuit,

71 Peter Clemoes, ed., "*In ascensione Domini*," in *Ælfric's Catholic Homilies*, EETS, s.s. 17 (Oxford, 1997), 345–53, at 350–1.

72 See Godden's discussion in "Saints' Lives and Miracles," 288–90.

73 Wulfstan, 6, *sanctum virum*, Ælfric, 71, *filium eius*; Wulfstan, 18, *sancto viro*, Ælfric, 73, *venerabili Æthelwoldi*; Wulfstan, 50, *vir sanctus*, Ælfric, 78, *episcopus*; Wulfstan, 52, *vir sanctus*, Ælfric, 78, *episcopum*. Note also Wulfstan, 48, *famulus Christi*, Ælfric, 77, *episcopus*; Wulfstan, 52, *vir Dei*, Ælfric, 78, *epsiscopus*. After Æthelwold's death in Ælfric, he is sometimes referred to as saint; see Wulfstan, 68, *sancti viri*, Ælfric, 79, *sancti Æthelwoldi*. Ælfric also refers to Æthelwold as a saint in the opening line.

74 Godden, "Saints' Lives and Miracles," 85.

> *adire* ecclesiam nequiret; *sed cum gemebunda orationi se dedisset*, subito inuenta est in ecclesia sedens cum infantulo ubi missam presbiter celebrabat.[75]
>
> [For it happened on a certain feast day, while his mother was seated in the house holding the infant on her bosom, such a strong tempestuous wind rose up that she was not able to go to church, as she had intended. However, when she had tearfully given herself to prayer, suddenly she found herself with the infant seated in the church where the priest was celebrating mass.]

In the passage above, Ælfric has changed a number of clauses *in toto*, rather than simply changing words sporadically, as he did elsewhere. Such wholesale revision can be seen in most of the miracles that Ælfric related.[76] These changes usually soften Wulfstan's exaggerated rhetoric. For instance, Ælfric said simply that "tempestuosam auram adsurgere" [a stormy wind rose up], while Wulfstan flamboyantly wrote that "ualidam inundantis pluuiae tempestatem erumpere"[77] [a great storm of inundating rain broke out]. The problem in this story, as stated by Ælfric, was that the storm did not allow the mother to go to church, while Wulfstan claimed that the storm was so strong "ut extra loci limen ... pedem movere non posset"[78] [that she was not able to move her feet out of doors]. The piety of the mother (nurse, in Wulfstan) is also overstated in Wulfstan, who claimed that "dum maerens amarissime fleret eo quod uotum piae intentionis soluere nequiret, caput humiliter omnipotentem Dominum rogatura declinauit et confestim diuina miseratione consolari promeruit"[79] [while the mournful girl bitterly cried because she was not able to fulfil the vow of her pious intention, she bowed her head humbly praying to the almighty God, and immediately she deserved to be consoled by divine pity]. Ælfric's text reads simply that "cum gemebunda orationi se dedisset" [when she had given herself to mournful prayer] she suddenly appeared in

---

75 Ælfric, 72.

76 The revision is especially interesting in the story of the thief, which Ælfric altered fairly radically by naming the guilty party and offering additional details. Lapidge and Winterbottom have suggested that the revisions result from Ælfric's personal knowledge of the event; see *Life of St Æthelwold*, 49 n. 6.

77 Wulfstan, 8.

78 Ibid.; Wulfstan attributed this miracle to Æthelwold's nurse, and not his mother; see Lapidge and Winterbottom, *The Life of St Æthelwold*, 72, n. 3.

79 Wulfstan, 8.

the church.[80] By making the storm less threatening and the nurse/mother less pious, Ælfric has made the miracle more dependent on the actions of God and less on the piety of humans. As Malcolm Godden has shown, Ælfric's miracles usually show God's approval for individuals on earth; they are not necessarily enacted by the agency of the humans with whom they are associated. This slight shift in focus to a miracle as proof of divine approbation, rather than as proof of an individual saint's power, appears throughout this *Life*.[81]

Furthermore, Ælfric has removed the reference comparing Æthelwold to Christ present in Wulfstan's text:

> Sicut enim propheta quondam ex Iudaea repente sublatus et in Chaldaea cum prandio est depositus, sic beatus puer Ætheluuoldus sub momento cum nutrice in templo est praesentatus, ut sicut ille refecit unum Dei hominem in lacu leonum, ita iste congruo tempore milia populorum pasceret in ecclesia sanctorum.[82]

> [For just as a prophet once was suddenly carried out of Judea into Chaldea and was deposited with food, thus the blessed child Æthelwold in a flash was presented in the temple with his nurse, just as the prophet fed one man of God in the den of lions, so at the appropriate time Æthelwold fed thousands of people in the church of the saints.]

This bizarre imagery comes from the fourteenth chapter of Daniel, where the prophet Habakkuk suddenly appeared to feed Daniel in the lion's den. Also, the phrase "*in templo prasentatus*" [presented in the temple] is reminiscent of the presentation in the temple of the infant Christ. Thus, Wulfstan joined these images in order to compare Æthelwold both to a prophet and to Christ. This kind of literary simile that mingles two distinct typological images and requires a great deal of active interpretation on the reader's part is precisely what Ælfric avoided both here and throughout his work.

80 The word *gemebunda* is especially interesting in this context, because it is a rare word (and rarer than any word that Wulfstan has used in this passage), but the obvious root *gemo* [to bemoan] makes the word self-explanatory.

81 Cf. the Life of St Swithun, where Swithun's miracles are attributed to divine approval of King Edgar, Bishop Æthelwold, and Archbishop Dunstan. See the introduction, pp. 10–12.

82 Wulfstan, 8.

Ælfric avoided typology, in part, because his narrative was more focused on Æthelwold's role as teacher and father to the monks, whereas Wulfstan's *Life* argued for Æthelwold's sanctity in more general and exaggerated terms. For instance, the following passage in Wulfstan's *Life* describes Æthelwold's character:

> Erat namque terribilis ut leo discolis *et peruersis*, humilibus uero et oboedientibus *se quasi agnum* mitissimum *exhibebat, ita serpentinae prudentiae temperans seueritatem ut* columbinae *simplicitatis non amitteret lenitatem. Quem si quando zelus rectitudinis cogeret ut iura disciplinae subiectis imponeret, furor ipse non de crudelitate sed de amore processit, et intus paterna pietate dilexit quos foris quasi insequens castigauit.* Pater erat *et pastor* monachorum, *peruigil sanctimonalium protector et uirginum*, uiduarum consolator, *peregrinorum susceptor*, ecclesiarum defensor, errantium corrector, pauperum recreator, *pupillorum et orphanorum adiutor*: quod plus impleuit opere quam *nostra paruitas* sermone possit euoluere.[83]
>
> [For he was as terrible as a lion to the wicked and the intractable, but to the humble and obedient, he showed himself to be as gentle as a lamb, tempering the severity of his snake-like wisdom in such a way that he did not lose the gentleness of dove-like simplicity. If ever the zeal for righteousness compelled him to place the laws of discipline on his subjects, his fury did not arise from cruelty, but from love, and inwardly he loved with paternal piety those whom he outwardly chastised as if he were attacking them. He was father and shepherd of the monks, the ever-watchful protector of nuns and virgins, the consoler of widows, the receiver of travellers, the defender of the church, the corrector of the wandering, reviver of the poor, helper of boys and orphans: he executed in deeds more than it is possible for my humbleness to relate with speech.]

This passage indulges in the hermeneutic tendency of *amplificatio*[84] to such an extent that it devolves into a series of titles that are not specific to Æthelwold, but could apply to many saintly men in his position. Furthermore, much of the rest of the passage is composed of artful literary allusions that are designed to showcase Wulfstan's wide reading more than

---

83 Wulfstan, 44.

84 For a discussion of amplification in Aldhelm, see Winterbottom, "Aldhelm's Prose Style," 62–70; see also Rebecca Stephenson, "Deliberate Obfuscation," 58–9. For a discussion in Byrhtferth, see ibid., 149–51.

Æthelwold's virtue. For instance, the phrases "serpentinae prudentiae" [snake-like wisdom] and "columbinae simplicitatis" [dove-like simplicity] arise from Matthew 10:5, which reads *estote ergo prudentes sicut serpentes et simplices sicut columbae* [be as wise as serpents and as simple as doves],[85] which Wulfstan has recast. When Ælfric compressed this passage, he removed many of the repetitive titles and literary allusions:

> eratque terriblilis ut leo inoboedientibus seu discolis, mitibus uero et humilibus mitior columba. Pater erat monachorum ac monialium, uiduarum consolator et pauperum recreator, ecclesiarum defensor, errantium corrector: quod plus opere impleuit quam nos possimus sermone enarrare.[86]
>
> [And he was as terrible as a lion to the disobedient or to the wicked, but to the humble and gentle, he was gentler than a dove. He was father of the monks and nuns, consoler of the widows, reviver of the poor, defender of the church, corrector of the wandering: he carried out in deeds more than I am able to tell with speech.]

In this passage, Ælfric focused much more specifically on Æthelwold's role as teacher and bishop. The list of titles, as reproduced in Ælfric, corresponds more closely to the role appropriate to a monastic bishop. He is the father of monks and nuns, he provides for those in need, he defends the church, and corrects those who wander from the faith.[87] All extraneous commentary that does not fit the model of a perfect saintly bishop has been excised, including references to Æthelwold's temper.[88] Furthermore, Ælfric replaces Wulfstan's cliché comparison between a lion and a lamb

---

85 Lapidge and Winterbottom, *Life of St Æthelwold*, 44.

86 Ælfric, 77.

87 Notably, Ælfric omits Wulfstan's *perversis*, replacing it with *inoboedientibus*, which Wulfstan lists as a positive virtue in the next clause. The replacement of *perversis* is especially odd in light of Ælfric's retention of the Grecism *discolis*, which means "perverse or wicked," a word that could be considered hermeneutic from its etymology. However, this word is latinized in the Vulgate at 1 Peter 2:18, and therefore was probably not considered esoteric by Ælfric.

88 Wulfstan's statement, "Quem si quando zelus rectitudinis cogeret ut iura disciplinae subiectis imponeret, furor ipse non de crudelitate sed de amore processit, et intus paterna pietate dilexit quos foris quasi insequens castigauit" [If ever the zeal for righteousness compelled him to place the laws of discipline on his subjects, his fury did not arise from cruelty, but from love, and inwardly he loved with paternal piety those whom he outwardly chastised, as if he were attacking them], finds no equivalent in Ælfric's passage.

with a more interesting comparison between a lion and a dove by compressing two of Wulfstan's statements. By removing the flamboyant redundancies of the paragraph, Ælfric is able to focus the narrative onto a single unified point, Æthelwold's excellence as teacher and bishop, important qualities to Benedictine reformers. Thus, Ælfric's precision in his vocabulary has an exact analogue in his single-minded narrative focus.

Although Ælfric tended to eliminate the diffuse literary allusions that are scattered throughout Wulfstan's prose, he did occasionally add a symbolic reference. Unlike Wulfstan's flowery and learned allusions, however, Ælfric's are focused and concise. For instance, when Bishop Ælfheah ordained Dunstan, Æthelwold, and Æthelstan, he predicted that two of them would become bishops. In Wulfstan's text, Æthelstan asks the bishop, "dicens, 'Num mihi continget esse unum ex duobus qui episcopali cathedra sublimandi sunt?'"[89] [saying, "Will it happen to me that I become one of the two who are elevated to the bishop's seat?"]. The bishop replied that not only would Æthelstan not become a bishop, but he would eventually leave the priesthood. Ælfric made a very slight intervention in Æthelstan's question, which heightens the sense of the latter's betrayal. In Ælfric's version, Æthelstan queried, "'sum ego,' inquit, 'ex illis duobus qui ad episcopalem dignitatem peruenturi sunt?'"[90] ["Am I," he asked, "one of the two who will arrive at the episcopal dignity?"]. By changing the *dicens* in Wulfstan's text to *inquit* Ælfric set the phrase *sum ego* apart from the rest of the sentence, thus highlighting simple words that otherwise would be insignificant.[91] The *sum ego* is reminiscent of the discussion during the Last Supper in which Jesus prophesied that one of his disciples would betray him. In response, Judas Iscariot asked, "numquid ego sum?" [Is it I?].[92] By this subtle change of only a few words, Ælfric compared Æthelstan's apostasy to Judas Iscariot's treachery. While this allusion does bring a symbolic level to the reading of this text, the symbol is well known and consequently controlled, with no space permitted for misinterpretation. A reference to Judas Iscariot can mean only one thing: betrayal.

Through his omissions and changes, Ælfric attempted to create a narrative that functioned at only a literal level. Allegory and typology are usually absent from Ælfric's writings. When symbolic literary allusions occur, they are powerful and clear, unlike the scattered and diffuse allusions that

89 Wulfstan, 12.

90 Ælfric, 72.

91 Since *inquit* is postpositive it cannot stand before the clause, as *dicens* does in Wulfstan's text, but must be embedded within the quoted statement.

92 Matthew 26:25.

occur throughout hermeneutic texts.[93] By the use of a logical sequence and controlled allusions (where such allusions exist), Ælfric was able to control the meaning of his text, limiting misinterpretation by focusing on the literal events of Æthelwold's life rather than the spiritual signification that these events could hold. In the same way that Ælfric preferred univalent words, he sought to create a univalent narrative without a hidden spiritual meaning or "gastlicum andgite," as he described it in his *Old English Preface to Genesis*.[94]

Dual Identity of English

An examination of Ælfric's abbreviation (and thus translation) practices calls us to reconsider his statements about English in his prefaces, which seem to inscribe two separate identities for English texts. They are texts that are both accessible and restricted at the same time. On the one hand, English is a simple language that "possit ad cor pervenire legentium vel audientium ad utilitatem animarum suarum" (*AP*, 107) [is able to penetrate to the heart of the reader or listener for the benefit of their soul]. In other words, it is an open language that can be read easily and has a more profound impact on Ælfric's English-language audiences. In another place, Ælfric described his English-language composition as "puris et apertis verbis linguę huius gentis" (*AP*, 107) [With pure and open words of this people's language], which he contrasts with Latin, described as "garrula verbositate aut ignotis sermonibus" (*AP*, 111) [babbling verbosity or unknown words]. The simplicity of English (described as "simplici locutione") is contrasted with the "artificiosi sermonis compositione," which has the double meaning both of something that has been carefully and skilfully crafted and of something that is artificial. Ælfric suggests that English-language composition is preferable for his native constituents because it is more natural than Latin, which is highly crafted and therefore contrived. The Latin texts cannot penetrate to the heart of the simple as the vernacular can.

Yet at the same time that the English text is open, it is also closed. Ælfric states: "Nec tamen omnia evangelia tangimus per circulum anni, sed illa tantummodo quibus speramus sufficere posse simplicibus ad animarum

93 Cf. Byrhtferth's digression on the word phylacteries in the *Enchiridion*, which consists of a series of literary allusions that constitute a learned digression on phylacteries that is not relevant to computus; see chap. 2, pp. 96–100.

94 Wilcox, *Ælfric's Prefaces*, 118.

emendationem" (*AP*, 107) [Nevertheless, we do not touch all the Gospels throughout the course of the year, but only those which we hope to be able to be sufficient for the emendation of the souls of the simple]. In other words, Ælfric will not translate all the biblical text, but only the parts that the "simple" can understand. This is not the only location in which Ælfric pointedly indicates that he has not and will not translate everything, but only those things that are safe for his audience to contemplate. Thus, English, despite its immediate visceral response from the reader, cannot approach nearly the same range of subjects that Latin texts can; full textual sources are available only to those who are literate in the ecclesiastical language. When we examine these comments in light of Ælfric's methodical translation practices, we see that he ensures that the range, not only of the subjects, but of the narrative possibilities of interpretation, remains limited.

Ælfric also presents English as a closed language when he refuses to translate, as he does at the end of the *Second Series of Catholic Homilies*, "ic næfre heononforð ne awende godspel oþþe godspeltrahtas of Ledene on Englisc. Gif hwa ma awendan wille ðonne bidde ic hine, for Godes lufon, þæt he gesette his boc onsundron fram ðam twam bocum ðe we awend habbað" (*AP*, 114) [I will never in the future translate a gospel or gospel explanations from Latin into English. If any wants to translate more, then I beg him for the love of God to set his apart from the two books which we have translated]. Of course, Ælfric does go on to translate further gospel passages, and the conflict between the promise and the later reality emphasizes other conflicts about the status of English, since this statement embodies two strongly dissimilar attitudes towards the vernacular. On the one hand, he has closed off the English language to future translation possibilities, at least as regards the Gospels (even though he did translate more later).[95] Yet at the same time, he wishes to assert an authority for his own English-language works that is perhaps unprecedented. Although it was common practice to mix together various homilies into one collection, Ælfric asks that his work be excluded from this tendency and stand apart in order to maintain a textual purity that would be more common in Latin-language pieces. Joyce Hill's studies of the dissemination of the *Catholic*

95 For a discussion of Ælfric's refusals to translate further biblical material and other issues related to the anxiety of his role as translator, see Robert Stanton, *The Culture of Translation in Anglo-Saxon England* (Cambridge, 2002), 156–66, esp. 156–7. I differ from this reading in that I emphasize the moments in which Ælfric's rhetoric differs from his practice, whereas Stanton pieces together the prefaces and the timeline in such a way as to explain away, in very specific terms, each of Ælfric's refusals.

Homilies prove that Ælfric's requests were not granted, and his homilies were mixed with other anonymous sources despite his concerns.[96] Nevertheless, he claims that his homilies deserve to be separate, because as the first series asserted, he is a fighter of heresy and thus deserves to be treated as a Latin authority, not merely as a vernacular author.

Again, Ælfric's status as a Latinate Benedictine monk, and therefore as a teacher to the laity, seems closely tied to the special position in which he places his own homilies. Wilcox argues that Ælfric saw his writings as a cohesive body of orthodox theology.[97] Peter Clemoes argued that this body of doctrine was carefully planned by Ælfric: "There is probably little that we do not know about Ælfric's plan as a whole. That it was a plan, consistently pursued, we can be certain from the way the parts take their place within the whole and because there is so little repetition. Moreover in spite of repeated misgivings, unlike many another literary enterprise the scheme was in all essentials carried to completion."[98] The perception of these scholars that Ælfric planned to produce a coherent canon in English suggests that this Anglo-Saxon writer considered himself to be an authority and that his English works were "equivalent in value to the patristic and Carolingian writers whom he lists as his sources."[99] If Ælfric is creating a body of vernacular, but orthodox, doctrine, then he is creating a work that threatens to supplant the text it is meant to open to a wider audience.[100] The inherent danger of writing in the vernacular comes from the

96 Joyce Hill, "Translating the Tradition: Manuscripts, Models and Methodologies in the Composition of Ælfric's *Catholic Homilies*, In Memoriam Peter Alan Martin Clemoes, 1920–1996," *Bulletin of John Rylands Library* 79 (1997): 43–65.

97 Wilcox, *Ælfric's Prefaces*, 1.

98 "The Chronology of Ælfric's Works," 57.

99 Wilcox, *Ælfric's Prefaces*, 70.

100 Rita Copeland discusses this effect of translation in *Rhetoric, Hermeneutics, and Translation in the Middle Ages*, Cambridge Studies in Medieval Literature 11 (Cambridge, 1991). Note similar discussion pertaining to Byrhtferth in chapter 1. I am not the first to apply Copeland's theories to Anglo-Saxon translation or to Ælfric, in particular. Robert Stanton succinctly summarized Copeland's argument thus: "Rita Copeland has recently shown how the practice of translation has never formed either an independent discipline nor an offshoot of poetics or language theory; rather it is inscribed in the institutional practices of classical antiquity and the Middle Ages, and straddles the margins of rhetoric and grammar. Specifically, Copeland traces the development of the practice of translation as rhetorical invention, which came to overshadow its periphrastic function in the teaching of *grammatica*. This disciplinary shift reflects an essential distinction between two aspects of translation: its replicative, preservative function on the one hand, and its inevitable tendency to create, and hence potentially to displace the source text, on the other." "Rhetoric and Translation," 139–40.

fact that the English-language text can both be widely read and effectively replace the Latin text that preceded it. Ælfric's English version of St Swithun's life epitomizes this truth, since it survives in three manuscripts, while his Latin epitome is extant in only one.[101] Lantfred's original Latin *Translatio* survives in only four manuscripts, a number which is comparatively low when you consider the greater survival of Latin texts in the post-conquest period.[102] While the small survival rate of any manuscript from Anglo-Saxon England makes it difficult to extrapolate readership based on extant manuscripts, it seems not a great leap to assert that Ælfric's English *Life of Swithun* was at least as important and as widely read as Lantfred's Latin original, if not more so.

The popular availability of the English-language text brings with it a considerable amount of risk, since the simple could misunderstand the English-language text, thinking it had pierced them to the heart, when in fact it had quite missed the mark. Ælfric's preface to the Old English translation of Genesis is the *locus classicus* for his anxieties about translation. He claims, "We secgað eac foran to þæt seo boc is swiþe deop gastlice to understandenne, and we ne writað na mare buton þa nacedan gerecednisse. Þonne þincþ þam ungelæredum þæt andgit beo belocen on þære anfealdan gerecednisse, as hit ys swiþe feor þam" (*AP*, 117) [We say also that the book has a very deep spiritual meaning, and we write no more than the naked narrative. Then, it seems to the uneducated that the meaning is locked in the singular narrative, but it is very far from that]. Again, Ælfric emphasizes that English is a closed language that limits interpretation, since it cannot translate the deeper spiritual meaning of the text, but only the "nacedan gerecednisse" [naked narrative], which he claims is "anfealdan," a word that can be translated as "singular," or in narrative terms might be more appropriate to term "univalent." The uneducated think they are getting access to the full meaning of the text through the English-language version, but as Ælfric warns us, that is far from the case. The reason English cannot contain the full meaning of the holy text seems to be that there is something sacred about the order of the Latin text, which Ælfric asserts "is swa geendebyrd, swa swa God silf hig gedihte þam writer Moise, and we ne durron na mare awritan on Englisc þonne þæt Liden hæfþ, ne þa endebirdnisse awendan, buton þam annum þæt þæt Leden and

101 For a discussion of the manuscripts of the English version, see Lapidge, *Cult of St Swithun*, 579–82; for the Latin epitome, see ibid., 555–7.

102 Lapidge, *Cult of St Swithun*, 238–42.

þæt Englisc nabbað na ane wisan on þære spræce fadunge" (*AP*, 118) [is ordered just as God himself dictated to the writer Moses, and we do not dare to write more in English than the Latin has, nor do we dare to translate the order except to say that Latin and English do not have the same manner in the arrangement of their speech]. Ælfric goes on to warn that "hit biþ swiþe gedwolsum to rædenne þam þe þæs Ledenes wisan ne can" (*AP*, 118) [it is very heretical for anyone to read who does not know how a Latin sentence is arranged]. By removing the sacred order of the Latin text Ælfric strips away many interpretive possibilities. This assertion cuts both ways for the status of the vernacular text. On the one hand, it limits the reader's permission to interpret the text, but, when read in context, Ælfric's statements present a cogent defence for sustained narrative translation, rather than an interlinear gloss, such as the kind that exist for the Psalms. Emphasizing the difference between the English and Latin order in this instance justifies separating the English text from the Latin and thus allows the vernacular version to circulate independently to be read without the limitations of the Latin text. In this way, Ælfric's writings are different from Byrhtferth's, since the latter author presented a bilingual text in which the English and Latin texts could not be separated, while Ælfric's English translations are independent, separated both from their source texts and from the epitomes that preceded them.

Perhaps as a result of Ælfric's fears for those who will misinterpret the spiritual meaning of the book of Genesis, he offers his readers a kind of short primer on interpretive techniques. For instance, he explains the plural forms for God in Genesis as reflecting the truth of the Trinity, "Oft ys seo halige þrinnys geswutelod on þisre bec, swa swa ys on þam worde þe God cwæð: 'Uton wyrcean mannan to ure anlicnisse.' Mid þam þe he cwæð 'Uton wyrcean' ys seo þrinnis gebicnod; mid þam þe he cwæð 'to ure anlicnisse' ys seo soðe annis geswutelod: he ne cwæð na menigfealdlice, 'to urum anlicnissum,' ac anfealdice, 'to ure anlicnisse'" (*AP*, 118) [Often the holy trinity is revealed in this book as it is in the words which God said, "Let us make man in our image." In that he said, "Let us make" the trinity is signified; in that he said, "in our likeness" is the true unity revealed: he did not say in the plural, "in our likenesses," but singularly "in our likeness"]. In this case the grammar of the passage reveals the holy mystery of the Trinity, in the implied plural subject of the three persons of the Godhead modified by the singular "anlicnisse" that they share. Therefore, grammar is "seo cæg ðe ðæra boca andgit unlicð" (*AP*, 115) [the key that unlocks the meaning of the book], as Ælfric stated in the preface to his *Grammar*. Ælfric further expounds the grammatical mystery of the

Trinity by another textual example in which the three angels came to Abraham and spoke as if they were one. This combination of grammatical analysis and textual exegesis provides a model for orthodox interpretation and opens up a text that Ælfric has repeatedly claimed is closed, with the spiritual meaning stripped away. This preface captures the dual identity of English most acutely, since it explicitly argues that a higher level of interpretation could be stripped away from a text in order to limit dangerous teachings; yet, at the same time, Ælfric offers brief instructions on how to go about unlocking grammatically rooted biblical exegesis in the vernacular.

While seeming to question the dangers of English-language interpretation, not only does Ælfric repeatedly fulfil his patron's request by completing the translation tasks assigned to him, but he even offers the reader a kind of interpretive key that could lead to an orthodox interpretation. While presenting English as a closed language, one with limited texts and limited interpretive possibilities, Ælfric's own translation project produced a substantial body of authoritative vernacular homilies and thereby opened a number of Latin texts to an English-language audience. While the act of translation allows Ælfric to disseminate the content of many sacred and religious texts that would not be available otherwise, it also effectively replaces the original Latin text with his translation for the vast majority of his English-speaking audience. This precarious status that English holds as a language that is both open and closed at the same time accords with what we have seen in Byrhtferth's vernacular writing, but Ælfric goes even farther than his contemporary in creating a substantial body of orthodox texts that obviate the need for equivalent Latin sources. While both authors openly diminish the status and value of English-language texts, their pedagogical practices tell a different story. While Ælfric's prefaces present a rich treasure hoard of Anglo-Saxon views on language and the appropriate use of the vernacular, these statements should always be read in the politically charged context of the post-reform period, in which Benedictines defined themselves by their learning and their skill in Latin. Furthermore, Ælfric's statements, in particular, must always be compared to his actual practices while translating, many of which conflict with his carefully crafted prefaces.

Conclusion

The quintessential trait of Ælfric's translation technique in his saints' lives and homilies is a condensation and compression of the source text that is so close to the wording of the original text that it is hard not to call it literal. But at the same time, the very closeness of the translation elides many subtle changes that he makes, many of which have much larger consequences, and these considerations are particularly important when Ælfric translates a contemporary work written in the hermeneutic style, such as the *Life of St Æthelwold* or the *Life of St Swithun*. To change the style of a text so profoundly has important ramifications. First, Ælfric's abbreviations reveal how much of the hermeneutic style is redundant and can be skipped. Therefore, they may offer a clue to how such texts were read. Perhaps medieval readers did not construe every word, as many of our interpretations assume, but merely strove to get the underlying idea and extrapolated the rest of the words from context. Given the relatively restricted circulation of scholarly texts, it seems entirely plausible that many medieval readers would not have access to the kinds of glossaries that allowed them to interpret the most esoteric vocabulary. Second, when we assume that Ælfric's *Life of St Æthelwold* was intended for English-language translation, or at least that Ælfric abbreviated in the same manner that he used for other works that were translated, then this study reveals the very real lengths Ælfric went to to control meaning in his text and to limit the potential for misinterpretation.

Ultimately, Ælfric's English-language works present a paradox. They greatly expand the use and purview of English, but at the same time limit what is disseminated in that language. Rhetorically in his prefaces, Ælfric emphasizes the limited status of English by reiterating how he is restricting the text in an effort to control and limit interpretation. Yet, the very act of translating as widely and comprehensively as he does belies Ælfric's concerns. A text once translated into English is a great deal more useful than one in an esoteric form of Latin. Thus, Ælfric's English-language homilies see enormous circulation, and these are the texts that fundamentally disseminate the political goals and messages of the monastic reformers to a broader population. As much as the reformers valued their Latin-language compositions, particularly those in the hermeneutic style, they needed Ælfric and his English-language homilies to disseminate the message more broadly in order to create the larger societal reforms they envisioned.

Conclusion

The English language occupied an uneasy position in late Anglo-Saxon England. On the one hand, its inferiority to Latin was repeatedly articulated and those readers requiring vernacular translations were stigmatized. On the other hand, it was used in a wide variety of pedagogical and instructional documents, many of which show evidence of wide distribution, such as Ælfric's homily collections. The utility of English stands in stark contrast to its apparent lack of perceived prestige. At the same time, the Latin language is moving in the opposite direction. It has very high prestige, but lacks the functional utility of English, a fact we see displayed throughout the *Enchiridion*, when the hermeneutic style is used to perform monastic identity formation but abandoned as the text turns to real instruction. It seems that the difficulty of the hermeneutic style requires an English-language translation, and a writer of hermeneutic saints' lives such as Byrhtferth needs a translator and abbreviator like Ælfric. In other words, the hermeneutic style needs English in order to function, but yet it requires Ælfric's and Byrhtferth's frequent reminders that Latin is more important, more prized, and more intellectual than English-language translations. These repeated vernacular assertions of the superiority of Latin cement both languages in the ideological positions dictated by the Benedictine Reform.

The linguistic ideology of Byrhtferth and Ælfric intersects in their treatment of the secular clergy, figures who, from a literary point of view, are not particularly important to the period. For Byrhtferth and Ælfric, however, these clerics create a foil of sorts that establishes a monastic identity, as they come to embody the undisciplined opposite of a good Benedictine monk. Lack of Latinity, especially mastery of the hermeneutic style, and reliance on vernacular language are important markers that signify other inabilities to maintain discipline in their lives. The real history of the secular clergy in Anglo-Saxon England remains to be written, but, at the very least, some of Byrhtferth's and Ælfric's insinuations about them have to be removed from the discussion of language and its appropriate uses in Anglo-Saxon England. Both of these monastic writers employed a caricature of the lazy secular cleric as an excuse for translating in the vernacular, even works that we otherwise know to have been beneficial to a monastic audience. Contained within the permission for writing in the vernacular that the illiterate (or at least unLatinate) priests provide is an implicit construction of identity for the monks, reminding them that good Benedictines can and should read Latin whenever possible.

As a result of the clear divergence between theory and practice shown throughout this book, modern scholars should not accept at face value Ælfric's description of the role of English in his prefaces nor Byrhtferth's explanation of his audiences. Although these statements are so clearly articulated that they are hard to disregard, the political and ideological posturing they encode cannot be ignored. When Byrhtferth or Ælfric attribute the need for translation to the laziness of the inobservant secular clergy,[1] these remarks must be read for what they tell us about monastic identity formation rather than as a realistic depiction of the historical realities of actual secular clerics. Above all, scholars must consider the real probability that the main audience for all Anglo-Saxon writing, in either English or Latin, was in fact monks, who had access to libraries and both the leisure and the requirement to read for their spiritual edification. This statement, however, should not be taken to dismiss the possibility of lay literacy or potential lay audiences for translated texts. Rather, I mean to suggest that we should temper the view that English is meant for the laity with the very real probability that many monks needed religious literature in their native tongue. Despite the repeated protestations that English texts are of lesser value, the writings of the late tenth and early eleventh century reveal a strong literary investment in English, as can be seen in Ælfric's extensive English-language writings, which Peter Clemoes and Jonathan Wilcox both interpret as a cohesive body of vernacular religious instruction. Byrhtferth's "hermeneutic English" and the *Enchiridion*'s vernacular translations of computistical material – both normally monastic preoccupations

1 Although Ælfric does not normally name secular clerics as an audience for translation (see chap. 4), he does catalogue their vices, including their lack of Latinity.

– also speak to a real and functionally important role for English in the late Anglo-Saxon period.

While Byrhtferth and Ælfric articulate very similar ideas about the relationship between English and Latin in late Anglo-Saxon England, they differ in their Latin writings. While the most difficult forms of Latin are not useful for either author's educational agenda, the hermeneutic style is an important part of the construction of an identity as a Latinate Benedictine monk. Beyond the *Enchiridion*, Byrhtferth is perhaps best known for his creation of saints' lives in a particularly elaborate form of the hermeneutic style.[2] Ælfric, by contrast, avoids the ambiguity connected to esoteric forms of Latin, and instead creates elaborate Latin and English prefaces that specifically articulate his Benedictine credentials. In other words, Byrhtferth performs his monastic identity through his style, while Ælfric states his explicitly.

The disjunction between the practices of these two writers may ultimately relate to a difference in audience. Nothing indicates that Byrhtferth ever imagined an audience for the *Enchiridion* much beyond his classroom at Ramsey. In the case of his Latin saints' lives, he may have potentially conceived of a wider monastic audience, but nothing about his works suggest that they were used by or useful to the laity. When speaking to an in-group of monks, the performance of his Benedictine credentials through his style is particularly important, potentially superseding even the explicit content of the saints' lives or the computistical material. Ælfric, by contrast, conceived of his role as teacher a bit more broadly and often seemed to have his eye on an ultimate lay audience who could have heard his sermons read aloud by the secular clergy. Even the majority of his Latin writings may have been intended for English translation and therefore cannot be considered apart from his vernacular work. There is also evidence to suggest that Ælfric had an even dimmer view of his monks' Latinity than Byrhtferth, since he abbreviated and simplified the standard monastic customary for the Benedictine Reform, the *Regularis concordia*, in his Latin *Letter to the Monks of Eynsham*.[3] As a primarily vernacular and pragmatic author, Ælfric needed to articulate his Benedictine identity

2 Michael Lapidge, ed., *Byrhtferth of Ramsey: The Lives of St Oswald and St Ecgwine*, Oxford Medieval Texts (Oxford, 2009).

3 Christopher A. Jones, ed., *Ælfric's Letter to the Monks of Eynsham*, Cambridge Studies in Anglo-Saxon England 24 (Cambridge, 1998).

and credentials clearly, since a performance of the hermeneutic style would likely not edify his audience.

This book began by considering the cult of St Swithun, since the different versions of his translation exemplify in microcosm the language dynamics of the reform. It is now useful to return to Ælfric's version of Swithun's narrative in order to illustrate the implications of this research for the study of English and Latin literature in the late Anglo-Saxon period. While most scholars agree that Ælfric's narrative provides a model for a Christian society ultimately subjugated to observant monks, the fundamental consideration of who was being educated by the English-language text has remained largely unexplored until now. Although Swithun's life could spread ideals of monasticism beyond the walls of the monastery – and it was dedicated to pious laymen – it is equally effective at inculcating a certain brand of monasticism among monks. One of the miracles concerned a local layman[4] whom Swithun warned in a dream that the monks failed to wake in the night to say prayers each time a miracle occurred, and thus were not sufficiently observant. This episode could be read as an encouragement to Æthelweard and Æthelmær, Ælfric's patrons, to oversee the monks in their jurisdictions, and it could also be read as encouraging a certain kind of identity formation among monks, since in an admonition to monks not to be lazy, we hear the echo of the diatribes against the secular clergy for their laziness. Good monks are those who rise at appropriate hours to fulfil their duties according to the Rule of St Benedict. That this admonishment and ensuing identity formation occurs in English is essential to understanding the role of the vernacular in England: while it may have been useful for educating the laity, it was also important in monastic education. Notably, the only complete surviving manuscript of Ælfric's *Lives of Saints* is found in Cotton Julius E.vii, which was kept in a monastery, despite its dedication to the lay nobles Æthelweard and Æthelmær.

The joining of Ælfric's English-language narrative to Lantfred's prior *translatio* shows the relative positions of Latin and English in the late Anglo-Saxon period. Both languages are necessary, but serve different purposes. The elevated style of Lantfred's version memorializes the act of unity that brought together the monks and the secular clergy. For the former secular clerics who wished to show their newfound monastic status and to prove their adherence to the Benedictine rule, the acquired skill of reading the very difficult hermeneutic style resulted from setting aside certain

4 Notably, it was a woman in Lantfred.

hours of the day for study, as required by the Rule. While the rigours of the hermeneutic style may have provided a litmus test for the sincerity of some, the average level of Latinity was never as high as the reformers would have us believe.[5] Ælfric's English version of the Swithun narrative is a useful document for spreading the social ideology of the reform, not just to pious laymen, but also to monks who needed to be encouraged to follow the rigid schedule of prayers prescribed in the Rule of St Benedict.

The wide circulation of Ælfric's English-language texts, especially his *Catholic Homilies*, proves the importance of vernacular religious education.[6] Saints lives composed in hermeneutic Latin enjoyed a relatively meagre distribution. Wulfstan of Winchester's *Life of St Æthelwold*, for instance, exists in only five manuscripts, none of which are extant before the twelfth century.[7] It is hard not to take the relatively infrequent copying and survival of manuscripts in the hermeneutic style as an indication that these texts were not used as often as their memorial function might imply. There is no question that the hermeneutic style was highly valued by the reformers. The creation of lives for Oswald, Dunstan, and Æthelwold in the hermeneutic style, and the use of the same style in the preface to the *Regularis concordia* prove the prestigious status placed on this form of Latin. Ideological importance, however, often does not accord with practical usefulness. These saints' lives appear in the lavish hermeneutic style because they were display pieces, in which the loftiness of the style encodes the importance of the people whom these works were intended to eulogize. At the same time that these texts glorify their subjects with lofty language, however, their audiences are limited to only an elite few, thus encouraging and almost requiring an English-language translation in order for the work to be further disseminated. For the ideals of the monastic reform to spread, a figure such as Ælfric had to translate important texts

5 Other scholars beginning with C.E. Hohler have also suggested that tenth-century Latinity would disappoint the leaders of the Benedictine Reform. "Some Service Books of the Later Saxon Church," in *Tenth-Century Studies: Essays in Commemoration of the Millennium of the Council of Winchester and* Regularis Concordia, ed. David Parsons (London, 1975), 60–83.

6 Joyce Hill, "Translating the Tradition: Manuscripts, Models and Methodologies in the Composition of Ælfric's *Catholic Homilies*, In Memoriam Peter Alan Martin Clemoes, 1920–1996," *Bulletin of John Rylands Library* 79 (1997): 43–65.

7 Michael Lapidge, "Textual Criticism and the Literature of Anglo-Saxon England," in *Textual and Material Culture in Anglo-Saxon England: Thomas Northcote Toller and the Toller Memorial Lectures*, ed. Donald Scragg (Cambridge, 2003), 116 n. 48.

into the vernacular, making them readily available, not just to the laity and to the secular clergy, but also to the vast majority of monks.

Almost universally, previous scholarship has accepted at face value the reformers' claim that monks could conduct their affairs in Latin. The evidence of the *Enchiridion*, however, argues exactly the opposite, since it is a primarily English-language text that was created for a monastic classroom and intended for monks with some proficiency in Latin. If these monks used a vernacular text to access computistical material, a subject closely connected to monastic identity, then they probably used English-language texts for other things as well. The circulation of many English-language translations suggests that monks may have been the primary audience for several translations, including those of the West Saxon Gospels and Ælfric's *Lives of Saints*, despite what the reformed abbot's prefaces might maintain.[8] If we read Old English texts of the Benedictine Reform, especially those of Ælfric, as intended first and foremost for a literate monastic audience – in addition to any other audience it might have had – then the status of English-language texts in the monastic reform takes on a much greater prominence then previous scholarship has afforded it.

I began this project as an attempt to understand the role and function of hermeneutic Latin in the monastic reform, but in many ways it has changed my understanding of the role of English in the late Anglo-Saxon period. Although reformers took great pride in their Latinity and disparaged English-language texts, their practices showed the high esteem in which they held all written documents, both English and Latin. The disparaging remarks about the incapacity of the English language and the monks' disdain for any language other than Latin must be read as both creating and reiterating a very specific kind of Latinate monastic identity, not reflecting the actual usage of these two languages in later Anglo-Saxon England. English-language texts were more widely accessible, to both monks and laity, for the vernacular played a primary role in spreading reformed ideals, while Latin texts, especially those in the hermeneutic style, served to

8 Roy Liuzza offered the "admittedly disappointing and predictable answer" that despite the temptation to imagine a lay audience for English translations of the Bible, "in all probability the Old English Gospels reached the general lay audience, if at all, in the voice of a narrator, as a gloss on a recited Latin liturgical reading rather than as an independent text." "Who Read the Gospels in Old English," in *Words and Works: Studies in Medieval English Language and Literature in Honour of Fred C. Robinson*, ed. Peter S. Baker and Nicholas Howe (Toronto, 1998), 15.

perform and constitute a specific Benedictine identity rather than to transmit specific ideas and information. It is also important to point out that Byrhtferth and Ælfric did not write in the heyday of the reform; they are both second-generation reformers, who were trained fairly consistently as Benedictine monks.[9] With the deaths of King Edgar and the major leaders of the reform, the political power of this movement weakened to a degree. It is during this period, the 990s and later, that we see in both Ælfric and Byrhtferth a strong monastic polemic against the secular clergy connected to their inability to read Latin. In this moment after the reform has lost its politically powerful leaders, the desire to develop a specific kind of monastic identity seems to have been particularly poignant, especially with a king who did not offer the monks the same level of royal support as his father. Since most late Anglo-Saxon literature was written or copied by reformed monks, an awareness of the contemporary political context must inform our reading of the entire corpus.

---

9 For the view that Ælfric began his life as a cleric, see Christopher A. Jones, "Ælfric and the Limits of 'Benedictine Reform,'" in *A Companion to Ælfric*, ed. Hugh Magennis and Mary Swan, Brill's Companions to the Christian Tradition 18 (Leiden, 2009), 67–108.

Bibliography

Note: *ASE* = *Anglo-Saxon England*

Primary Sources

Alcuin. *De Grammatica*, *Library of Latin Texts – Series A: Database for the Western Latin Tradition*. Online. Brepols, 2009.

Aristotle. *Rhetoric and Poetics*. Trans. Rhys Roberts. New York: Modern Library, 1954.

Baker, Peter S., and Michael Lapidge, eds. *Byrhtferth's Enchiridion*. EETS, s.s., 15. Oxford: Oxford University Press, 1995.

Bately, Janet, ed. *The Anglo-Saxon Chronicle: A Collaborative Edition*. Vol. 3, *MS. A*. Cambridge: D.S. Brewer, 1986.

Blake, Martin, ed. *Ælfric's De temporibus anni*. Anglo-Saxon Texts 6. Woodbridge: D.S. Brewer, 2009.

The Calendar and the Cloister: Oxford, St John's College MS17. Montreal: McGill University Library, Digital Collections Program, 2007. http://digital.library.mcgill.ca/ms-17.

Campbell, Alistair, ed. *The Chronicle of Æthelweard*. London: Nelson, 1962.

– *Frithegodi monachi breuiloquium uitae beati Wilfredi et Wulfstani cantoris narratio metrica de Sancto Swithuno*. Zurich: Thesaurus Mundi, 1950.

Clemoes, Peter, ed. *Ælfric's Catholic Homilies: The First Series*. EETS, s.s., 17. London: Oxford University Press, 1997.

Colgrave, Bertram, and R.A.B. Mynors, eds. *Bede's Ecclesiastical History of the English People*. Oxford: Clarendon Press, 1969.

Crawford, S.J. *Byrhtferth's Manual*. EETS, o.s., 177. London, 1929.

Dolbeau, F. "Le *Breuiloquium de omnibus sanctis*: Un poème inconnu de Wulfstan, chantre de Winchester." *Analecta Bollandiana* 106 (1988): 35–98.

Ehwald, R., ed. *Aldhelmi Opera*. Monumenta Germaniae historica, Auctores antiquissimi 15. Berlin, 1919.

Fehr, B., ed. *Die Hirtenbriefe Ælfrics in altenglischer und lateinischer Fassung*. With a supplement by P. Clemoes. Bibliothek der angelsächsischen Prosa 9. Darmstadt, 1966.

Garmonsway, G.N., ed. *Ælfric's Colloquy*. 2nd ed. London, 1947.

Giles, J.A. *Vita Quorundum Anglo-Saxonum*. Publication of the Caxton Society 16. London, 1854.

Godden, Malcolm, ed. *Ælfric's Catholic Homilies: Introduction, Commentary, and Glossary*. EETS, s.s., 18. London: Oxford University Press, 2000.

– *Ælfric's Catholic Homilies: The Second Series*. EETS, s.s., 5. London: Oxford University Press, 1979.

Günzel, Beate, ed. *Aelfwine's Prayerbook: London, British Library, Cotton Titus D. XXVI + XXVII*. Henry Bradshaw Society 108. London: Henry Bradshaw Society, 1993.

Gwara, Scott, ed. *Aldhelmi Malmesbiriensis prosa de virginitate cum glosa Latina atque Anglosaxonica*. Corpus Christianorum Series Latina 124, 124A. Turnhout: Brepols, 2001.

Gwara, Scott, ed., and David W. Porter, trans. *Anglo-Saxon Conversations: The Colloquies of Ælfric Bata*. Woodbridge: Boydell, 1997.

Henel, Heinrich, ed. *Ælfric's De temporibus anni*. EETS, o.s., 213. London, 1942.

Jones, Christopher A., ed. *Ælfric's Letter to the Monks of Eynsham*. Cambridge Studies in Anglo-Saxon England 24. Cambridge: Cambridge University Press, 1998.

Langefeld, Brigitte, ed. *The Old English Version of the Enlarged Rule of Chrodegang: Edited together with the Latin Text and an English Translation*. Münchner Universitätsschriften, Texte und Untersuchungen zur Englischen Philologie 26. Frankfurt: P. Lang, 2004.

Lapidge, Michael, ed. *Byrhtferth of Ramsey: The Lives of St Oswald and St Ecgwine*. Oxford Medieval Texts. Oxford: Oxford University Press, 2009.

– *The Cult of St Swithun*. Winchester Studies 4.2. Oxford: Clarendon Press, 2003.

Lapidge, Michael, and Michael Herren, trans. *Aldhelm: the Prose Works*. Cambridge: D.S. Brewer, 1979.

Lapidge, Michael, and Michael Winterbottom, eds. Wulfstan of Winchester, *The Life of St Æthelwold*. Oxford Medieval Texts. Oxford: Clarendon Press, 1991.

– "Ælfric's Vita S. Æthelwoldi." In Wulfstan of Winchester, *The Life of St Æthelwold*. Oxford Medieval Texts. Oxford: Clarendon Press, 1991.

Lindsay, W.M., ed. *The Corpus, Épinal, Erfurt, and Leyden Glossaries*. Publications of the Philological Society 8. London: Oxford University Press, 1921.

– *Isidori Hispalensis episcopi etymologiarum sive originum libri XX*. Oxford, 1911.
McCann, Justin, ed. and trans. *The Rule of St Benedict*. Westminster, MD: Newman Press, 1952.
McGurk, P., ed. *An Eleventh-Century Anglo-Saxon Miscellany*. Early English Manuscripts in Facsimile 21. Copenhagen: Rosenkilde and Bagger, 1983.
Morris, R., ed. *The Blickling Homilies*. EETS, o.s., 58, 63, and 73. London, 1874–80. Reprinted as a single volume. London: Oxford University Press, 1967.
Muir, Bernard James, ed. *A Pre-Conquest Prayer-Book (BL MSS Cotton Galba A.xiv and Nero A.ii (ff. 3–13))*. Henry Bradshaw Society 103. Woodbridge: Boydell, 1988.
Plummer, Charles, ed. *Two of the Saxon Chronicles Parallel*. Vol. 1. 1892. Reprinted Oxford: Clarendon, 1952.
Prescott, Andrew. *The Benedictional of St Æthelwold: A Masterpiece of Anglo-Saxon Art*. London: British Library, 2002.
Raine, J., ed. *The Historians of the Church of York*. Vol. 1. Rolls Series 71. London, 1879.
Scragg, Donald, ed. *The Vercelli Homilies and Related Texts*, EETS, o.s., 300. London: Oxford University Press, 1992.
Skeat, Walter W., ed. *Ælfric's Lives of Saints*, EETS, o.s., 76, 82, 94, 114. London, 1881–1900. Reprinted as 2 volumes. London: Oxford University Press, 1966.
Stubbs, W., ed. *Memorials of St Dunstan*. Rolls Series 63. London, 1874.
Sweet, Henry, ed. *King Alfred's West Saxon Version of Alfred's Pastoral Care*. EETS, o.s., 45 and 50. London, 1871.
Symons, T., ed. *The Monastic Agreement of the Monks and Nuns of the English Nation*. London: Nelson, 1953.
Symons, T., S. Spath et al., eds. "Regularis concordia Anglicae nationis." In *Consuetudinum saeculi X/XI/XII monumenta non-Cluniacensia*, ed. Kassius Hallinger, 61–147. Corpus Consuetudinum Monasticarum 7.3. Siegburg: F. Schmitt, 1984.
Wallis, Faith, trans. *Bede: The Reckoning of Time*. Translated Texts for Historians 29. Liverpool: Liverpool University Press, 1999.
Wilcox, Jonathan, ed. *Ælfric's Prefaces*. Durham Medieval Texts 9. Durham: Durham Medieval Texts, 1994.
Winterbottom, Michael, ed. *Three Lives of English Saints*. Toronto Medieval Latin Texts. Toronto: Centre for Medieval Studies by the Pontifical Institute of Mediaeval Studies, 1972.
Zupitza, J., ed. *Ælfrics Grammatik und Glossar: Text und Varienten*. Sammlung englischer Denkmäler in kritischen Ausgaben 1. Berlin, 1880. Reprinted with an introduction by Helmut Gneuss. Hildesheim: Weidmann, 2001.

Secondary Sources

Baker, Peter S. "Byrhtferth's *Enchiridion* and the Computus in Oxford, St John's College 17." *ASE* 10 (1982): 123–42.

– "The Inflection of Latin Nouns in Old English Texts." In *Words and Works: Studies in Medieval English Language and Literature in Honour of Fred C. Robinson*, ed. Peter S. Baker and Nicholas Howe, 187–206. Toronto: University of Toronto Press, 1998.

– "The Old English Canon of Byrhtferth of Ramsey." *Speculum* 55 (1980): 22–37.

Barrow, Julia. "The Clergy in English Dioceses c.900–c.1066." *Pastoral Care in Late Anglo-Saxon England*, ed. Francesca Tinti, 17–26. Anglo-Saxon Studies 6. Woodbridge: Boydell Press, 2005.

– "The Community of Worcester, 961–c.1100." In *St Oswald of Worcester: Life and Influence*, ed. N. Brooks and C. Cubitt, 84–99. Studies in the Early History of England 2. Leicester: Leicester University Press, 1996.

Bately, Janet M. "The Alfredian Canon Revisited: One Hundred Years On." In *Alfred the Great: Papers from the Eleventh-Centenary Conferences*, ed. Timothy Reuter, 107–20. Studies in Early Medieval Britain 3. Aldershot: Ashgate, 2003.

– "Did King Alfred Actually Translate Anything? The Integrity of the Alfredian Canon Revisited." *Medium Ævum* 78 (2009): 189–215.

– "The Literary Prose of King Alfred's Reign: Translation or Transformation?" In *Old English Prose: Basic Readings*, ed. Paul Szarmach, 3–27. Basic Readings in Anglo-Saxon Prose 5. New York: Garland, 2000. First delivered as inaugural lecture in the Chair of English Language and Medieval Literature delivered at University of London King's College, 4 March 1980. Reprinted as *Old English Newsletter Subsidia* 10 (1984).

– "Old English Prose before and during the Reign of Alfred," *ASE* 17 (1988): 93–138.

– "Uþwita/Philosophus Revisited: A Reflection on OE Usage." In *Essays on Anglo-Saxon and Related Themes in Memory of Lynne Grundy*, ed. Jane Roberts and Janet Nelson, 16–36. London: King's College London, Centre for Late Antique and Medieval Studies, 2000.

Berry, Mary. "What the Saxon Monks Sang: Music in Winchester in the Late Tenth Century." In Yorke, *Bishop Æthelwold*, 149–60.

Berry, Reginald. "'*Ealle þing wundorlice gesceapen*': The Structure of the *Computus* in Byrhtferth's Manual." *Revue de l'Université d'Ottawa* 52 (1982): 130–41.

Bishop, T.A.M. *English Caroline Minuscule*. Oxford Paleographical Handbooks. Oxford: Clarendon Press, 1971.

Blair, John. *The Church in Anglo-Saxon Society*. Oxford: Oxford University Press, 2005.

– "Secular Minster Churches in Domesday Book." In *Domesday Book: A Reassessment*, ed. Peter Sawyer, 114–25. London: Edward Arnold, 1985.

Bosworth, J., and T. Northcote Toller. *An Anglo-Saxon Dictionary*. Oxford, 1898.

Brookes, Stewart. "Reading between the Lines: The Liturgy and Ælfric's Lives of Saints and Homilies." *Leeds Studies in English* 42 (2011): 17–28.

Brooks, Nicholas. *The Early History of the Church of Canterbury: Christ Church from 597–1066*. Leicester: Leicester University Press, 1984.

Bullough, D.A. "The Educational Tradition in England from Alfred to Ælfric: Teaching *utriusque linguae*." *Settimane di studio del Centro italiano di studi sull'alto medioevo* 19 (1972): 453–94.

Busse, Wilhelm G. "*Sua gað ða lareowas beforan ðæm folce, & ðæt folc æfter*: The Self-Understanding of the Reformers as Teachers in Late Tenth-Century England." In *Schriftlichkeit im frühen Mittelalter*, ed. Ursula Schaefer, 58–106. ScriptOralia 53. Tübingen: Gunter Narr, 1993.

Chapman, Don. "Uterque Lingua / Ægôer Gereord: Ælfric's Grammatical Vocabulary and the Winchester Tradition." *JEGP* 109 (2010): 421–45.

Clayton, Mary. "Centralism and Uniformity versus Localism and Diversity: The Virgin and Native Saints in the Monastic Reform." *Peritia* 8 (1994): 95–106.

– *The Cult of the Virgin Mary in Anglo-Saxon England*. Cambridge Studies in Anglo-Saxon England 2. Cambridge: Cambridge University Press, 1990.

– "Homiliaries and Preaching in Anglo-Saxon England." *Peritia* 4 (1985): 207–42.

Clemoes, Peter. "The Chronology of Ælfric's Works." In *Old English Prose: Basic Readings*, ed. Paul E. Szarmach, 29–72. Basic Readings in Anglo-Saxon England 5. London: Garland, 2000. First published in *The Anglo-Saxons: Studies in Some Aspects of Their History and Culture Presented to Bruce Dickins*, ed. Peter Clemoes. London: Bowes and Bowes, 1959.

Constable, Giles. "Monasteries, Rural Churches, and the *cura animarum* in the Early Middle Ages." *Settimane di studio del Centro italiano di Studi sull'alto medioevo* 28 (1982): 349–89.

Copeland, Rita. *Rhetoric, Hermeneutics, and Translation in the Middle Ages: Academic Traditions and Vernacular Texts*. Cambridge Studies in Medieval Literature 11. Cambridge: Cambridge University Press, 1991.

Cubitt, Catherine. "Ælfric's Lay Patrons." In Magennis and Swan, eds, *Companion to Ælfric*, 165–92.

– "Images of St Peter: The Clergy and the Religious Life in Anglo-Saxon England." In *The Christian Tradition in Anglo-Saxon England: Approaches to Current Scholarship and Teaching*, ed. Paul Cavill, 41–54. Christianity and Culture: Issues in Teaching and Research. Cambridge: D.S. Brewer, 2004.

Dahan, Gilbert. *The Christian Polemic against the Jews*. Trans. Jody Gladding. Notre Dame, IN: University of Notre Dame Press, 1998.

de Jong, Mayke. *In Samuel's Image: Child Oblation in the Early Medieval West*. Brill's Studies in Intellectual History 12. Leiden: Brill, 1996.

Derolez, René. "Those Things Are Difficult to Express in English ..." *English Studies* 70 (1989): 469–76.

Deshman, Robert. *The Benedictional of St Æthelwold*. Studies in Manuscript Illumination 9. Princeton, NJ: Princeton University Press, 1995.

– "*Benedictus Monarcha et Monarchus*: Early Medieval Ruler Theology and the Anglo-Saxon Reform." *Frühmittelalterliche Studien* 10 (1976): 204–40.

– "*Christus rex et magi reges:* Kingship and Christology in Ottonian and Anglo-Saxon Art." *Frühmittelalterliche Studien* 10 (1976): 367–405.

Dictionary of Old English, Old English Corpus [electronic resource]. Ed. Antonette diPaolo Healey. Ann Arbor: University of Michigan Press, 1998.

Discenza, Nicole Guenther. *The King's English: Strategies of Translation in the Old English* Boethius. Albany, NY: SUNY Press, 2005.

– "Wealth and Wisdom: Symbolic Capital and the Ruler in the Translational Program of Alfred the Great." *Exemplaria* 13 (2001): 433–67.

– "Writing the Mother Tongue in the Shadow of Babel." In *Conceptualizing Multilingualism in England 800–1250*, ed. Elizabeth M. Tyler, 33–55. Studies in the Middle Ages. Turnholt: Brepols, 2011.

Drout, Michael D.C. *How Tradition Works: A Meme-Based Cultural Poetics of the Anglo-Saxon Tenth Century*. Medieval and Renaissance Texts 306. Tempe: Arizona Center for Medieval and Renaissance Studies, 2006.

– "Re-Dating the Old English Translation of the Enlarged Rule of Chrodegang: The Evidence of the Prose Style." *JEGP* 103 (2004): 341–68.

Dumville, David. "Beowulf Come Lately: Some Notes on the Paleography of the Nowell Codex." *Archiv für der neueren Sprachen und Literaturen* 225 (1988): 49–63.

– "The Catalogue Texts." In McGurk, *An Eleventh-Century Anglo-Saxon Miscellany*, 55–8.

– *English Caroline Script and Monastic History: Studies in Benedictinism, A.D. 950–1030*. Studies in Anglo-Saxon History 6. Woodbridge: Boydell Press, 1993.

Fisher, D.J.V. "The Early Biographers of St. Ethelwold." *English Historical Review* 67 (1952): 381–91.

Foot, Sarah. "Anglo-Saxon Minsters: A Review of Terminology." In *Pastoral Care before the Parish*, ed. John Blair and Richard Sharpe, 212–25. Leicester: Leicester University Press, 1992.

– "Language and Method: The Dictionary of Old English and the Historian." In *The Dictionary of Old English: Retrospects and Prospects*, ed. M.J. Toswell,

73–87. Old English Newsletter Subsidia 26. Kalamazoo, MI: Medieval Institute, Western Michigan University, 1998.

– *Monastic Life in Anglo-Saxon England, c. 600–900*. Cambridge: Cambridge University Press, 2006.

– *Veiled Women*. 2 vols. Studies in Early Medieval Britain. Aldershot: Ashgate, 2000.

Gatch, Milton McC. *Preaching and Theology in Anglo-Saxon England: Ælfric and Wulfstan*. Toronto: University of Toronto Press, 1977.

George, Judith W. *Venantius Fortunatus: A Latin Poet in Merovingian Gaul*. Oxford: Clarendon Press, 1992.

Gill, Paramjit S., Tim B. Swartz, and Michael Treschow. "A Stylometric Analysis of King Alfred's Literary Works." *Journal of Applied Statistics* 34.10 (2007): 1251–8.

Gneuss, Helmut. *Handlist of Anglo-Saxon Manuscripts: A List of Manuscripts and Manuscript Fragments Written or Owned in England up to 1100*. Medieval and Renaissance Text Studies 241. Tempe: Arizona Center for Medieval Renaissance Studies, 2001.

– *Hymnar und Hymnen im englischen Mittelalter*. Buchreihe der Anglia 12. Tübingen: De Gruyter, 1968.

– "The Origin of Standard Old English and Æthelwold's School at Winchester." *Anglo-Saxon England* 1 (1972): 63–83.

– "The Study of Language in Anglo-Saxon England." In *Textual and Material Culture in Anglo-Saxon England: Thomas Northcote Toller and Toller Memorial Lectures*, ed. Donald Scragg, 78–88. Publications for the Manchester Centre for Anglo-Saxon Studies 1. Cambridge: D.S. Brewer, 2003. First published in *Bulletin of the John Rylands University Library of Manchester* 72 (1990): 1–32.

Godden, Malcolm R. "Ælfric's Changing Vocabulary." *English Studies* (1980): 206–23.

– "Ælfric's Saints' Lives and the Problem of Miracles." In *Old English Prose: Basic Readings*, ed. Paul Szarmach, 287–309. Basic Readings in Anglo-Saxon England 5. New York: Garland, 2000. First published in *Leeds Studies in English*, n.s., 16 (1985): 83–100.

– "Apocalypse and Invasion in Late Anglo-Saxon England." In *From Anglo-Saxon to Early Middle English: Studies Presented to E. G. Stanley*, ed. M. Godden, D. Gray, and T. Hoad, 130–62. Oxford: Clarendon Press, 1994.

– "The Development of Ælfric's Second Series of *Catholic Homilies*." *English Studies* 54 (1973): 209–16.

– "Did King Alfred Write Anything?" *Medium Ævum* 76 (2007): 1–23.

– "Experiments in Genre: The Saints' Lives in Ælfric's *Catholic Homilies*."

In *Holy Men and Holy Women*, ed. Paul E. Szarmach, 261–87. Albany: SUNY Press, 1996.

– "Literary Language." In *The Cambridge History of the English Language: Vol. 1, The Beginnings to 1066*, ed. Richard M. Hogg, 490–535. Cambridge: Cambridge University Press, 1992.

Godman, Peter. "The Anglo-Latin *opus geminatum*: From Aldhelm to Alcuin." *Medium Ævum* 50 (1981): 215–29.

Gransden, Antonia. "Traditionalism and Continuity during the Last Century of Anglo-Saxon Monasticism." *Journal of Ecclesiastical History* 40 (1989): 159–207.

Gretsch, Mechthild. *Ælfric and the Cult of Saints in Late Anglo-Saxon England.* Cambridge Studies in Anglo-Saxon England 34. Cambridge: Cambridge University Press, 2005.

– "Ælfric, Language and Winchester." In Magennis and Swan, *Companion to Ælfric*, 109–37.

– "Æthelwold's Translation of the *Regula Sancti Benedicti* and Its Latin Exemplar." *ASE* 3 (1974): 125–51.

– "The Benedictine Rule in Old English: A Document of Bishop Æthelwold's Reform Politics." In *Words, Texts, and Manuscripts: Studies in Anglo-Saxon Culture Presented to Helmut Gneuss on the Occasion of His Sixty-fifth Birthday*, ed. Michael Korhammer, Karl Reichl, and Hans Sauer, 131–58. Cambridge: D.S. Brewer, 1992.

– *The Intellectual Foundations of the Benedictine Reform.* Cambridge Studies in Anglo-Saxon England 25. Cambridge: Cambridge University Press, 1999.

– "The Junius Psalter Gloss: Its Historical and Cultural Context." *ASE* 29 (2000): 85–121.

– *Die Regula Sancti Benedicti in England und ihre altenglische Übersetzung.* Texte und Untersuchungen zur englischen Philologie 2. Munich: W. Fink, 1973.

– "Winchester Vocabulary and Standard Old English: The Vernacular in Late Anglo-Saxon England." *Bulletin of the John Rylands University Library of Manchester* 83.1 (Spring 2001): 41–87.

Hall, Thomas N. "Ælfric as Pedagogue." In Magennis and Swan, *Companion to Ælfric*, 193–216.

Hart, Cyril. "Byrhtferth and His Manual." *Medium Ævum* 41 (1972): 95–109.

Henel, Heinrich. *Studien zum altenglischen Computus.* Beiträge zur Englischen Philologie 26. Leipzig: Bernhard Tauchnitz, 1934.

Hill, Joyce. "Ælfric: His Life and Works." In Magennis and Swan, *Companion to Ælfric*, 35–65.

– "Ælfric's Grammatical Triad." In *Form and Content of Instruction in Anglo-Saxon England in the Light of Contemporary Manuscript Evidence*, ed.

Patrizia Lendinara, Loredana Lazzari, and Maria Amalia D'Aronco, 285–307. Fédération Internationale des Instituts d'Études Mediévales, Textes et Études du Moyen Age 39. Turnhout: Brepols, 2007.

– "Authority and Intertextuality in the Works of Ælfric." *Proceedings of the British Academy* 131 (2005): 157–81.

– "The Benedictine Reform and Beyond." In *A Companion to Anglo-Saxon Literature*, ed. Phillip Pulsiano and Elaine Treharne, 151–69. Blackwell Companions to Literature and Culture 11. Oxford: Blackwell, 2001.

– "Reform and Resistance: Preaching Styles in Late Anglo-Saxon England." In *De l'homelie au sermon: Histoire de la prédication médiéval*, ed. Jacqueline Hamesse and Xavier Hermand, 15–46. Textes, Études, Congrès 14. Louvain-la-neuve: Institut d'études médiévales de l'Université Catholique de Louvain, 1993.

– "The '*Regularis concordia*' and Its Latin and Old English Reflexes." *Revue Bénédictinc* 101 (1991): 299–315.

– "Saint George before the Conquest." *Report of the Society of the Friends of St George's and the Descendants of the Knights of the Garter* 6 (1987): 284–95.

– "Translating the Tradition: Manuscripts, Models and Methodologies in the Composition of Ælfric's *Catholic Homilies*. In Memoriam Peter Alan Martin Clemoes, 1920–1996." *Bulletin of John Rylands Library* 79 (1997): 43–65.

Hofstetter, Walter. *Winchester und der spätaltenglische Sprachgebrauch: Untersuchungen zur geographischen und zeitlichen Verbreitung altenglischer Synonyme*. Münchener Universitäts-Schriften, Philosophische Fakultät, Texte und Untersuchungen zur englischen Philologie 14. Munich: W. Fink, 1987.

– "Winchester and the Standardization of Old English Vocabulary." *ASE* 17 (1988): 139–61.

Hohler, C.E. "Some Service Books of the Later Saxon Church." In *Tenth-Century Studies: Essays in Commemoration of the Millennium of the Council of Winchester and* Regularis Concordia, ed. David Parsons, 60–83. London: Phillimore, 1975.

Hollis, Stephanie. "Scientific and Medical Writings." In *A Companion to Anglo-Saxon Literature*, ed. P. Pulsiano and E. Treharne, 188–208. Blackwell Companions to Literature and Culture 11. Oxford: Blackwell, 2001.

Irvine, Martin. *The Making of Textual Culture: "Grammatica" and Literary Theory, 350–1100*. Cambridge Studies in Medieval Literature 19. Cambridge: Cambridge University Press, 1994.

Janson, Tore. *Latin Prose Preface: Studies in Literary Conventions*. Studia Latina Stockholmiensia 13. Stockholm: Almqvist and Wiksell, 1964.

– *Prose Rhythm in Medieval Latin from the 9th to the 13th Century*. Studia Latina Stockholmiensia 20. Stockholm: Almqvist and Wiksell, 1975.

Jayatilaka, Rohini. "The Old English Benedictine Rule: Writing for Women and Men." *ASE* 32 (2003): 147–87.

John, Eric. "The King and the Monks in the Tenth-Century Reformation." In *Orbis Britanniae and Other Studies*, 154–80. Leicester: Leicester University Press, 1966.

Jones, Charles W. "A Legend of St Pachomius." *Speculum* 18 (1943): 198–210.

Jones, Christopher A. "Ælfric and the Limits of 'Benedictine Reform.'" In Magennis and Swan, *Companion to Ælfric*, 67–108.

– "Ælfric's Pastoral Letters and the Episcopal Capitula of Radulf of Bourges." *Notes and Queries* 42.2 (June 1995): 149–55.

– "*Meatim Sed et Rustica*: Ælfric of Eynsham as a Medieval Latin Author." *Journal of Medieval Latin* 8 (1998): 1–57.

Katz, Jacob. *Exclusiveness and Tolerance: Studies in Jewish–Gentile Relations in Medieval and Modern Times*. Oxford: Oxford University Press, 1961.

Ker, N.R. *Catalogue of Manuscripts Containing Anglo-Saxon*. Oxford: Clarendon Press, 1957.

– "Two Notes on Ashmole 328 (Byrhtferth's Manual)." *Medium Aevum* 4 (1935): 16–19.

Keynes, Simon. *The Diplomas of King Æthelred "The Unready," 978–1016: A Study in Their Use as Historical Evidence*. Cambridge: Cambridge University Press, 1980.

– "Edgar, *Rex Admirabilis*." In *Edgar: King of the English 959–975: New Interpretations*, ed. Donald Scragg, 3–59. Publications of the Manchester Centre for Anglo-Saxon Studies. Woodbridge: Boydell, 2008.

– "England, c. 900–1016." In *The New Cambridge Medieval History, vol. 3, 900–1024*, ed. Timothy Reuter, 456–84. Cambridge: Cambridge University Press, 1999.

Kiernan, Kevin. *Beowulf and the Beowulf Manuscript*. New Brunswick, NJ: Rutgers University Press, 1981.

– "The Eleventh Century Origin of *Beowulf* and the *Beowulf* Manuscript." In *Anglo-Saxon Manuscripts: Basic Readings*, ed. Mary P. Richards, 277–99. Basic Readings in Anglo-Saxon England 2. New York: Routledge, 1994.

Knappe, Gabriele. "Classical Rhetoric in Anglo-Saxon England." *ASE* 27 (1998): 5–29.

– *Traditionen der klassischen Rhetorik im angelsächsischen England*. Anglistische Forschungen 236. Heidelberg: C. Winter, 1996.

Knowles, David. *The Monastic Order in England: A History of Its Development from the Times of St Dunstan to the Fourth Lateran Council, 940–1216*. 2nd ed. Cambridge: Cambridge University Press, 1963.

Langefeld, Brigitte. "*Regula canonicorum* or *Regula monasterialis uitae*? The Rule of Chrodegang and Archbishop Wulfred's Reforms at Canterbury." *ASE* 25 (1996): 21–36.

Lapidge, Michael. "Æthelwold as Scholar and Teacher." In Lapidge, *Anglo-Latin Literature, 900–1066*, 183–211. First published in Yorke, *Bishop Æthelwold*, 89–117.

– *Anglo-Latin Literature, 900–1066*. London and Rio Grande, OH: Hambledon Press, 1993.

– *The Anglo-Saxon Library*. Oxford: Oxford University Press, 2006.

– "*B.* and the *Vita S. Dunstani.*" In Lapidge, *Anglo-Latin Literature, 900–1066*, 279–91. First published in *St Dunstan and His Times*, ed. Nigel Ramsay, T.W.T. Tatton-Brown, and Margaret Sparks, 251–63. Woodbridge: Boydell Press, 1992.

– "Byrhtferth and Oswald." In *St Oswald of Worcester: Life and Influence*, ed. N. Brooks and C. Cubitt, 63–84. Studies in the Early History of England 2. Leicester: Leicester University Press, 1996.

– "Byrhtferth and the *Vita S. Ecgwini.*" In Lapidge, *Anglo-Latin Literature, 900–1066*, 293–315. London: Hambledon Press, 1993. First published in *Mediaeval Studies* 41 (1979): 331–53.

– "Byrhtferth at Work." In *Words and Works: Studies in Medieval English Language and Literature in Honour of Fred C. Robinson*, ed. Peter S. Baker and Nicholas Howe, 25–43. Toronto: University of Toronto Press, 1998.

– "A Frankish Scholar in Tenth-Century England: Frithegod of Canterbury / Fredegaud of Brioude." In Lapidge, *Anglo-Latin Literature, 900–1066*, 157–81. First published in Lapidge, *Anglo-Saxon England* 17 (1988): 45–65.

– "The Hermeneutic Style in Tenth-Century Anglo-Latin Literature." In Lapidge, *Anglo-Latin Literature, 900–1066*, 105–49. First published in *ASE* 4 (1975): 67–111.

– "Israel the Grammarian in ASE." In Lapidge, *Anglo-Latin Literature, 900–1066*, 87–104. First published in *From Athens to Chartres: Neoplatonism and Medieval Thought*, ed. H.J. Westra, 97–114. Leiden: Brill, 1992.

– "Knowledge of the Poems of Venantius Fortunatus in Early Anglo-Saxon England." In Lapidge, *Anglo-Latin Literature, 600–899*, 399–407. First published in *ASE* 8 (1979): 287–95.

– "Poeticism in Pre-Conquest Anglo-Latin Prose." *Publications of the British Academy* 129 (2005): 321–37.

– "Schools." In *The Blackwell Encyclopaedia of Anglo-Saxon England*, ed. Michael Lapidge, John Blair, Simon Keynes, and Donald Scragg, 409. Oxford: Blackwell, 1999.

– "Schools, Learning and Literature in Tenth-Century England." In Lapidge, *Anglo-Latin Literature, 900–1066*, 1–48. First published in *Settimane di studio del Centro italiano di Studi sull'alto medioevo* 38 (1991): 951–98.

– "Some Latin Poems as Evidence for the Reign of Æthelstan." In Lapidge, *Anglo-Latin Literature, 900–1066*, 49–86. First published in *ASE* 9 (1981): 61–98.

– "The Study of Latin Texts in Late Anglo-Saxon England." In Lapidge, *Anglo-Latin Literature, 600–899*, 455–98. First published in *Latin and the Vernacular Languages in Early Medieval Britain*, ed. N.P. Brooks, 99–140. Leicester: Leicester University Press, 1984.

– "Textual Criticism and the Literature of Anglo-Saxon England." In *Textual and Material Culture in Anglo-Saxon England: Thomas Northcote Toller and the Toller Memorial Lectures*, ed. Donald Scragg, 107–36. Cambridge: D.S. Brewer, 2003. First published in *Bulletin of the John Rylands University Library of Manchester* 73 (1991): 17–45.

– "Three Latin Poems from Æthelwold's School at Winchester." In Lapidge, *Anglo-Latin Literature, 900–1066*, 225–77. First published in *ASE* 1 (1972): 85–137.

Lendinara, Patrizia. "The Third Book of the *Bella Parisiacae urbis* by Abbo of Saint-Germain-des-Prés and Its Old English Gloss." *ASE* 15 (1986): 73–89.

Liuzza, Roy M. "Anglo-Saxon Prognostics in Context: A Survey and Handlist of Manuscripts." *ASE* 30 (2001): 181–230.

– "In Measure, Number, and Weight: Writing Science." In *The Cambridge History of Early Medieval English Literature*, ed. Clare A. Lees. Cambridge: Cambridge University Press, 2013.

– "Who Read the Gospels in Old English." In *Words and Works: Studies in Medieval English Language and Literature in Honour of Fred C. Robinson*, ed. Peter S. Baker and Nicholas Howe, 3–24. Toronto: University of Toronto Press, 1998.

Lockett, Leslie. "An Integrated Re-examination of the Dating of Oxford, Bodleian Library, Junius 11." *ASE* 31 (2002): 141–73.

Lockwood, Richard. *The Reader's Figure: Epideictic Rhetoric in Plato, Aristotle, Bossuet, Racine and Pascal.* Histoire des idées et critique littéraire 35. Geneva: Librairie Droz, 1996.

MacCormack, Sabine G. *Art and Ceremony in Late Antiquity.* The Transformation of the Classical Heritage 1. Berkeley and Los Angeles: University of California Press, 1981.

Magennis, Hugh. "Ælfric Scholarship." In Magennis and Swan, *A Companion to Ælfric*, 5–34.

– "Audience(s), Reception, Literacy." In *A Companion to Anglo-Saxon Literature*, ed. Phillip Pulsiano and Elaine Treharne, 84–101. Blackwell Companions to Literature and Culture 11. Oxford: Blackwell, 2001.

Magennis, Hugh, and Mary Swan, eds. *A Companion to Ælfric.* Brill's Companions to the Christian Tradition 18. Leiden: Brill, 2009.

Marsden, Richard. "Ælfric as Translator: The Old English Prose *Genesis.*" *Anglia* 109 (1991): 319–58.

McGurk, P. "The Computus." In McGurk, *Eleventh-Century Anglo-Saxon Miscellany*, 51–5.

Menzer, Melinda. "Ælfric's English *Grammar.*" *JEGP* 103 (2004): 106–24.

Moore, R.I. *The Formation of Persecuting Society: Power and Deviance in Western Europe, 950–1250*. Oxford: Blackwell, 1987.

Nelson, Janet L. "Parents, Children and the Church in the Earlier Middle Ages." In *The Church and Childhood: Papers Read at the 1993 Summer Meeting and the 1994 Winter Meeting of the Ecclesiastical History Society*, ed. Diana Wood, 81–114. Studies in Church History 31. Oxford: Blackwell Publishers, 1994.

Neuman de Vegvar, Carol. "Saints and Companions to Saints: Anglo-Saxon Royal Women Monastics in Context." In *Holy Men and Holy Women: Old English Prose Saints' Lives and Their Contexts*, ed. Paul E. Szarmach, 51–94. SUNY Series in Medieval Studies. Albany: State University of New York Press, 1996.

O'Brien O'Keeffe, Katherine. *Stealing Obedience: Narratives of Agency and Identity in Later Anglo-Saxon England*. Toronto: University of Toronto Press, 2012.

Ogawa, Hiroshi. "Sententia in Narrative Form: Ælfric's Narrative Method in the Hagiographical Homily on St Martin." *Leeds Studies in English* 42 (2011): 75–92.

Parkes, M.B. "The Contribution of Insular Scribes of the Seventh and Eighth Centuries to the 'Grammar of Legibility.'" In *Scribes, Scripts, and Readers: Studies in the Communication and Dissemination of Medieval Texts*, 1–18. London: Hambledon Press, 1991.

Polheim, K. *Die Lateinische Reimprosa*. Berlin: Weidmann, 1925.

Porter, David W. "The Latin Syllabus in Anglo-Saxon Monastic Schools." *Neophilologus* 78 (1994): 463–82.

Raw, Barbara C. *Anglo-Saxon Crucifixion Iconography and the Art of the Monastic Revival.* Cambridge Studies in Anglo-Saxon England 1. Cambridge: Cambridge University Press, 1990.

Riché, Pierre. *Education et culture dans l'occident barbare*. Patristica sorbonensia 4. Paris: Éditions du Seuil, 1962.

Robinson, J.A. *The Times of Saint Dunstan*. Oxford, 1923.

Ruff, Carin. "The Perception of Difficulty in Aldhelm's Prose." In *Insignis Sophiae Arcator: Essays in Honour of Michael W. Herren on his 65th Birthday*, ed. Gernot Wieland, Carin Ruff, and Ross G. Arthur, 165–77. Publications of the Journal of Medieval Latin 6. Turnhout: Brepols, 2006.

Rumble, Alexander R. *Property and Piety in Early Medieval Winchester: Documents Relating to the Topography of the Anglo-Saxon and Norman City and Its Minsters*. Winchester Studies 4.3. Oxford: Clarendon Press, 2002.

Sato, Kiriko. "Ælfric's Lexical Alterations in His Adaptations from the Old English Boethius." *Neophilologus* 95 (2011): 305–11.

Scheil, Andrew P. *The Footsteps of Israel: Understanding Jews in Anglo-Saxon England*. Ann Arbor, MI: University of Michigan Press, 2004.

Scragg, Donald. "Ælfric's Scribes." *Leeds Studies in English* 37 (2006): 179–89.

Scragg, Donald, ed. *Edgar, King of the English, 959–975: New Interpretations*. Publications of Manchester Centre for Anglo-Saxon Studies. Woodbridge: Boydell, 2008.

Semper, Phillipa. "Doctrine and Diagrams: Maintaining the Order of the World in *Byrhtferth's Enchiridion*." In *The Christian Tradition in Anglo-Saxon England: Approaches to Current Scholarship and Teaching*, ed. Paul Cavill, 121–37. Cambridge: D.S. Brewer, 2004.

Shaw, Philip, and Rebecca Stephenson. "Early Medieval." *YWES* 91 (2012): 1–29.

– "Early Medieval." *YWES* 92 (2013): 1–35.

Sheerin, D.J. "The Dedication of Old Minster, Winchester, in 980." *Revue Bénédictine* 88 (1978): 261–73.

Sims-Williams, Patrick. *Religion and Literature in Western England, 600–800*. Cambridge Studies in Anglo-Saxon England 3. Cambridge: Cambridge University Press, 1990.

Smetana, Cyril L. "Ælfric and the Early Medieval Homiliary." *Traditio* 15 (1959): 164–204.

Smyth, A.P. *King Alfred the Great*. Oxford: Oxford University Press, 1996.

Stafford, Pauline. "The King's Wife in Wessex 800–1066." *Past and Present* 91 (1981): 3–27.

– *Unification and Conquest: A Political and Social History of England in the Tenth and Eleventh Centuries*. London: Edward Arnold, 1989.

Stanton, Robert. *The Culture of Translation in Anglo-Saxon England*. Cambridge: D.S. Brewer, 2002.

– "Rhetoric and Translation in Ælfric's Prefaces." *Translation and Literature* 6 (1997): 135–48.

Steen, Janie. *Verse and Virtuousity: The Adaptation of Latin Rhetoric in Old English Poetry*. Toronto: University of Toronto Press, 2008.

Stenton, F.M. *Anglo-Saxon England.* 3rd ed. Oxford: Clarendon Press, 1971.
Stephenson, Rebecca. "Ælfric of Eynsham and Hermeneutic Latin: *Meatim Sed et Rustica* Reconsidered." *Journal of Medieval Latin* 16 (2006): 111–41.
– "Byrhtferth's Enchiridion: The Effectiveness of Hermeneutic Latin." In *Conceptualizing Multilingualism in England, 800–1250*, ed. Elizabeth M. Tyler, 121–44. Studies in the Early Middle Ages. Turnhout: Brepols, 2011.
– "Deliberate Obfuscation: The Purpose of Hard Words and Difficult Syntax in the Literature of Anglo-Saxon England." Unpubl. PhD diss., University of Notre Dame, 2004.
– "Reading Byrhtferth's Muses: Emending Section Breaks in Byrhtferth's 'Hermeneutic English.'" *Notes and Queries* 252.1 (March 2007): 19–22.
– "Scapegoating the Secular Clergy: The Hermeneutic Style as a Form of Monastic Self-Definition," *ASE* 38 (2009): 101–35.
Stock, Brian. *The Implications of Literacy: Written Language and Models of Interpretation in the Eleventh and Twelfth Centuries.* Princeton, NJ: Princeton University Press, 1983.
Stodnick, Jacqueline. "'Old Names of Kings or Shadows': Reading Documentary Lists." In *Conversion and Colonization in Anglo-Saxon England*, ed. Catherine E. Karkov and Nicholas Howe, 109–31. Medieval and Renaissance Texts and Studies 318 .Tempe: Arizona Center for Medieval and Renaissance Studies, 2006.
Stotz, Peter. *Handbuch zur lateinischen Sprache des Mittelalters.* 5 vols. Handbuch der Altertumswissenschaft, Abteilung 2, Teil 5. Munich: C.H. Beck'sche Verlagsbuchhandlung, 1998.
Stow, Kenneth R. *Alienated Minority: The Jews of Medieval Europe.* Cambridge, MA: Harvard University Press, 1992.
Swan, Mary. "Identity and Ideology in Ælfric's Prefaces." In Magennis and Swan, *Companion to Ælfric*, 247–69.
Thornbury, Emily. "Aldhelm's Rejection of the Muses and the Mechanics of Poetic Inspiration in Early Anglo-Saxon England." *ASE* 36 (2008): 71–92.
Upchurch, Robert. "A Big Dog Barks: Ælfric of Eynsham's Indictment of the English Pastorate and Witan." *Speculum* 85 (2010): 505–33.
– "For Pastoral Care and Political Gain: Ælfric of Eynsham's Preaching on Marital Celibacy." *Traditio* 59 (2004): 39–78.
– "Shepherding the Shepherds in the Ways of Pastoral Care: Ælfric and Cambridge University Library, MS Gg.3.28." In *Saints and Scholars: New Perspectives on Anglo-Saxon Literature and Culture in Honour of Hugh Magennis*, ed. Stuart McWilliams, 54–74. Cambridge: D.S. Brewer, 2012.
Wallis, Faith. "Background Essay: St John's College 17 as a Computus Manuscript." In *The Calendar and the Cloister.*
– "Location and Dating." In *The Calendar and the Cloister.*

Whatley, E. Gordon. "*Pearls before Swine*: Ælfric, Vernacular Hagiography, and the Lay Reader." In *Via Crucis: Essays on Medieval Sources and Ideas in Memory of J.E. Cross*, ed. Thomas N. Hall with Thomas D. Hill and Charles D. Wright, 158–84. Medieval European Studies 1. Morgantown: West Virginia University Press, 2002.

Whitelock, Dorothy. "The Old English Bede." *Proceedings of the British Academy* 48 (1962): 57–90.

Wieland, Gernot. "Geminus Stilus: Studies in Anglo-Latin Hagiography." In *Insular Latin Studies: Papers on Latin Texts and Manuscripts of the British Isles, 550–1066*, ed. Michael W. Herren, 113–33. Toronto: Pontifical Institute of Mediaeval Studies, 1981.

Wilcox, Jonathan. "Ælfric in Dorset and the Landscape of Pastoral Care." In *Pastoral Care in Late Anglo-Saxon England*, ed. Frencesca Tinti, 52–63. Anglo-Saxon Studies 6. Woodbridge: Boydell Press, 2005.

– "The Audience of Ælfric's Lives of Saints and the Face of Cotton Caligula A. xiv, fols. 93–130." In *Beatus Vir: Studies in Early English and Norse Manuscripts in Memory of Phillip Pulsiano*, ed. A.N. Doane and Kristen Wolf, 228–63. Medieval and Renaissance Texts and Studies 319. Tempe: Arizona Center for Medieval and Renaissance Studies, 2006.

Winterbottom, Michael. "Aldhelm's Prose Style and Its Origins." *ASE* 6 (1977): 39–76.

– "The Style of Æthelweard." *Medium Ævum* 36 (1967): 109–18.

Wormald, Patrick. "Æthelwold and His Continental Counterparts: Contact, Comparison, Contrast." In Yorke, *Bishop Æthelwold*, 13–42.

Yorke, Barbara. "Æthelwold and the Politics of the Tenth Century." In Yorke, *Bishop Æthelwold*, 65–88.

– *Bishop Æthelwold: His Career and Influence*. Woodbridge: Boydell Press, 1988.

– "The Women in Edgar's Life." In Scragg, *Edgar, King of the English*, 143–57.

Zetzel, James E.G. *Marginal Scholarship and Textual Deviance: The Commentum Cornuti and the Early Scholia on Persius*. Bulletin of the Institute of Classical Studies Supplement 84. London: Institute of Classical Studies, School of Advanced Study University of London, 2005.

Index

Toronto Anglo-Saxon Series

1 *Preaching the Converted: The Style and Rhetoric of the Vercelli Book Homilies*, Samantha Zacher
2 *Say What I Am Called: The Old English Riddles of the Exeter Book and the Anglo-Latin Riddle Tradition*, Dieter Bitterli
3 *The Aesthetics of Nostalgia: Historical Representation in Anglo-Saxon Verse*, Renée Trilling
4 *New Readings in the Vercelli Book*, edited by Samantha Zacher and Andy Orchard
5 *Authors, Audiences, and Old English Verse*, Thomas A. Bredehoft
6 *On Aesthetics in* Beowulf *and Other Old English Poems*, edited by John M. Hill
7 *Old English Metre: An Introduction*, Jun Terasawa
8 *Anglo-Saxon Psychologies in the Vernacular and Latin Traditions*, Leslie Lockett
9 *The Body Legal in Barbarian Law*, Lisi Oliver
10 *Old English Literature and the Old Testament*, edited by Michael Fox and Manish Sharma
11 *Stealing Obedience: Narratives of Agency and Identity in Later Anglo-Saxon England*, Katherine O'Brien O'Keeffe
12 *Traditional Subjectivities: The Old English Poetics of Mentality*, Britt Mize
13 *Land and Book: Literature and Land Tenure in Anglo-Saxon England*, Scott T. Smith
14 *Writing Women Saints in Anglo-Saxon England*, edited by Paul E. Szarmach
15 *Anglo-Saxon Manuscripts: A Bibliographical Handlist of Manuscripts and Manuscript Fragments Written or Owned in England up to 1100*, Helmut Gneuss and Michael Lapidge

16 *The King's Body: Burial and Succession in Anglo-Saxon England*, Nicole Marafioti
17 *From Lawmen to Plowmen: Anglo-Saxon Legal Tradition and the School of Langland*, Stephen Yeager
18 *The Politics of Language: Byrthferth, Aelfric, and the Multilingual Identity of the Benedictine Reform*, Rebecca Stephenson

www.ingramcontent.com/pod-product-compliance
Lightning Source LLC
LaVergne TN
LVHW090158080826
844660LV00013B/861/J